HOW GENDER STUDIES BROKE THE UNIVERSITY

HOW GENDER STUDIES BROKE THE UNIVERSITY

Cynthia Burack

Pitchstone Publishing
Durham, North Carolina

Pitchstone Publishing
Durham, North Carolina
www.pitchstonebooks.com

Library of Congress Cataloging-in-Publication Data

Names: Burack, Cynthia, 1958- author
Title: How gender studies broke the university / Cynthia Burack.
Description: Durham, North Carolina : Pitchstone Publishing, [2025] | Includes bibliographical references and index. | Summary: "A political theorist and professor of women's, gender and sexuality studies tells the story of how gender studies and other progressive disciplines undermine free speech, academic freedom, and intellectual diversity in universities. As a decades-long insider, the author demonstrates how faculty and administrators foment student anger, promote radical identity-based activism, and institutionalize illiberal and authoritarian practices, and she calls on her colleagues to desist in order to resuscitate the reputation of higher education"— Provided by publisher.
Identifiers: LCCN 2024062095 (print) | LCCN 2024062096 (ebook) | ISBN 9781634312806 paperback | ISBN 9781634312813 ebook
Subjects: LCSH: Women's studies | Gender identity—Study and teaching (Higher) | Universities and colleges—Sociological aspects
Classification: LCC HQ1180 .B87 2025 (print) | LCC HQ1180 (ebook) | DDC 305.4—dc23/eng/20250507
LC record available at https://lccn.loc.gov/2024062095
LC ebook record available at https://lccn.loc.gov/2024062096

CONTENTS

Acknowledgements

I'd like to thank Felon, my bang-up friend and roomie, for helping me think about being politically unhoused and for suggesting the frame of "tribing times." Amos Brigham provided technological assistance at a crucial moment in the process. Jeff Mann and Suzanne Franks went above and beyond by reading the manuscript and gently pointing out my errors. Suzanne can't believe that "academemoir" doesn't name an established genre. Craig Gibson, who shared many excellent pieces of literature with me, was just the conversation partner I needed as I wrote this book.

I'm grateful to The Ohio State University for a 2023–24 sabbatical that provided time to write.

I'm especially grateful for the Foundation for Individual Rights and Expression (FIRE), whose Faculty Legal Defense Fund provided me an attorney in an Equal Employment Opportunity investigation that commenced in the summer of 2020 and wasn't resolved until early 2022. I'm also happy to acknowledge the important role of the Academic Freedom Alliance in standing up for this value and inviting me to become a member.

No part of this book was published before now.

Preface

What follows is in one respect the story of a working-class girl who grew up to become a professor. This isn't the book I intended to write at this late stage in my career. I've always been fascinated by the how, what, and why of belief. I'd written about the American political right for many years when, in 2013, I started to work on a project about how prayer is used as a vehicle for delivering political messaging.

Then I changed my mind. I interrupted that research to investigate the Obama administration's efforts to support international sexual orientation and gender identity (SOGI) human rights. But I also set out to analyze domestic US opposition to these efforts. For the first time, I found it necessary to critically examine the beliefs and advocacy of the academic left—my people—and what I found demoralized but didn't surprise me.

After Donald Trump won the 2016 presidential election, and feeling certain I would document the dismantling of US support for LGBTI human rights, I continued to study US SOGI foreign policy. Then a funny thing happened: while I was writing *How Trump and the Christian Right Saved LGBTI Human Rights*, I learned I was the target of an Equal Employment Opportunity (EEO) investigation. I kept writing as I defended myself against accusations of harassment leveled by a group of gender studies grad students and joined by the chair of my department.

To cut to the chase, in a graduate seminar on feminist methodologies, I used an article by a feminist anthropologist in part to raise an important question: why is it necessary to identify the possibility of our own *positive* biases and the ways these can distort our research? Scholars in many social justice–oriented fields—I counted myself as one of these—do research "on" or "about" groups with which we feel an affinity. Given our affinities, how can we ensure that we're conducting our research in a way that maximizes our ability to get to the truth and not be distracted by our own convictions and attachments?

The initial set of accusations was anchored by one central claim: that the empirical example I used to demonstrate this ethical dilemma in research was actually aimed at students—or at particular students; sometimes it was hard to tell—as a form of harassment. I suspect that equally, if not more, offensive was my implicit suggestion that partisan advocacy for a group on "our" side could ever violate the trust conferred on us as scholars.

In recent years, some academics have written about the experience of being accused by their institutions of discriminating against or harassing students. These accounts fruitfully inform the uninitiated about the combination of threat, secretiveness, and assumption of guilt that characterizes these processes. I recognize every one I've seen.

Because "my" investigation went on for a year and a half, a full account of what transpired could fill its own book. But I won't put you through that. As the investigation proceeded, I learned a great deal about the ways in which the process itself treats the accused as confirmed bigots while tying their hands with a set of policies designed to keep them quiet and prevent them from mounting an effective defense.

Throughout the ordeal, it occurred to me over and over that when universities subject faculty to accusations such as those many of us hear and read about, they really don't want anyone in the outside world to know what they're doing. Think about how many universities have been caught with their bad behavior hanging out since 2020. Even if we just kept track of the universities that have had to make or retract public statements, pay damages, or reverse illegal or unconstitutional policies, we would be very busy, indeed!

Although I didn't expect to become a target of investigation, of course,

I already knew I didn't share many of the views expected and required of faculty in gender studies. I never confessed my sins against the reigning conception of social justice, but my grad students knew it too. One thing that distinguishes grad students in progressive fields from most of the undergrads who pass through our classrooms is that grad students are on their way to becoming the next generation of well-socialized activist scholars. They can spot a garden-variety-free-speech-and-scientific-method-respecting heretic a mile away.

As late as the early months of 2023, I intended to resume my research project on the politics of prayer in the United States. I'd been gathering an archive to do just that. But I'd also been putting together another archive—of threats to academic freedom. I didn't know that I'd do anything with this latter collection of books, articles, quotes, and thoughts—no prayers—but I believed I should pay close attention to what was being wrought.

As I weighed the merits of these projects, one memory bugged me. Before the Covid pandemic, I was a member of an LGBT professional committee when an eminent scholar (hereafter, the Scholar) delivered a talk on the possibility of effecting some compromise with Christian conservative bakers and florists who refused to lend their skills and businesses to the consecration of same-sex marriages. A YouTube video of the talk circulated among LGBTQ academics, many of whom reacted with anger and a sense of having been betrayed.

Not me. By the time the talk made the rounds, I'd been trying for a while to imagine a compromise that might enable small proprietors not to be fined out of business because they refuse to participate in celebrating same-sex marriages. I confess that in addition to my concern about ordinary citizens losing their livelihoods because they chose to act in accordance with their conscience, I knew that each person at the center of these cases had become a martyr to the Christian conservative movement. And rightly so! Had they been on the other side, we would have feted the hell out of them.

In spite of the campaign that was building steam behind the scenes against the Scholar, I found his talk cogent and helpful to my own thinking about the issue. As you might guess, this was not the position of many of my colleagues.

The episode came to a head with the decision of the LGBT committee to draft a public letter condemning the Scholar's choice to deliver the talk at a time when LGBTQ people were under threat from right-wing political forces. I explained to the chair of the committee why I wouldn't sign such a letter. I suggested that members of the committee could sign as individuals or that the letter could indicate that it had been drafted by a majority of the committee rather than issuing from the committee as a whole.

In the brief, civil back-and-forth that ensued, the committee chair objected to the timing of the Scholar's talk. I responded that I disagreed with this take and believed the timing was appropriate.

In fact, I couldn't imagine when would be a good time to talk about compromise. If not when there were bitter disputes about rights, would it be when, in some utopian future, we'd won decisively and vanquished all our adversaries? I don't know why but, in the end, the committee decided not to draft a public letter of disapproval.

The incident crystallized knowledge I'd had for some time: that I'm a poor fit for the most progressive redoubts of academia. In fact, I've become un-fit. Which, when it comes down to it, is what the students and the chair of my department meant when they reported me to the university as a bigot in progressives' clothing.

This all brings me to the present moment. Because I won't bore you with the details of a nineteen-month investigation into my nefarious pedagogical activities, some of the information I acquired by way of participant observation at the EEO investigation may go to waste. As for this book, I'll tell you what I often told my students: I hope something you find here is useful to you.

HOW GENDER STUDIES BROKE THE UNIVERSITY

Introduction: Tribing Times

FIRE Alarm

Memories of decades of faculty meetings mostly run together. However, this moment I remember. It's 2017, and I'm seated at a conference table next to the chair of my department. As the meeting breaks up, a colleague stops to sympathize about an online drubbing the chair has recently received. The chair and an outrage mob of mostly women academics have tried to force a feminist journal to retract an article with which the academics disagreed and to apologize for having published the article in the first place.[1]

My chair's defense of that effort in the preeminent magazine of American higher education does not play well with scholars who don't share her politics or her enthusiasm for shutting down speech of which she and her associates disapprove. The exchange is brief. Although I'm close, I miss the first couple of words of the chair's response. But the last three words are plainly audible: burn it down.

Burn it down.

To be fair, maybe I've never heard that phrase at any other time in gender studies. Except I have. For example, a scholar my department invited to give a lecture during the Covid pandemic described teaching her students that capitalism sucks. The goal of her teaching, she explained, was for students to want to burn everything down.

So, there you are. It's not just the MAGA and alt-right that want to burn "it" down. Gender studies professors also think burning it down and bragging to each other about teaching students to burn it down are fine things that nobody in the leftyist precincts of American academia could possibly disapprove of. And too often, we don't.

In this story, nobody blows the whistle. There are no shredded documents, clandestine meetings, or burner phones. There's no grand jury. No one flees to Russia. I can't blow the whistle because in recent years the secrets have spilled out. This book is a story, in part my story, about far-left academic progressivism and the field of gender studies, which I've come to believe cheats students intellectually and damages higher education.

It's not just gender studies, of course. Much of what I've written here also applies to the broader institutional contexts in which the "interdiscipline" of gender studies is embedded: the humanities, sectors of the sciences and social sciences, and—to the extent that universities came to parrot and enforce the worldview of gender and other identity-based "studies"—US higher education. I occasionally offer examples from universities abroad because when America sneezes, the world catches a cold.[2]

Over time, I've fallen out of love with women's studies and its successor "studies" fields and academic units: feminist; gender; queer; sexuality. As painful as it has been to come to this place, I think that universities, students, and the academic enterprise would be better off if women's and other identity-based "studies" had never been institutionalized in US higher education. These "studies" didn't cause the affective polarization and political extremism that plague the United States, but they exacerbate the enmity of our trib[e]ing times.

Needless to say, I didn't always see it this way, and it probably took me too long to get here. There was, as many academics like to say, a liminal period in which I saw the problems I'll lay out clearly but thought they were irritating deviations from a mostly virtuous norm. That was self-deceiving.

My estrangement from the field that's now often called gender studies has had three broad causes. One is that, over time, I've come to think differently about some issues, and most of those changes have propelled me away from the monoculture of progressive doctrine and pedagogy. The second is that academic women's studies changed over time, from the comparative intellectual free-for-all that prevailed across the nascent discipline to the expunging of disfavored theories, methods, approaches, pedagogies, and issue positions that gender studies has become.[3]

Third is that my gender studies colleagues' wildest dream came true: their ideology became the official belief system of US higher education, codified in university policies and enforced against all challengers. As Harvard psychologist Steven Pinker put it in 2023, "vast regions in the landscape of ideas are no-go zones, and dissenting ideas are greeted with incomprehension, outrage, and censorship."[4] As I write this book, I can't think of a core gender studies belief, ideal, demand, conviction, or standard that didn't become part of the de facto doctrine of US universities by 2022.

In what follows, I offer claims and evidence that constitute my case against gender studies and official academic progressivism. But the big argument of the book is this: gender studies had a key role in creating an alarmingly effective habitat for anti-intellectualism, political dogmatism, and populist left-wing authoritarianism. Gender and other "studies'" fingerprints are all over illiberal higher ed trends, acts, goals, beliefs, ideas, and instruction. Until political backlash commenced, we didn't even try to hide it.

Who created this habitat? In the academy, the face of left-wing populist authoritarianism is female. Journalist Tara Henley is among those who note that as women achieved greater parity with men in cultural and intellectual institutions, they became "increasingly comfortable calling for censorship of other perspectives," often "with remarkable force."[5]

I don't want to be misunderstood as saying "all women" or, for that matter, "all men." But there is empirical evidence of *tendencies* of female and male faculty with regard to the principle of academic freedom. Cory Clark, a psychologist and executive director of the Adversarial Collaboration Project at the University of Pennsylvania, cites some of this evidence, drawing conclusions from analysis of her own data. She writes that

> men are more tolerant of controversial and potentially offensive scientific findings being pursued, disseminated, and discussed, and women are more willing to obstruct or suppress science perceived to be potentially harmful or offensive. Put more simply, men are relatively more interested in advancing what is *empirically correct*, and women are relatively more interested in advancing what is *morally desirable.*

How has the increase in the number of women faculty and administrators—a goal pursued by generations of women who valued education—helped to put us where we are today?

> [O]n average, women are more willing to suppress science for moral reasons, and men are more willing to allow offensive or even potentially harmful ideas to be shared. As the population of academia shifts from one dominated by men to one that is more balanced or disproportionately female, support for including moral and harm concerns into the scientific and publishing process is likely to increase, and support for academic freedom is likely to decline.[6]

Specific characteristics of the higher ed landscape suggest why sex matters in our current crisis. For some time, women have outpaced men in university enrollment and lean more to the left than men in their political identification. As an empirical matter, most gender studies professors are women, most gender studies students are women, and a high percentage of faculty in the other radical/progressive programs and departments are women. Women have made impressive inroads in the humanities and the humanities subfields of social science disciplines in recent decades. And it's in these spaces that we find some of the densest pockets of the illiberalism that plagues the academy.

Women are much better represented in university and professional organization administration than they were when I started my career. In fact, women have been successful enough in attaining the highest positions in higher ed that a Congressional hearing on campus antisemitism in December 2023 featured women presidents of Harvard, MIT, and the University of Pennsylvania. Finally, women predominate among human resources and student affairs personnel, and investigators of allegations of civil rights violations. Thus, a queer, decolonial, antiracist activist ethos with a female face normalizes many of the beliefs and practices I describe in this book.[7]

At the risk of being labeled a misogynist, I can't unsee the womanness of our academic predicament. It wouldn't strike many of my colleagues in the humanities as scurrilous to point out that the ethos of the populist, authoritarian right in the United States is masculine and, as many would no doubt conclude, toxically so. Somehow, this close attention to detail fails us when we turn our attention to the academy.

Scratch the surface of the worldview I criticize or challenge it directly, and you trigger justifications of policies and practices based on historically gendered conceptions of care and harm. Thus, I will in due course take a stab at how, in relatively short order, we moved on from academic feminists formulating theories of care to other academic feminists deploying pro-social, care-based justifications for left-wing illiberalism.

I want to stipulate up front that US higher ed is in a parlous state for many reasons. Others, better positioned than me, have written incisively about these problems. So, I'm going to explore what I know best when it comes to higher ed: the consequences of the cobbling together of inaccessible poststructuralist theories, critical theories, identity-based activist demands, narratives of lived experience, and progressive intuitions to produce an ideology incubated by faculty in gender studies and other cognate disciplines.

This ideology came to represent the common sense of intellectual elites. It was translated into university policies and then imposed on those who might be inclined to resist.

Before I go farther down this road, I need to clarify a few things. First, am I going to acknowledge my personal responsibility for what women's studies and its successors have become? Yes, I am. It may not seem sufficient, but my regret is real. Second, am I blaming all gender studies and other left-leaning faculty—an indictment that would sweep up full-time, part-time, contingent, and affiliated/associated faculty members? No, I'm not, so let me say in advance: #NotAllFaculty. Third, am I suggesting that all women faculty are to blame for our current predicament? Of course not! So, #NotAllWomen. Finally, am I tarring students who have taken women's studies courses, majored or minored in the field, received a certificate or graduate minor, or had a graduate degree in the field conferred upon them? Again, no, so: #NotAllStudents.

Speaking of students, many Americans have come to believe that US higher education pits radical students against faculty and administrators. There are reasons why so many embrace this explanation, including that "71 percent [of students surveyed] are in favor of reporting professors for saying something deemed offensive."[8] Here's my take, which I'll say more about as we go on: the problem here isn't the students. It's us: faculty and administrators; the adults, not the "kids."[9] Oh, the kids are not alright, but what's in the chapters to come isn't primarily their fault.

Students have an important role to play, though. Faculty tasked students with being front-line workers in the trade of academic illiberalism, prepared to equate much intellectual inquiry with injury. When individual cases erupt into public view, we might be tempted to diagnose evidence of young adult fragility. Adolescents and young adults may, indeed, have become more anxious and fragile over time.[10] But we can get a good purchase on what's afoot if we see these as cases of students absorbing esoteric "knowledge"; achieving intellectual closure and certainty;[11] bolstering "groupish" identities as activists and allies;[12] and enforcing crude versions of their elders' grand theories to reap the social rewards these acts can yield.[13]

Now look behind those students. In the cases generated in recent years, we've seen faculty and administrators encouraging students' complaints and activism. As the psychologist Lee Jussim puts it, "the threat to academic freedom [comes] from academics."[14] Hence, any analysis of left-wing illiberalism on American campuses must reckon with the fact that academics lurk in the background when their colleagues or students are being punished or threatened with punishment for exercising academic freedom.

This very dynamic prompted the cultural theorist Laura Kipnis, investigated twice by Northwestern University for criticizing Title IX investigations, to wonder, "why are scholars such snitches?"[15]

For these developments, many will blame young adults who point out malefactors like crime victims at a line-up. Or, as at Stanford Law School, dress up as black bloc protesters and make their best effort to intimidate a disobedient administrator.[16] By all means, let's criticize this behavior. But let's also remain focused on the adults behind the curtain.

As a depressive realist, I'm not hopeful that the dilemma of dueling authoritarianisms of right and left can be rectified in a way that would pave a path for truth-seeking in the academy and other cultural institutions. But maybe you can, as my friend Alayna likes to say, prove me wrong.

In the meantime, in this Introduction, I provide an overview of the problem of left-wing illiberalism in academia. First up, you'll find a brief account of academic freedom, the gold standard that we in the academy have touted—especially when we're threatened by outside intervention and sometimes even as we're violating it.

Next, I explain some of the choices of nomenclature I make throughout this book. I always strive for clarity. If I succeed, what I've written will be clear enough that any motivated reader can spot what I might have gotten wrong. A quick primer on language and concepts may help with such an effort. Finally, I outline what the rest of the book has to offer. Feel free to treat the chapters as a buffet and skip anything that doesn't appeal.

A Very Short Course on Academic Freedom

Commentators use different terms and refer to somewhat different concepts in discussing threats to freedom in cultural institutions, including free speech, free inquiry, value pluralism, and academic freedom. In this book, I primarily use the concept of academic freedom, which the United Nations Educational, Scientific and Cultural Organization (UNES-

CO) has defined as

> the right, without constriction by prescribed doctrine, to freedom of teaching and discussion, freedom in carrying out research and disseminating and publishing the results thereof, freedom to express freely their opinion about the institution or system in which they work, freedom from institutional censorship and freedom to participate in professional or representative academic bodies.[17]

Student speech can be threatened in some of the same ways as faculty speech. I strongly support the principle that students should enjoy freedom of speech in academic contexts, subject to reasonable constraints regarding, for example, threats and true disruptions to the learning environment. Specious claims of harm shouldn't be deployed to prevent political and intellectual disagreements among students.

Academic freedom isn't just an abstract principle. It's been elucidated in a variety of documents produced by faculty and legal experts. These documents represent systematic reflections on what it is, why it's important, and how to achieve it. I won't address them in this brief introduction, but courts have also produced decisions that have helped to define boundaries and justifications of academic freedom.[18]

Two foundational documents are statements of principles endorsed by the American Association of University Professors (AAUP): the 1915 Declaration of Principles on Academic Freedom and Academic Tenure and the 1940 Statement of Principles of Academic Freedom and Tenure. That was the old AAUP, not the one we have now.[19]

Other key statements include: in 2014, the University of Chicago Report of the Committee on Freedom of Expression (also known as the Chicago Statement or Chicago Principles); and, in 2023, the Princeton Principles for a Campus Culture of Free Inquiry (also known as the Princeton Principles). Finally, and with a somewhat different focus, there is the University of Chicago's 1967 Report on the University's Role in Political and Social Action, also known as the Kalven Report.

The first of these, the 1915 Declaration of Principles, surveys a number of actors and issues that relate to academic freedom. It lays out the prime functions of professors in institutions of higher education, which are: "a. to promote inquiry and advance the sum of human knowledge; b. to provide general instruction to the students; and c. to develop experts for various branches of the public service." These functions can't be adequately fulfilled "without accepting and enforcing to the fullest extent the principle of academic freedom." Thus, the Declaration argues that "it is in the public interest that the professorial office should be one both of dignity and of independence."[20]

The 1940 Statement of Principles is more succinct and less florid in its language. It sets forth the argument made by many contemporary critics that higher ed should serve the common good and that "the common good depends upon the free search for truth and its free exposition." The Statement lays out three core principles of academic freedom, which I shorten below but which are more fully rendered in the original document.

> 1. Teachers are entitled to full freedom in research and in the publication of the results . . . ,
> 2. Teachers are entitled to freedom in the classroom in discussing their subject . . . .
> 3. College and university teachers are citizens, members of a learned profession, and officers of an educational institution. When they speak or write as citizens, they should be free from institutional censorship or discipline . . . .

In 1970, an additional set of "interpretive comments" was added to the 1940 Statement as footnotes.[21]

The Chicago Statement, published in 2014, addresses the ideals of the University of Chicago and constitutes an intervention into contentious debates over speech on US campuses.[22] By 2014, a number of incidents of cancellation had signaled a turn to intolerance of speech with which university community members disapproved. The Statement acknowledges that "the ideas of different members of the University community will often and quite naturally conflict" but declares that

> it is not the proper role of the University to attempt to shield individuals from ideas and opinions they find unwelcome, disagreeable, or even deeply offensive. . . . [C]oncerns about civility and mutual respect can never be used as a justification for closing off discussion of ideas, however offensive or disagreeable those ideas may be to some members of our community.

Subject to restrictions regarding the "the time, place, and manner of expression," the Chicago Statement clarifies that universities should not suppress or punish even "offensive, unwise, immoral, or wrong-headed" speech and ideas.[23] According to the Foundation for Individual Rights and Expression, by 2024, one hundred and seven universities had endorsed Chicago or a "substantially similar statement."[24]

The Princeton Principles "affirm" the Chicago Statement "while expanding its scope." Specifically, the Principles claim that "universities have a *special fiduciary duty* to foster freedom of thought for the benefit of the societies that sustain them." In a few deft sentences, the Principles explain how US universities came to "stifle free inquiry" by prioritizing the avoidance of "harm" to students. And they link the telos of universities—"to pursue truth, advance knowledge, and encourage artistic excellence wherever the quest may lead"—to democracy and citizenship: "a culture of free inquiry is essential to any education that aims to form free citizens and promote the growth of students."[25]

Although the Chicago and Princeton Principles seem to have in common their provenance as official university statements, the latter statement was issued by the James Madison Program in American Ideals and Institutions and wasn't officially endorsed by Princeton University.

Of all the historical and contemporary academic freedom statements and declarations, it was the Kalven Report that suddenly became famous in 2023. At the time, universities faced a public reckoning over their refusal to condemn pro-Hamas speech on campuses after years of having declared themselves prolifically on other issues.

Kalven's innovation is its case for insulating universities from "political fashions, passions, and pressures" by maintaining institutional neutrality. Its most quoted passage distinguishes between the proper roles of universities and individuals, declaiming that "the instrument of dissent and criticism is the individual faculty member or the individual student. The university is the home and sponsor of critics; it is not itself the critic" The report provides humorous support for disputation in higher ed, arguing that "a good university, like Socrates, will be upsetting."[26]

Until 2023, many departments and universities, including mine, generated position statements on a host of social and political issues. Most, if not all, of these expressed anxiety about the psychological state of students and positioned the university as a mitigator of harm caused by extramural events.

Many issue statements highlighted therapeutic reflections on policy issues and the faculty's preoccupation with students' feelings. One example came to public attention in late 2023 when Barnard College embraced its inner Kalven and removed a women's, gender, and sexuality studies (WGSS) department statement regarding the October 7 attacks and the Israeli military response from the university's website.[27]

WGSS core faculty responded by creating a WordPress website to host the exiled statement. They named their project, "In This Moment," a portentous phrase that seems to function to rally progressives much as "for such a time as this" functions to rally Christian conservatives.[28] The "decolonial feminist scholars and educators" of the WGSS department stood "in solidarity with [their] students who have experienced a wide variety of emotions and reactions following the disturbing events that have occurred in recent weeks and over multiple decades."[29]

Implicitly rejecting the idea that Barnard should be "the home and sponsor of critics" rather than "itself the critic," the WGSS faculty also declared themselves "here to protest increasing curtailment of free speech and academic freedom at colleges and universities across the US." I can only imagine what would transpire on the WordPress webpage if another department at Barnard had hazarded a less decolonial take on the conflict in the Middle East. I have no reason to think that WGSS would zealously champion that department's right to "free speech and academic freedom."

The Barnard WGSS statement raises the possibility of an alternative reading of Kalven: that it prohibits administrators speaking for faculty but "exten[ds] [the principle] of neutrality beyond the central administration to include all sub-units and faculty departments of a college." John K. Wilson's position is that extending neutrality to departments—prohibiting departments from taking positions on political issues—constitutes "the most dangerous betrayal of the Kalven Report's principles."

I agree with Wilson that Kalven is "a monument to faculty power."[30] I just believe that the faculty it should empower are individuals, not units or departments. There's no better way for a faculty member to out herself as a heretic spoiling for punishment than to object to her department's position on a nonnegotiable social justice issue.

In early 2023, as Republican state legislators circled, my university did something that many other US universities did that year: after having endorsed the Chicago Principles in 2022, it publicly (re)committed itself to academic freedom.[31] The Board of Trustees duly affirmed that the new policy was utterly consistent with the university's "shared values."[32] Even if we set aside the timing, the claim that there was nothing to see here wasn't terribly convincing.

I'll say more about the resort to "shared values" later. Suffice it to say that, at least in many cases, a vigorous defense of academic freedom isn't consistent with the potpourri of "values"—to say nothing of the related "principles" and "behaviors"—our universities direct us to share.

In October 2023, not long after the Hamas attack, many universities, including mine, rushed to embrace the principle of institutional neutrality. Gone would be the issue statements of old, some of which read as though they'd been produced by artificial intelligence responding to a prompt to blend the syntax of poststructuralism with that of the Symbionese Liberation Army. Faculty at my university were apprised that our Kalvenesque policy, which would apply to colleges and departments as well as to the university itself, would severely limit issue statements.[33]

The about face on issue statements revealed anxiety about the possibility that our statements might leak to the world off campus. Institutional leaders offered a template for chairs, not to speak to outside stakeholders about extramural events, but to speak to their own units.

Even communications to a department's students and faculty would be required to use the template and be submitted to the university's office of Marketing and Communications before being circulated.

The policy was conceived in anxiety about the possible repercussions of institutional issue statements that affirmed progressive faculty unanimity. Predictably, it overcorrected by placing a campus administrative office in control of faculty speech—one of the very problems Kalven was created to resolve.

Even if all universities endorsed principles of academic freedom, we'd still have to make judgments and have difficult discussions. For example, on the Kalven report: some hold that university administrators and officers should speak about events of the day only as individuals.[34] Others insist that administrators and officers should speak for their institutions, not to take sides on contentious issues but to "affirm human decency."[35] Let's have this debate, which is an improvement over the slew of progressive institutional statements on contentious questions that preceded it.

Anytime we take up debates over academic freedom, a question may present itself: What is the constituency for academic freedom? Is academic freedom crucial to the wider project of US democracy, or is it a recondite matter that need only concern pinheads, eggheads, and talking heads?

I agree with those who regard academic freedom as essential to the success of liberal democracy. For the historian and Canadian elected official Michael Ignatieff, academic freedom isn't "a privilege of a liberal elite" with "no constituency beyond academia." In Ignatieff's view, "universities—like courts, a free press, and independent regulatory bodies—are essential restraints on majoritarian rule that keep us all free." Universities simply can't fulfill their function as "guardrails of democracy" without academic freedom.[36]

The conservative writer Lorenzo Warby comes to a similar conclusion about the threat to liberal democracy posed by the erosion of academic freedom for different reasons. Warby argues that progressive academic "information bubbles" reinforce "tribal beliefs" and inevitably result in "a loss of contact with other people's concerns, with what they believe and why." This "persistent, self-protecting unawareness—particularly among the cultural elite—is fatal to democratic health, indeed to a resilient society, over the long run."[37]

One reason I wrote this book is my conviction that we in the academy must change course for there to be a chance that we can appeal to American citizens to support liberal democratic institutions. If we fail, the alternative is a feast for right-wing illiberals: increasing enmity between gown and town, working-class Americans defecting to an illiberal Republican Party, and right-wing authoritarians cracking down on universities, a process that's well underway.[38]

Many of my colleagues beg to differ. For a substantial subset of these, the struggle between a morally pure and virtuous left and an authoritarian right is a matter of faith. They speak a particular language, incant progressive "magic words," and sniff out unacceptable signs of moral, political, or intellectual ambiguity.[39]

I've known for many years that the failure or refusal to speak this language, incant the magic words, and avoid ambiguity will be taken as signs of, at best, moral turpitude and, at worst, full-blown treason. Rather than soft-pedaling the transformation that's brought so many colleges and universities to this place, let's take left-wing illiberalism literally and seriously. Because, as bad as things are for higher ed, they can get even worse.

Let's start by nailing down some key terms and concepts.

Foundations

"How can we have a proper debate when we no longer speak the same language?" Richard Dawkins is one of many academics who has expressed concern about how challenging it is to engage in intellectual debate and deliberation when siloed elites and groups speak an esoteric language.[40]

Naturally, we don't just find this problem in higher ed. Media and politics are filled with broad- and narrow casting. In *Sin, Sex, and Democracy: Antigay Rhetoric and the Christian Right*, I argue that one marker of the Christian conservative right's maturation as a movement was its elites' success in directing biblical condemnations of same-sex sexuality to ingroup believers while using—and teaching believers to use—rights and majoritarian democratic arguments to defend the movement's positions in public.[41]

Domains of knowledge often require technical language shared by specialists. I'll write more about the language of academic progressivism in chapters to come. For now, here are some terms and ideas you should keep in mind as you read. A phrase you'll see regularly in these pages is "my colleagues," so I want to clarify to whom I refer. Generally speaking, I use this term for progressive faculty and the broader academy that translated their particular—at times, peculiar—views into university policy.

In other words, the phrase, "my colleagues," only denotes faculty colleagues in my department or university when the context so clarifies. I also refer to "my university" and "Flagship State University," and otherwise redact references to the institution where I spent the majority of my career. I've made this choice because the problems I highlight in this book are widely shared and not the preserve of any particular college or university. Not being an elite institution, my university may have been a little late to the game of illiberalism. As progressive illiberalism represents a cutting edge of praxis, some colleagues in such institutions worked very hard to catch up.[42]

In classes and scholarship, I tried to communicate respectfully about ideas to which I don't subscribe and the groups that hold those ideas. As I'll discuss later, in gender studies classrooms, such a practice can cause problems. At times, I've been encouraged by some colleagues to refer to these groups by "our" understandings of their beliefs—for example, to use "anti-choice" as nomenclature for those who oppose a right to abortion instead of "pro-life."

Nevertheless, I've usually rejected terms that would valorize my politics and made an effort to refer to groups using language they prefer. Reviewers of my manuscripts have commented on my propensity to treat those with whom I disagree with respect. I'm not sure this was always a compliment.

Another term I use here is one my students would recognize: fellow citizens. In the classroom, I consistently alluded to those with whom "we" disagree as fellow citizens. Some people we disagree with may do very bad things, such as pumping conspiracy theories and propaganda into political discourse and scheming to subvert the Constitution and the rule of law.

However, I don't talk about even right-wing authoritarian followers as permanent enemies. Instead, I try to think of them as some intellectuals and political leaders regarded the majority of adversaries after conflicts such as the US Civil War and World War II: as people who, if we're lucky, will be reincorporated as members of a politically-diverse polity, ideally on peaceful and democratic terms.

Having taught twentieth century political ideologies, I'm aware of the history and defining attributes of fascism, including its early warning signs. I don't believe that everyone to my right—much less to the right of my progressive colleagues—is a fascist. But my standard bears little resemblance to the one that has prevailed in swaths of academia. There, academic freedom and value pluralism are often regarded with suspicion or equated with a covert agenda to inject antifeminism, white supremacy, or some other brand of virulent hatred into research and teaching.[43]

For the record, because casting everyone who doesn't profess the tenets of the progressivism I'll challenge as bigots or fascists has been commonplace in the academy, I'm neither fascist nor a bigot. Most of my faculty colleagues probably know it's unlikely that deep-cover fascists have successfully burrowed into gender studies or a cognate field, waiting years or decades for the perfect moment to sabotage agendas of justice and liberation. Unfortunately, when the chips are down, many have acted as though they don't know how unlikely such a scenario is.

I suspect that the belief that fascism or bigotry may be revealed at any time in the form of a reading, a question, a term, or a piece of information that doesn't fit the preferred doctrine serves a purpose for those who fall for it. Like the identification of witches in other eras, it confirms *that there really are witches, fascists, and bigots among us.* They look like "us," but they are not us. Thus, they pose a greater threat than those who wear their reactionary identity on their sleeve.

Having said this, I have a confession: In the process of thinking through challenging questions, I've relied on the work of thinkers who would be anathema to my colleagues. Some of these thinkers identify as conservative or libertarian. In some quarters, they would *be* identified as much, much worse. I'm neither morally polluted by proximity to these authors and ideas nor bothered by the fact that I disagree with them on some issues.

An example of one such figure I've referred to in my writing is the late Michael Gerson. Gerson was a speechwriter for George W. Bush and a *Washington Post* opinion columnist from 2007 until his death in 2022. Before Trump captured the Republican Party, I disagreed with Gerson much of the time. In the time of Trump, however, I saw Gerson as an ally. Even as he was dying, he continued to explain his heretical views on Trump and race to fellow conservatives—especially Christian conservatives—and beg them to reconsider their allegiance to the man who referred to himself as their "favorite president."

For his trouble, Gerson was branded a "liberal" by the leader of a prominent Christian conservative organization.[44] Because the tactic of smearing everyone to a movement's right *or* left is a common way to delegitimize those who can call into question the movement's fundamental righteousness.

Another such figure is the former member of Congress and co-chair of the House Select Committee to Investigate the January 6th Attack on the United States, known to my friends as my girlfriend, Liz Cheney. If I were straight, the venerable jurist J. Michael Luttig and the attorney George Conway—with whom I would no doubt disagree on many issues—might be my secret boyfriends.

Although some viewpoints have been effectively proscribed in the academy, I support the proposition that it's perfectly okay—even edifying—for us to disagree and walk away to contend another day.

Rather late in my career, my research agenda required that I confront a dilemma for the first time. What should I call the left-wing belief system shared by many of my colleagues that would preemptively prohibit the US government from supporting the human rights of vulnerable groups such as gender and sexual minorities abroad on the grounds that any such support would inevitably serve sinister—usually imperialist or neoliberal—ends?

In *Because We Are Human*, I call the class of scholars who represent what I now understand as populist left-wing authoritarianism a "thought community" or "thought collective," and those in the academy who I believe it's necessary to criticize for their dogmatic political commitments and frequent lack of empiricism, "radical humanities scholars."[45] I use the term "radical" descriptively rather than pejoratively, as many scholars understand their politics and thought in this way and use the term to differentiate themselves from liberals.[46]

Admittedly, the distinction between liberals, leftists, radicals, and progressives is inside baseball and might puzzle our fellow citizens who don't speak dialects of academese or high activism. Confusion isn't resolved by the tendency of political commentators and survey researchers to refer to liberals as those who lean farthest left on the left-right continuum.

Many thinkers can facilitate our understanding of this distinction between progressivism and liberalism, but the journalist Pamela Paul does so accessibly, listing

> liberal values, many of them products of the Enlightenment, [that] include individual liberty, freedom of speech, scientific inquiry, separation of church and state, due process, racial equality, women's rights, human rights and democracy.

She adds that "liberals do not see government as the problem, but as a means to help the people it serves."[47]

Well, yes, governments can do many things, positive and negative. Although we wouldn't know it from many progressive polemics against "the state," the federal government is always doing many things at once, some contradictory. No single nefarious motive lies behind the decisions made in Congress, the White House, the Executive Branch agencies, and the Judiciary every day and over the course of American history. Part of our job, should we accept it, is to analyze the multitude of acts, policies, and outcomes that point in many different directions and give reasons why we regard them as positive or negative and for whom. In this way, serious colleagues can check our work.

Anyone who would like to understand what's happened in universities should start with the fact that it's not just, or even primarily, conservatives who find themselves at odds with illiberal progressives. After all, conservatives are a minority in academia. Instead, faculty and administrators who identify as a progressive vanguard inside cultural institutions "openly reject *liberalism* as a form of oppression."[48] As a result, "liberal professors are running scared."[49]

For academic progressives, liberals are an—sometimes even *the*—enemy. Though possibly well-meaning, they knowingly or unknowingly collude with conservatives to uphold rapacious capitalism and undermine social justice. You may associate them with "status-quoists" and "anti-woke centrists."[50] Just for good measure, and to acknowledge that there are many negative euphemisms for those perceived as fence sitters in a binary world, other possibilities include the "lukewarm" whom John the Apostle suggests God will "spue . . . out of [his] mouth."[51] Research confirms that the unambivalent don't like those they perceive as ambivalent on contentious political issues.[52]

Facing the terminological dilemma of how to refer to those I criticize in this book, some writers have recurred to the "intersectional," "social justice," or "critical social justice" left, all of which are terms used by the reference group. More snide and dismissive is "woke," Woke/ism, and "The Great Awokening." Although there's precedent within a particular community for woke and its variations, it's not a fraternal gesture when critics employ it. Calling illiberal academics "fundamentalists" links academic progressivism with dogmatic religious faith.

Academic versions of terminology include the political commentator Wesley Yang's "successor ideology" and the political scientist Yascha

Mounk's "identity synthesis."[53] Both "successor" and "synthesis" are polite and respectful—an intellectual olive branch to a belief system whose practices and effects can be illiberal.

I'm still comfortable referring to those who cleave to the worldview I'll criticize as a thought community. But, just as there might be a variety of successor ideologies or identity syntheses, there are many possible thought communities. I want to be able to be more specific about the one that was incubated in gender (and other identity) studies before it emerged into public view as the primary ideology of higher education.

More content-specific terms to characterize this ideology and those who embrace it include post-liberal progressivism and post-Enlightenment progressivism.[54] Many old school economic progressives disapprove, but it's difficult to deny that the belief system of the US academy is a form of progressivism.[55] Its adherents would no doubt agree that it means to kill off such elements of Enlightenment liberalism as freedom of speech and moral universalism when they conflict with the tenets of its worldview.[56] For simplicity, throughout this book, I'll use combinations of the following terms: academic progressive illiberalism.

I'm concerned about the widespread conviction on the left that this worldview should occupy a privileged position in cultural and intellectual institutions.[57] Hence, I want to be clear about how it produces and champions forms of illiberalism that can target a range of enemies, including conservatives and left-of-center turncoats.

Even those whose progressive credentials have been—until just that moment—unimpeachable haven't been safe. One such scholar is Vincent Lloyd, professor and director of the Center for Political Theology at Villanova University and an academic with a long vita of scholarship and instruction on race and racism. In 2022, Lloyd taught a Telluride Association summer seminar for high school students entitled "Race and the Limits of Law" that started well but deteriorated until, by the end, most of his students had gone AWOL.

Accused of perpetrating microaggressions and compromising students' safety, Lloyd concluded that the seminar came to bear the hallmarks of a cult. One charge among many lodged against Lloyd was, as he characterized it, that he "invited [students] to think about the reasoning of both sides of an argument, when only one side was correct."[58] Lloyd refers to the ideology that came to dominate his seminar as "anti-racism," but his story suggests that it was a hybrid of diverse influences.

I'll say more about the worldview that animates academic illiberalism as we go on, but for now, let me offer a simile and see if it illuminates. In geology, a conglomerate is a "clastic" rock, "composed of fragments, or clasts, of . . . older rocks." These broken pieces become embedded in a matrix of ordinary sediment, such as sand. The matrix cements the disparate pieces together, creating a new rock.[59]

I think of academic progressive ideology as being like a conglomerate: composed of pieces of at times pre-existing, unrelated ideas, convictions, axioms, theories, and exhortations—what the historian Simon Sebag Montefiore calls a "historically nonsensical mix."[60] The internal contradictions are obvious to anyone who looks.

Briefly, while poststructuralist theories tend to pave a path to relativism, identity activisms promote doctrinaire demands and truth claims. Critical theories are a grab bag of relativisms and doctrinaire truth claims.[61]

It's really not difficult to expose logical and empirical problems with the offspring of this polyamorous marriage of disparate theories with activism. The only thing that can distract us from the contradictions and empirical inadequacy is its defense couched in the language of care and harm. And, indeed, what holds the disparate elements of this conglomerate together is a matrix of care or at least claims about what's required to provide care and protect from harm.

These claims are delivered in the form of declarative statements about what is or is not essential to avoid harm. Of course, such declarations are debatable even when those making the statements assert that they're not.

I'm going to argue that gender studies, its "studies" brethren, the humanities, other disciplines and subfields, and whole universities embraced and entrenched left-wing populist authoritarianism, so I'll briefly explain what I mean by adopting this terminology. Throughout, I'll also refer to "illiberalism" in the academy, most of which is correlated with positions and acts that purveyors understand as required to achieve care, equity, inclusion, belonging, or social justice. My use of this term should be regarded as an alternative way to refer to populist left-wing authoritarianism, which is a mouthful.

Populism + Authoritarianism

As critics have pointed out, left-wing "illiberalism did not come out of nowhere: it was born on elite college campuses and has trickled down to nearly every university."[62] The illiberal moment in higher ed is often dated as having begun between 2011 and 2014.[63] But there's a caveat: If you're in a field that helped to produce these ideas and practices, you will have gotten in on the ground floor well before 2011.

I begin with populism. Among recent scholars of populism, Jan-Werner Müller has made an argument of the sort that attracts disapprobation from progressive academics for not distinguishing between bad *right*-wing populism and good *left*-wing populism, also known as democracy. I don't agree with this perspective, and I think the clarity of Müller's analysis of populism vitiates these critiques.

Müller lays out a parsimonious set of features characteristic of the populisms that threaten democracy and human rights in many parts of the world, including the United States. In Müller's analysis, populism: insists "that a part of the people *is* the people"; moralizes politics and political conflict in a way that discredits and demonizes opponents and compromise with those opponents; and treats political opponents as "enemies of the people."[64]

Left- and right-wing versions of populism exhibit the same features because populism isn't an ideology with consistent tenets but, rather, a "political logic"; "a way of formulating demands, rather than a set of demands."[65] The political theorist Margaret Canovan argues that populism emerges from "tensions" within democracy, including between "pragmatic" (liberal, constitutional, rules-based, minority-protecting) governance and "redemptive" (people-powered, "action-based," even "revivalist") politics.[66] Redemptive political impulses can arise from either end of the political continuum.

The populist playbook gives us Donald Trump telling his followers that he's their proxy and tribune. That he stands between the enemies they share and those who believe in him, and that the blows he absorbs he takes in their stead. Because, at least as Trump tells it, his enemies really want to harm real Americans who can't defend themselves.

My colleagues' version goes something like this: when the racists, bigots, phobes, and tools of fascism and neoliberalism disagree with and criticize us, they are really harming you, our beloved students. When you hear these dangerous words, speak up; we'll step between you and them.

The authoritarian move that complements this populist message is similar: we'll use the tools at our disposal to silence and destroy those who want to harm you. Which brings us to authoritarianism.

The modern study of authoritarianism was born during the rise and consolidation of Nazism in Europe. *The Authoritarian Personality* examined social factors responsible for the formation of an "authoritarian personality" predisposed toward antisemitism and fascism.[67] Scholars have criticized the studies' methods, its roots in psychoanalysis and Marxist theory, and the F-Scale derived from the research and intended to measure dispositions toward authoritarianism.[68]

A major innovation in the field is the Right-Wing Authoritarianism (RWA) scale, created by the psychologist Bob Altemeyer.[69] On the strength of decades of research, Altemeyer summarized his findings and the political consequences of authoritarianism for a more general audience in *The Authoritarians* and, with John Dean, in *Authoritarian Nightmare: Trump and his Followers*.[70]

Unlike right- and left-wing versions of populism, right- and left-wing versions of authoritarianism manifest quite differently. Twenty years ago, Altemeyer held that left-wing authoritarianism was rare in the United States. On this score, his analysis has been overtaken by events. There is a left-wing authoritarian movement in the United States, and its characteristics are the inverse of right-wing authoritarianism.

The characteristics of left-wing authoritarianism described by psychologist Thomas H. Costello and his colleagues bear an uncomfortable similarity to what we do and how we do it in gender studies and the progressive academy. Costello and his colleagues

> predicted that individuals high in LWA are generally dogmatic, hostile toward the present hierarchy, prejudiced and punitive toward perceived enemies, disposed toward moral absolutism, and tolerant of political violence. Our results point to the fruitfulness of a tripartite conceptualization of LWA comprising three correlated dimensions—*antihierarchical aggression, top-down censorship, and anticonventionalism.*[71]

These three dimensions of left-wing authoritarianism both contrast and overlap neatly with the three key dimensions of right-wing authoritarianism Altemeyer identifies: "1) a high degree of submission to the established, legitimate authorities in their society; 2) high levels of aggression in the name of their authorities; and 3) a high level of conventionalism."[72]

Just to recap before we move on, while right-wing authoritarians are very attached to authorities (the dear leader), the psychologist Luke Conway points out that left-wing authoritarianism functions through demands for submission to illiberal beliefs and an illiberal agenda, not particular leaders.[73] While right-wing authoritarianism insists on conventionality, left-wing authoritarians want to level (or reverse) hierarchies and hold conventionality in contempt. Both right- and left-wing authoritarians are more likely than non-authoritarians to use or condone aggression to get what they want.

If left-wing populism isn't all good, and authoritarianism can emerge from the political left as well as the right, those of us who care about the future of higher ed should take illiberalism within universities more seriously than we are. That is, we shouldn't count on public advocacy and litigation from free speech advocacy organizations, and right-wing attacks to "right" the ship of intellectual inquiry.

On the political right as well as the left, support for authoritarianism and political violence has risen in the United States.[74] Academics may be relieved about the not unexpected news that support for both is higher on the political right than it is on the political left. But that's cold comfort for those committed to both higher ed and democracy.

To preemptively address a question I've been asked, I care very much about the dangers of right-wing authoritarianism. I just don't believe that intensifying right-wing illiberalism in our politics is a sufficient justification for hiding criticisms of illiberalism in the academy under a bushel.[75]

Indeed, the fact that partisans and many elites of one of two major political parties in the United States cheerfully embrace a personality-disordered right-wing authoritarian as their permanent leader doesn't absolve the academic left of its various coercions. I believe it's valuable and necessary to point out injustices and illiberalisms wherever we find them. In this, I agree with the journalist Cathy Young, who argues that "resisting illiberalism in all its forms, including the 'progressive' ones, is all the more important at this moment when the free world is uniting in defense of its values against the authoritarian tide."[76]

Put another way, no matter what happens on the political right, universities shouldn't get a free pass to enshrine an official belief system and harass those who disapprove. Having long cited the political right as justification for their own demands for compliance, many of my colleagues forcefully argue to the contrary.

I find myself caught between illiberalisms of the left and right. Like many others, I believe without reservation that the right-wing variant is a greater threat to Americans and to the citizens of many other countries in the twenty-first century. I found a pithy way to express the dilemma in a tweet from Tom W. Ferguson: "Coming to grips with [the] fact that, at 79, I will spend the rest of my life having to align with Insufferables to beat back Deplorables." Reflecting on Ferguson's plight, the political commentator Charlie Sykes dubs those in this predicament, which includes many Never-Trump conservatives like him, "The Inconsolables."[77]

We'll examine particular aspects of left-progressive academic illiberalism in the chapters to come, but I suspect that a claim of progressive support for violence might be a sticking point. If so, let's address that now.

Left-Wing Authoritarianism and Violence

Do campus progressives condone violence? On October 7, 2023, Hamas fighters based in Gaza invaded Israel and murdered approximately 1,200 Israeli citizens, most civilians. The Hamas attack provided something of a natural experiment to help answer this question about academic progressivism and attitudes toward violence. Recall that, before October 7, especially on the political left, pleas and anecdotes by critics of academic illiberalism were often dismissed as hyperbole. Or they were explained away as the tantrums of college students who would inevitably grow into more mature forms of thought. It has ever been thus, we were told.

Before October 7, I would have pointed to the academic progressive insistence that a wide range of viewpoints and arguments on a host of issues constitute violence against abject, oppressed, vulnerable groups. The predictable result is that the most easily triggered or offended students defined the boundaries of expression, inside the classroom and out. These students and the faculty who inform and succor them exercised a discomfort veto under the pretext that words are violence.

I would have pointed to the fact that if progressives believe what they say they believe, their own verbal denunciations of foes and generous suggestions for punishment of speech and disagreement must also constitute violence. Such an approach has the virtue of taking left-wing illiberal claims seriously and applying them in an even-handed way even if progressives prefer not to.

Returning to Dawkins' concern about being able to debate in the absence of consensual meaning, one of his examples is "violence." Dawkins cites the Oxford Dictionary definition of violence to underscore the difference between his own sense of its meaning and the redefinition of " 'violence' to include the non-physical." He uses the following example: "If someone calls you 'she' when you prefer 'they,' I might see it as a mild discourtesy. But if you see it as a 'violent' threat to your very existence, then our interpretations of 'incitement to violence'—and hence of freedom of speech—are going to diverge sharply."[78]

After October 7, critics and skeptics of the academy had more to work with. I assume there's no need to rehearse the details of left-wing joy that broke out on social media and campuses after the attacks. Lest we forget, celebrations on campuses and in progressive enclaves across the United States included paeans to "our martyrs," and stupefying Hamas-inspired parades of "queers for Palestine." Images of hang-gliding fighters "posted by everyone from Black Lives Matter/Chicago to neo-Nazi groups, . . . g[ave] intersectionality a whole new meaning."[79]

Later, expert spin masters declared that no Israeli girls or women were raped or sexually tortured and that the operation was actually a false flag.[80] These claims were duly repeated by followers with an interest in exculpating those responsible for the attacks. Thus, the completion of a common extremist sequence of arguments was achieved: it didn't happen. And if it did, it was either well deserved or perpetrated by the oppressors to frame the oppressed. Such arguments have utility because speakers don't need to choose among them; they can use whichever claim suits them at a particular moment.

Among critics of academia, responses ranged from horror to vindication. Aghast at the spectacle that unfolded on American university campuses, many commentators pointed out the disorienting contradiction between the demand for emotional safety within universities and the ebullience with which some faculty and students regarded the torture, murder, and kidnapping committed by Hamas fighters against civilians.

There was, for example, the philosopher Christopher Freiman's hot take: "Campuses that routinely cancel talks by conservative speakers in the interest of creating a safe space for everyone are apparently very permissive about campus speech that amounts to endorsement of the murder of Jewish civilians."[81] In *The Atlantic*, the journalist Michael Powell concluded that "the notion that Indigenous violence is inevitable, even liberatory, has gained chilling traction on the American left,"[82] and the journalist Conor Friedersdorf entitled his analysis of the campus response to Hamas violence, "Students for Pogroms in Israel."[83]

The former Republican Senator Ben Sasse, then president of the University of Florida, was perceptive on the question of speech as violence when he pointed out that while, for campus progressives, both "an oppressor's speech" and "an oppressor's silence" are violence, "for the oppressed, even violence is just speech."[84] Critics had been trying to warn about threats to ideas and speech in American higher ed for some time. But—perhaps persuaded by progressives' depiction of their critics as fascist sock puppets—many hadn't listened.

What You Get

In recent years, scholars who hail from different intellectual traditions have taken a crack at constructing "stories of continuity between a contemporary left-wing movement and a past cadre of supposedly corrupting left-wing thinkers."[85] These origins include, but aren't limited to, the radical intellectual crucible of the sixties (in which the Frankfurt School critical theorist Herbert Marcuse looms large),[86] an obsession with difference and diversity,[87] intersectionality,[88] political correctness,[89] hostility to science,[90] civil rights law,[91] postmodernism/poststructuralism,[92] antiracism/critical race theory,[93] and even nationalism.[94] Many accounts, including Helen Pluckrose and James Lindsay's *Cynical Theories*, identify and trace multiple precursors.[95]

In addition to intellectual lineages, investigators have suggested that social, cultural, and economic factors bear some responsibility for helping to produce our illiberal form of progressivism. Factors cited include: the dramatic expansion of higher ed during the era of anti-Vietnam and identity activisms; the shift from a manufacturing to an information society; changes in child rearing practices; the proliferation of cell phones; the internet and social media; the decline of trust in institutions; the Great Recession; economic inequality and declining economic mobility; rising right-wing authoritarianism and democratic backsliding; changing national demographics; increased (especially affective) polarization;

police violence against black boys and men and/or the Black Lives Matter movement; and climate change/disasters and efforts to mitigate climate change.

I'm drawn to this kind of project of intellectual history, which could keep large numbers of scholars busy and out of trouble for decades. A hazard for intellectual genealogies is that they can provide too neat a conceptualization of academic progressive illiberalism. The reality, which many critics of the academy understand, is that there are multiple sources of this ideology, some of which are at odds with each other.

I'd like to think that if we're setting our sights on fundamentally contradictory ideas, we'll figure that out and correct ourselves. But there's no reason to think that academic progressivism is self-correcting. For one thing, many scholars who have embraced illiberalism aren't interested in making an effort to falsify the tenets of their belief system. Or even to acknowledge that what they share is a belief system.

But, in part because of its anarchic sourcing and in part because many academic progressives hold that logic and empiricism are synonymous with patriarchal, colonizing white supremacy, the ideology contains internal contradictions. I suspect that punitive demands for obedience arise, at least in part, from this very reality. Protecting oppressed groups that are threatened by enemies may require "heroic striving for 'evidence' to prove that the unbelievable is the only thing that can be believed."[96]

Hence, instead of origins and theoretical lineages, in this book I focus on outcomes, consequences, and everyday life in the most social justice-oriented recesses of US higher ed. In these spaces, shared belief has been both assumed and aggressively policed. And "value minorities" have been identified for repercussions.[97] But so have those who treated diverse viewpoints with respect. As you will see, I regard illiberal academic progressivism primarily as a social movement rather than a philosophy.

Like other social movements, academic progressivism came, implicitly or explicitly, to require those under its purview to substitute the beliefs of the group for their own judgment.

As critics have demonstrated, my progressive colleagues analyze social, economic, and political issues through particular lenses of power and identity. It would be a mistake to assume that these lenses are merely *available* for those who wish to use them. Instead, academic progressives believe that scholars and teachers should be barred from investigating alternatives to progressive orthodoxies out of respect for students' identities, compelling allegiance using the specter of harm.

Thus, in a world that some academic progressives cast as constituted of relations, networks, registers, nodes, discourses, and narratives of power, only they possess truth. And because the world of power and oppression is so hazardous for those designated oppressed, they believe that only those cognizant of, and willing to attest to, the truth should be allowed to speak. Really—it's as simple as this.

This means that the very scholars who have labored most to condemn totalizing theories and binary accounts of every issue are some of the most binary, totalizing, and moralizing thinkers I've ever encountered. And I spent my suggestible early years, first as a child Catholic and, later, as a teenaged Southern Baptist! Rejecting "truth"—and ironizing it in quotation marks—they believe that the views they propagate constitute truth.

Complications that dissenters are enjoined not to investigate inevitably arise.

In Chapter 1, "Mea Culpa," I relate relevant aspects of my background and acknowledge my complicity in the project that became gender studies. Mind you, it's not that I was important or that my renunciation signals a moment of reckoning. As we know from watching the—first, slow, and then shockingly quick—debasement and authoritarianification of the conservative movement and Republican Party in the United States, every such movement needs its leaders and ideologues. These leaders and ideologues set the party line and define boundaries of what's acceptable and what's required.

In addition to leaders, movements require loyal followers. As we know from studying today's political right, they don't have to be a majority to damage institutions and frighten would-be nonconformists.

Also in this chapter, I remind readers about the history of the founding and institutionalizing of women's studies in American universities. I follow with an initial pass at some obvious ways in which the ideology I criticize mimics its sworn enemies. Far from being a complete critique, this section is just a preview of what's to come. And I return to early criticisms of women's studies to assess how they've held up approximately thirty years on.

To structure Chapters 2 through 4, I use Müller's model of populism. In reading these chapters, bear in mind my contention that we can fruitfully interpret what's become of the progressive academy as what transpires when left-wing authoritarians are behind the higher ed steering wheel and ordinary identity progressives fill the car.

In Chapter 2, "The People," I look more closely at "the people" of the gender studies project that began to displace women's studies in the nineties. There's nothing intrinsically right or wrong about, as we women's/gender studies scholars have been wont to say, "centering" particular groups in our politics and scholarship. You do you, and all that.

But interrogating this centering is also completely legitimate, including questioning premises, evidence, conclusions, and intellectual lineages. Suppressing the freedom of scholars and students to question progressive scholarship and pedagogy is a problem. Indeed, it's one of the problems that's brought us to this fraught point in the history of higher ed.

To understand how gender studies and other academic progressives have organized universities to serve the people and ideology at the center of their project, it's necessary to examine controversial Diversity, Equity, and Inclusion (DEI) practices. Information about these practices that universities would have preferred to conceal has been exposed in public records requests. Also revealing are practices of recent years that fit under the heading of "inclusive pedagogy."

Chapter 3, "Moralizing Politics," sets the stage for the "top-down censorship" that enabled progressives to institutionalize and police the moralizing of politics. The first task of moralizing politics is implicitly denying that conversations we're all having about contentious issues are *political* conversations. For this point, I'll turn to the Christian right, another socio-political movement with a habit of denying that its positions in contentious debates are political.

As many scholars and writers have pointed out, for decades care and its violation, harm, have been central to left politics and feminist thought. Thus, I provide a very quick overview of the centrality of care and harm to women's and gender studies. I then suggest that we don't have to wonder what happens when care goes bad; the answer is right in front of us.

Illiberal academic progressives do what Christian conservatives have long done with regard to the concept of harm: stretch the boundaries of what they understand as causing and constituting "actual harm" that must then be interdicted. John Stuart Mill foresaw this likelihood and is impossible to dispense with as a thinker.

Chapter 4, "Enemies of the People," is the point in my story when academic progressivism turns decisively against academic freedom. Progressives in gender studies and in other precincts of the university are free to identify and center the people they believe matter, moralize political choices, and criticize ideas of which they disapprove.

I'd prefer that they perform these tasks honestly—for example, not lazily attribute all disagreement to bigotry and incipient fascism. And I'd prefer that universities offer a range of thinking about all contentious issues, which we too often haven't done by design. Even so, centering, moralizing, and attributing are all protected by principles of academic freedom.

Engaging in retribution against those deemed to be enemies of the people isn't. Still, in recent years, punishment, threats of punishment, and strategies for avoiding punishment for ideological transgressions became mundane features of life in the academy. So much so that prominent scholars one might think could weather student boycotts and the accusations of peers have confessed that they trim their teaching and public comments to avoid blowback. A high percentage of their peers have expressed the same anxiety.[98]

In this chapter, I explore the phenomenon of liberals and liberalism as enemies of academic progressives, highlight the concerns of critics who are expatriates from authoritarian or totalitarian states, explain the roots of my pessimism about universities being able to reorient themselves away from academic illiberalism, and offer a modest suggestion to my progressive colleagues for achieving their political goals without destroying the academy in the process.

Finally, in Chapter 5, "Critical Thinking," I explore the state of critical thinking pedagogy through the stark difference between higher ed traditionalism and academic progressivism. Both "sides" in this debate value critical thinking; they just mean completely different things by it. Understanding this difference can help us make sense of fractious arguments in which both sides claim the high ground of the critical.

Except for the literary scholar Daphne Patai, most critics of the belief system and methods of gender studies have been academics who are outside gender studies and other identity "studies" fields looking in. By contrast with the many critics who have taken on the illiberal progressive academy, my criticisms don't just come from inside the house. They come from inside one of the rooms in which these politics and practices were refined.

In many disciplines, the goal has been to make sure that students never hear, much less seriously consider, alternative explanations or analyses of the issues academic progressives consider lie within their domain. Effectively, this means all issues upon which there's disagreement. Alternative, heterodox, or offensive ideas must be smothered in their cradle—kept from being expressed by implicit or explicit threats of punishment.

If this weren't the goal, gender and other "studies," humanities departments, and a range of other spaces across the university would be able to tolerate the odd heretic in their midst. But as became abundantly clear, they could not and mostly would not. Tabia Lee discovered this reality when she was fired as the director of Diversity, Equity, and Inclusion at De Anza Community College in Cupertino, California. Accused of " 'white speaking,' 'whitesplaining' and supporting white supremacy," among her missteps was not referring to people of Latin American descent as "Latinx."[99] With the professor of rhetoric Erec Smith and others, Lee went on to found Free Black Thought.

Progressives in academia don't want to tolerate the heretic even if she's perfectly happy for all colleagues to perform work in their own way and makes no effort whatever to interfere with any, or all, of her colleagues. Her mere possession of a title, an office, or a teaching assignment carries the danger that at any moment she might raise a question or convey some piece of knowledge inconsistent with the view of the faculty-as-a-whole.

Across many disciplines, faculty have been selecting for progressive beliefs for some time, and this process of selection has reinforced the single-mindedness of the professoriate. My colleagues invite people like me—cranks, rebels, defectors, and misfit toys—to acknowledge the obvious: that we are a minority destined to be swept away by death, retirement, or public disapprobation.

It appears that those of us who kept hanging around in progressive disciplines, leftovers from an earlier time in which less specific criteria for selection prevailed, are a "transitional generation." That's how Aunt Lydia describes the first batch of women shipped to the re-educational Red Center in Margaret Atwood's dystopian novel, *The Handmaid's Tale.* Aunt Lydia concedes that life is hard for this initial group of Gileadean hostages because they've known freedom but promises that "for the ones who come after, it'll be easier."[100]

Let's not allow being pressured to abide by an illiberal creed to get easier. When I was young, I rejected the moralizing dictates of God, my family, and prevailing community standards. Unbeknownst to me, those years were, as my father often noted of hardship, "good training" for the twilight of my career as an academic. Not all students and citizens want better than what we've given them, but all deserve better.

I'll say more about students I've taught later, but I want to end this chapter with a story: A few years ago, a gender studies major who was preparing to graduate came to see me one afternoon for office hours. I don't recall the reason for her visit. A shy international student, she looked down into her lap for much of our conversation. But toward the end of our meeting, she suddenly looked up, held my gaze, and said, "I regret every day I choose this major." What could I say? I'll tell you what I told her, with real sadness for not being able to change the past: I'm sorry.

1 Mea Culpa

What's My Story?

In 2022, I was invited to contribute a chapter to an anthology on the January 6, 2021 assault on the Capitol in Washington, DC. Directed to consider the question, "what should we do to prevent another January 6?," I wrote something I knew the editors were unlikely to welcome: suggestions for what *we*—lefties, academic and otherwise—might do to try to lower the temperature of American political discourse. Not until I received positive feedback on my chapter from the two reviewers solicited by Oxford University Press did I conclude the chapter wouldn't be cut from the volume.[1]

One reviewer identified a factor that contributes to the ideological gulf between academia and America: if most academics hail from well-educated and economically comfortable families, we truly may not understand our fellow citizens. This referee suggested that at some point in the future, I might want to address how this disjunction contributes to the polarization between right and left that's a defining feature of US politics. That reviewer was singing my song, and I lightly revised the chapter to integrate the theme.

Let me start with some background. We olds recall that in 1988, Senator Joe Biden mounted a Democratic primary campaign for President. On the stump, he told audiences that he'd come from a long line of coal miners and that he was the first member of his family to attend college. The problem was that it wasn't *his* story. Inexplicably, Biden had borrowed the bio from British Labour leader Neil Kinnock. When the truth came to light, the Senator terminated his campaign.

I was in grad school at the time, and I joked that if this narrative was a winning campaign bio, I should run for president. Like Kinnock, I come from coal miners and, when I went to college in 1976, I was the first person in my family to do so.

My grandparents received some primary education. My paternal grandfather was born in Poland and came to the United States as a toddler; my grandmother's family emigrated from Hungary a few years before she was born. My father grew up in a small coal mining town in Southwestern Pennsylvania. To escape the mines and help support his family, he dropped out of high school to join the Army and completed his GED as a soldier.

My mother grew up not far away, in a holler in northern West Virginia where her ancestors on one side had lived since the eighteenth century. My maternal grandmother died in childbirth with her sixth child when my mom was nine years old. Having completed the eighth grade in a one-room school, my mom moved to the nearby big city of Morgantown and, as a teenager, worked in a clothing factory to help support her family. In the eighties, as she neared fifty, she received her GED and became a licensed practical nurse.

When I was growing up in my working-class family, few professional role models were close at hand. In elementary school, I wanted to be either an archeologist, a geologist, or a paleontologist. In other words, I wanted to dig things out of the ground. To this day, I keep rockhounding tools and a metal detector in my car, and my idea of the best possible day is one spent scurrying down to the foreshore of the River Thames to mudlark as the high tide recedes.

I spent much of my childhood and adolescence reading from lists of canonic literature—my awkward path to forms of culture that were outside my experience. While I had strong interests in literature and history, by adolescence my main avocation was singing: in church, in the high school choir, and in vocal competitions. It is indeed possible to letter in choir, even in the football state of Texas.

I went off to college in the bicentennial year. In those days, it wasn't common for universities to create programs to support "first gen" students. Academic naif that I was, it never occurred to me that I might benefit from some special handling. Instead, I learned everything I know about higher education on the street. I began college as a music major and ended up in history.

Regardless of my major, by then I assumed I'd make my living as a teacher. After all, in my sixties childhood and seventies adolescence, I saw women being moms, retail workers, nurses, and teachers. During high school, at a time when women were being mainstreamed in the US Army, I received buckets of literature encouraging me to enroll in ROTC for officer training.

Because I'd been a military dependent, the Army knew everything there was to know about me except what I was just figuring out: that I was a lesbian. I didn't consider a career in the military.

A scrapbook I created during my first year of college reminds me that, at least in some respects, I haven't changed much. I matriculated in the aftermath of what came to be called, variously, the Kanawha County, West Virginia "textbook controversy" and "textbook war." A dispute over school textbooks conservatives called blasphemous and anti-American began locally but eventually was nationalized as Charleston became a site of what would come to be dubbed the "culture war."[2] There's a case to be made that the controversy was the first major skirmish in that war.

In my censorship scrapbook, I collected articles about the Kanawha County controversy as well as other efforts to prevent students, especially high school students, from gaining access to books and subjects. Weighing the likelihood that I'd wind up on the bad end of such a controversy, I determined that I wasn't cut out for K–12 teaching.

My interest in political theory was sparked by two classes I took as an undergrad: one in political science and one in philosophy. I had no interest in politics, *per se*. Political theory offered me the opportunity to immerse myself in abstract theorizing that was in part a refuge from the forms of labor I associated with life in the working class. I didn't really understand what it meant to get a PhD or become an academic, but I couldn't have been more grateful to get paid to read, write, and teach.

I became involved in women's studies in grad school. I took two of the few courses then offered, including the university's first graduate seminar in women's studies. I sneaked away from the political science department to serve as a teaching assistant in women's studies courses without pay or credit and joined the fledgling network that connected grad students across the university who shared an interest in women's studies.

Enthusiastic to contribute to the progressive refashioning of political science, as a grad student, I designed and instructed the first workshops for political science grad student instructors in my department on the significance of race and gender in the classroom.

Against the advice of my advisor, I wrote my dissertation in feminist theory. I didn't hold his effort to persuade me to pursue a more marketable topic against him. Political science students incautious enough to specialize in theory at a mid-grade public university were few and far between, and he wanted me to succeed. I also didn't tell my professors that I spent a not insignificant chunk of my time as a grad student singing in a chorus. I knew that having this knowledge would have obliged them to regard me as someone who was not a serious student.

As it is, I cherish memories of performing with a chorus that took me to many cities in Europe and to the Soviet Union. To this day, I credit the fall of the USSR not to the failure of Soviet communism or to Reagan's deft leadership but to my chorus's cultural diplomacy, to wit: performing Beethoven's *Missa Solemnis* mass—his plea for peace—in Moscow, Dresden (GDR), London, and West Berlin in the summer of 1988 under the direction of Maestro Antal Doráti. Because of the chorus, I also know that practice is a necessary if not a sufficient condition for getting to Carnegie Hall.

In my first job after graduation, I directed a first-year honors program in politics and ethics. In addition, I functioned as an official core faculty member in women's studies even though my non-tenure track position was in political science. I taught women's studies courses in the summer, mentored students, and served on committees. From there, I moved on to a joint position in women's studies and political science, where I continued teaching courses in political ideologies, feminist theory, and the history of political thought.

My final berth was in a department of women's studies that transitioned to women's, gender and sexuality studies. I started out teaching courses that were somewhat related to my training and research. By the end, I was mostly instructing courses in literature. That wasn't because I thought my intellectual mastery extended to the literary arts. It was because teaching about politics had become hazardous. It made sense to minimize my exposure to denunciation.

If I couldn't lead students to examine different perspectives and consider a variety of ways of thinking about how to organize our world, I couldn't teach political theory. I could do my best to convey a love for literature and place fiction and some genres of non-fiction in social and historical context.

Because, as a scholar, I wanted to think and write about issues I cared about, I studied the intellectual history of theories of women's moral development; and lesbian and black feminist thought and politics. For most of my career, I studied the Christian conservative movement's worldview and activism. My research in religion and politics focused on abortion rights, LGBTQ rights in the United States, and the sexual orientation and gender identity (SOGI) foreign policy of the US government.

I've never written critically about women's or gender studies, and I wouldn't be doing it now if not for the effort invested by members of my community to see me punished for my deviations. I've had the great privilege of being able to process questions about the world through study and writing, so here we are.

From Women's to Gender Studies

Advocacy for women's studies programs and curricula at US colleges and universities began in the political context of sixties movements of the political left, including women's, black, Chicano, gay and lesbian, and indigenous rights. For our purposes, I divide the history of women's/gender studies into two phases. I don't mean for this rough taxonomy to be irrefutable—just useful.

The first phase of women's studies began with the inception of the field in the seventies and lasted into the nineties. The second phase encompasses the transition to gender studies.

There are many silences in gender studies where debate could flourish. One of these ellipses is in the history of our own discipline. There have been many histories of women's studies and feminist theory. However, although we occasionally talk about that history, we're usually careful not to do so in terms that might reveal the ways in which many current and future faculty would repudiate the early version of the discipline as faulty and even embarrassing. Perhaps I can help.

Women's Studies

Women's studies didn't come first. It followed the founding of Black/African American studies. The first black studies program was created in 1968 at San Francisco State. Advocacy for and achievement of black studies helped provide a template for other identity "studies" programs and departments to come.

The first women's studies program was also founded in California, at San Diego State in 1970. Activism for a program in women's studies emerged from the political ferment of the era and its numerous movements for rights and liberation, including the women's liberation movement. Feminist students worked with faculty and members of the community to persuade the university to create the program, which became a department in 1975.[3]

Like other identity studies, women's studies was established as both a space for scholarship on issues related to women and as the academic arm of the women's movement. Those of us who became involved in women's studies in the seventies and eighties enlisted in the enterprise with a variety of motives. Some of us believed women's studies would help solve problems that women confronted in the real world. Some saw women's studies as a space in which to develop basic theory that most male scholars weren't interested in. Our politics were all over the place, from the quest to make the United States live up to liberal democratic values to a desire to spark left-wing revolution.

In the early years, women faculty, staff, and students created women's studies classes and programs on their own time and mostly without institutional resources. These women, who advocated for other women, faced down male administrators, and created programs in disused spaces, were tough cookies. The ones I met sometimes terrified me with their sense of righteous outrage and ability to get shit done.

The original women's studies classes, minors, and majors didn't result from careful curricular planning as much as they reflected the availability, research agendas, and teaching interests of women faculty who were willing to instruct a course with content on women, sometimes as an overload. Considering how long it can take for new disciplines to emerge and become institutionalized, women's studies grew relatively quickly, attracting students to individual classes before it was possible for them to minor and major in the field.

Undergrad and grad curricula, majors, minors, certificates, and grad degrees were established piecemeal. Women faculty and administrators coordinated programmatic knowledge and strategy by way of formal and informal networks. Faculty hires began to be made in joint positions and full-time lines.

The process of achieving these milestones was one many radical movements strive mightily to achieve and regard ambivalently. This is a movement's institutionalization, also known as the process of becoming the establishment that radical thinkers and actors define themselves against. There were many important markers of the institutionalization of women's studies. One was the founding of the National Women's Studies Association (NWSA) in 1977. Another, which extended the reach of a virtual women's studies community, was the creation of the international women's studies email list, WMST-L, in 1991.[4]

A third was the establishing over time of many journals, some of which integrated academic research with political organizing and activism. Early journals included *Feminist Studies*, *Frontiers: A Journal of Women's Studies*, the *National Women's Studies Journal* (since 2010, *Feminist Formations*), and *Women's Studies Quarterly*. The most unique of the women's studies periodicals was *off our backs*, founded in 1970 and run until 2008 by a volunteer feminist collective that included academics and non-academics.[5] Today, women's/gender studies journals are published in the United States and abroad. Journal focuses include countries and geographic regions, academic disciplines, particular topics, and target audiences.

It took 20 years after the founding of a women's studies program for the first PhD program in women's studies to get up and running. Emory University admitted its first PhD students in 1990; in 2024, the National Women's Studies Association listed 23 PhD programs in women's/gender/feminist/sexuality studies in the United States but, because of the many forms taken by women's, queer, feminist, and gender studies, this is almost certainly an undercount.[6]

There were some concerns about a women's studies PhD, even among those who were well disposed toward the discipline. In *Cultivating Humanity: A Classical Defense of Reform in Liberal Education*, the philosopher Martha Nussbaum defended the promise of women's studies to fill gaps in humanist education and to help form world citizens. Still, even Nussbaum conceded that it was "imprudent to offer" a women's studies PhD for two reasons: because women's studies doctoral students wouldn't be employable and because such scholars wouldn't achieve "mastery of any single discipline."[7]

When women's and gender studies faculty developed and marketed the women's/gender studies PhD to upper administration and trustees, our pitch took several forms, including that a women's/gender studies PhD would enhance the research profile of the university and serve students clamoring for an opportunity to acquire a doctorate in a hot, cutting-edge field.

Over 20 years ago, my department awarded its first honorary doctorate to Martha Nussbaum. She wouldn't make the cut today.

Employability hasn't been as much of a problem as Nussbaum feared. One key difference between the early period of women's studies and later gender studies is that, before the proliferation of women's/gender/ethnic studies PhD programs, women's studies faculty were trained in traditional disciplines. This was to be expected in the first three decades or so of women's studies; where else would women studies faculty have come from if not existing disciplines?

As women's studies departments inaugurated doctoral programs, they produced PhDs who were now trained in the field instead of having to be socialized and incorporated into it from what some no doubt regarded as politically questionable disciplines. At last, we could produce the kinds of prospective faculty who could be counted on to be ideologically aligned. As women's and gender studies programs, departments, and grad programs expanded and proliferated, their faculty conscientiously solicited, interviewed, and hired these PhDs.

Beginning in the nineties, gender studies programs also benefited from the growth and political homogeneity of other identity studies disciplines. These units provided additional pools from which gender studies faculty could safely—politically speaking—be selected.

Nussbaum's other concern, that women's studies PhDs wouldn't develop mastery in a discipline, expresses a traditional disciplinary perspective that a doctorate requires specialized training in a set of theories and methods employed in a bounded branch of knowledge. In this traditional perspective, disciplines are necessary for *inter*disciplinarity.

The innovation of the progressive academy was to moot disciplinary boundaries, especially in the humanities, by training students in theories that enable scholars to claim authority across the widest possible range of knowledge. When such a system is in place, few questions can arise anywhere, in any field, that these faculty don't know the answer to. The answers are always already there in the theories.

In such a system, what passes for intellectual diversity is that faculty are practicing queer or anti-racist or post-colonial theory in criminology, public health, literature, political theory, law, social work, or some—

any—other discipline. Imagine faculty teaching diverse subjects and yet somehow managing to converge on the same correct answers to all social, political, and economic questions.

From time to time over the years, students in my gender studies department complained that their classes were repetitive. We faculty conjured different fixes for this problem while side-stepping the likely culprit: the intellectual homogeneity we built.

Nussbaum needn't have worried that the gender studies PhD wouldn't be successful. She might have worried instead about its success in chasing out alternative theories, methods, and perspectives. That is, what its success would do to the university.

Even in the first generation, from the inception of women's studies in the seventies into the nineties, women's studies faculty weren't all relying on the same perspectives or pursuing the same agenda. Some were most interested in developing and disseminating cultural, literary, and political thought and praxis on a variety of topics. These included the absence and representation of women in texts of all kinds; war, colonialism and imperialism; discrimination based on sex and non-normative sexuality; and violence, discrimination, and harassment based on race and/or sex.[8]

Other students and faculty were interested in projects of excavation or measurement—discovering and documenting the situation of women in many times and places. One set of these scholars searched history for evidence of women's lives, achievements, obstacles to achievement, and experience. They found foremothers, pioneers, missing women of achievement, the revaluing of women's productive and reproductive work, and accounts of women's lives in every place and time that we could fill in through careful study of often neglected records

Another set searched and analyzed contemporary records for data that would enable them to disaggregate and study women and men in every domain: social, legal, political, and economic. Or they devised and executed methodologies for producing such data for analysis.

We should also account for a third draw that can overlap with other agendas. This is what the political scientist Michael Barkun refers to as "stigmatized knowledge": "knowledge claims that have not been accepted by those institutions we rely upon for truth validation." Most often identified with conspiracy theories, stigmatized knowledge comes in many forms and, as Barkun acknowledges, "only a permeable membrane now separates the fringe from the mainstream."[9]

Stigmatized knowledge—about the sources, faces, and nuances of oppression, for example—was one draw of women's studies. Such secret knowledge provided initiates with a key to unlock what might otherwise remain stubborn, even bewilderingly insoluble, social, political, economic, and interpersonal problems.

Like the knowledge that circulates in movements such as Christian conservatism, such knowledge isn't just intellectually, but also emotionally and spiritually, satisfying. The Hungarian author and journalist Arthur Koestler captures the process of acquiring this knowledge in his account of his conversion to communism:

> The new light seems to pour from all directions across the skull; the whole universe falls into pattern like the stray pieces of a jigsaw puzzle assembled by magic at one stroke. There is now an answer to every question, doubts and conflicts are a matter of the tortured past—a past already remote, when one had lived in dismal ignorance in the tasteless, colorless world of those who *don't know*.[10]

Stigmatized knowledge has always been part of the allure of women's, gender, and other studies. Who doesn't want to peek behind the curtain and understand why things are really the way they are?

A caveat to generalizations about women's and feminist studies is the fact that most women academics who have understood themselves or their work as feminist since the seventies haven't been in women's studies programs or departments. Feminist scholars in women's studies and traditional disciplines investigated women's art, literature, history, health, childbearing/rearing, paid and unpaid labor, psychology, political behavior, religious practices, and sexuality.

They knew what they were doing was likely to be regarded as dispensable in traditional disciplines. Worse, they might lose opportunities for tenure and promotion because they pursued such pedestrian topics.

In this respect, scholars who did research on women had some experiences in common with those who focused on minority or disfavored groups.[11] The first generation of scholars in such research areas took a chance that their work would be rewarded by their peers. Some succeeded, while the careers of others faltered. Many remain unknown or underappreciated for their contributions. Yet, they persisted, and those who came later benefitted from that persistence as topics and fields became academically respectable.

These two agendas—one an explicitly radical political project and the other a project of excavation and measurement—were in tension with each other from the beginning. It's possible to pursue both at the same time. However, the first agenda is politically leftist and—in this period—often originated in Marxism, socialism, or anarchism.

By contrast, unless we preemptively define all objectives of the intellectual arm of the women's movement as "political"—something we did and do quite a lot of—the second agenda could be relatively politically anodyne. Indeed, even feminist theorizing could be politically anodyne. For example, I would have been hard pressed to identify the political significance of my dissertation, which was later published as *The Problem of the Passions: Feminism, Psychoanalysis, and Social Theory*. My project was to examine several prominent feminist accounts of women's moral psychology for what I believed were tendencies in some to delete or downplay women's "disagreeable passions," a concept I borrowed from the philosopher David Hume. I thought there were interesting questions at stake, but this wasn't an incendiary political program that spoke truth to power.

Most people who knew I was using feminist theory in my dissertation assumed I was writing about differences between women and men. But no, I was shining a light on the effort of some feminist theorists to depict women as morally different from, and superior to, men. That is, not saddled with, and motivated by, disagreeable passions.[12] In retrospect, my skepticism toward a view of women as paragons of empathic virtue could have been a sign of problems to come that I ignored in my enthusiasm for a feminist life of the mind.

I found the project of excavation and measurement on which many feminist scholars had embarked exhilarating. Accounts of what women's studies did for those of us who found it in its early period included restoring previously excluded and denigrated lives and experiences to the intellectual record. We also saw ourselves reflected in the intellectual milieu generated by women's studies. I recognize that heady stuff in students' enthusiasm for gender studies today.

In retrospect, I have no doubt that this experience, which validated our identities, helped to mask illiberal tendencies that women's studies' early critics warned about.

Even though women's studies was forged in the political activism of the sixties and seventies, the course of women's studies didn't run smooth. Indeed, in its early period, there were, as the title of a feminist anthology from the early nineties had it, many "feminist nightmares" consisting of "women at odds."[13]

Women's studies constituencies clashed heatedly and repeatedly over sexuality, race, particular social and political issues of the day, and topics located in the weeds of women's studies discourse and politics. Giddy with excitement over all this intellectual ferment, and busy fashioning myself as a feminist scholar, I didn't see signs that were right in front of me. Starting in grad school in the eighties, I was enthusiastic about women's studies. Over time, the scales fell from my eyes. To mix metaphors, there was no going back to laboring in the progressive vineyard.

Illiberal Signs in Women's Studies

The first takedowns of women's studies were published in the nineties, approximately ten to twenty years after the birth of women's studies programs in US universities. The most famous of these were written by Daphne Patai, her collaborator, the philosopher Noretta Koertge, and Christina Hoff Sommers, a philosopher and Senior Fellow at the American Enterprise Institute.

Sommers, the author of several books about women's studies and feminism, was a relatively distant figure to most academic feminists, and she was easy to dismiss as conservative. By contrast, Daphne Patai seemed to enjoy being a vexatious presence among women's studies faculty. Patai was affiliated with women's studies, so she knew the field as an insider. In the nineties, as she researched *Professing Feminism: Cautionary Tales from the Strange World of Women's Studies* (co-authored with Koertge) and *Heterophobia*, Patai attended NWSA meetings and haunted the Women's Studies Listserv with barbed commentaries on women's studies discourse and shenanigans.

Patai and Koertge challenged women's studies and feminist scholars directly, wondering, for example, what arguments could be adduced for the existence of women's studies if the field did "not promote, indeed, d[id] not stand for, open inquiry, critical exploration of multiple perspectives (even threatening ones), and scholarship not tethered to the political passions of the moment."[14]

Women's studies scholars responded to Patai's challenges not with empirical data or rigorous arguments, but with the force of numbers, assertions of abject identity, and what passed in the field as law-like generalizations. I can't pretend I didn't participate in the groupthink of the era because I know that on at least one occasion in the nineties, I trolled Patai on the WMST-L.

Looking back, it's easy to see how the social, political, institutional, and intellectual milieu in which women's studies developed set conditions for the illiberal ideas and practices to follow. Those ideas and practices were there nearly from the beginning. As time passed, we grew them to maturity.

First, by the eighties, many women's studies scholars adopted a popular intellectual strategy for investigating women's lives and identities. This was the philosopher Sandra Harding's suggestion to "start off thought" from the perspective of particular abject groups.[15] By this, Harding and other feminist theorists meant placing marginalized group members, including their narrated experiences, material conditions, and oppressions, at the center of analysis.

The standpoint epistemology associated with Harding and other feminist theorists helped to establish the authority of "lived experience" that's prevailed ever since, even as the feminist literature of that era went out of fashion.

Depending on your perspective, the dictum to "start off thought" has enabled empathy toward and comprehension of disfavored groups or has undercut the possibility of questioning personal testimonies of harm. As the philosopher Patrick J. Casey points out, this conception of "experience" collapses two different definitions: "practical wisdom" that "accumulates over time" and "experience that is living and immediate."[16]

When progressive scholars and teachers advanced the authority of lived experience, they didn't mean experience as wisdom. They asserted and demanded acquiescence to the interpretations of members of oppressed groups about their subjective and intersubjective lives.

Complicating the authority of lived experience is prodigious evidence from psychology that, in significant respects, we don't have privileged insight into our own minds, actions, motivations, choices, and perceptions. Adding insult to our delusions of perspicacity, we often misunderstand others' minds, actions, motivations, choices, and perceptions as well. But consult women's studies back in the day or gender studies today, and you'll be informed that members of oppressed groups do have unique access to this information, about themselves and others.

A second dimension of our thought and practice was, like the first, also related to identity. This one was, broadly, about the authority held by people of marginalized or historically underrepresented identity groups. So, for example, who has standing to choose texts, design assignments, deliver lectures (if one still does that sort of thing), lead discussions, and assign grades? Who has standing to write about particular disfavored groups or issues that some may connect with those groups? There were even debates over who can perform research and write *with* members of marginalized groups.[17]

If we strove for political consistency, purity, and egalitarianism, the answer was usually that allies in the movement should stand down, listening to and following the lead of students, colleagues, and activists from what the psychologist Jonathan Haidt calls "sacralized victim groups."[18] Debates such as these—mostly contained among small groups of like-minded colleagues—set the stage for later disputes over inclusive instruction, allyship, and cultural appropriation.

Third, from its inception, women's studies had an ambivalent—at times even an adversarial—relationship with science and the scientific method. Some women's studies pioneers were trained in the natural and social sciences. There were, and are, feminist scientists, of course. But women's studies was dominated by qualitative scholars whose perspective on scientific method ranged from skepticism to outright defiance.

To share a sense of what I mean, I've heard colleagues declare that it isn't appropriate to use or support the use of scientific method to test or redescribe indigenous knowledge because indigenous knowledge has its own standards for verification. Science, many argue, is central to colonialism and capitalism and is a kind of settler euro-heteropatriarchal system. It's no surprise, then, that women's and gender studies faculty have sometimes remonstrated with female STEM students about their choice to study science instead of gender studies.

Fourth, unanimity and consensus were overvalued and socially enforced in a variety of ways. As in other social movements, "disagreement [wa]s viewed as betrayal."[19] But the upside is the reward of emotional and intellectual concord: the high of individual boundaries dissolving into the group. Early adopters of women's studies may well remember interminable meetings, the goal of which was to reach a nirvana of consensus.

Aldous Huxley noted that "there is intoxication to be found in a crowd. For it is good to be one of many, all doing the same thing."[20] We weren't always of one mind, but we were intoxicated a lot of the time.

What we didn't value enough was intellectual diversity, also known as intellectual pluralism. If there's one thing I've come to appreciate more over the course of my career, it's this kind of diversity. As the university has become more homogeneously progressive, we've lost the input of people we believe—or know, just *know*—are wrong. In too many spaces, we've even lost the capacity to hear their concerns, perspectives, and arguments as others might render them in good faith.

I agree with Eboo Patel, the founder of Interfaith America, that

> a university is about intellectual pluralism—the exploration of the diversity of reality through a variety of methods, the testing of different explanatory frameworks, the consideration of a range of moral claims. It is also about civic pluralism: bringing together people of diverse identities and divergent ideologies in considerate conversation.

Patel contrasts commitments to "some version of intellectual and civic pluralism" on the part of university presidents and their immediate senior administrators with "student-facing staff seek[ing] to inculcate a single, ideologically narrow version of social justice."[21]

The assumption in women's studies that we were insurgents battling dominant—also known as wrong—ideas never changed, even when universities adopted our perspectives.

Fifth, from the beginning, women's studies placed trauma at the heart of the field. Oppressed by sexism, racism, homophobia, labor exploitation, and violence, including sexual assault, we understood ourselves to suffer from trauma. Trauma psychology was a prolific source of meaning and perspective, even for women's studies scholars whose research didn't focus on the topic.

Understanding women as trauma victims became an organizing principle of the field. Before demands for "safe spaces" and "trigger warnings" were incorporated into the repertoire of inclusive academics, we had the therapeutic prescriptions produced by trauma theorists and clinicians. This emphasis on trauma is now baked into progressive disciplines, regardless of the actual experiences of students. Many aspects of inclusive pedagogy, including microaggressions, safe spaces, and trigger warnings, spring directly from the conviction that students are traumatized in ways that require mothering, monitoring and redress.

Sometimes we can look back on a particular event as a historical turning point, even if it didn't cause what followed. For the contemporary LGBTQ movement in the United States, the Stonewall riot in the summer of 1969 in New York City is such an event. In her recounting of the moment in 1969 when the gay liberation movement ignited in New York City, the memoirist and former English professor Karla Jay writes that "Stonewall was a catalyst or a flashpoint, and its historical significance rests on incidental factors, such as time and place .... The tenor of the country was such that it was impossible for a radical gay and lesbian movement not to emerge at that pivotal moment in time."[22]

For women's studies, a likely suspect event that has been cited as such a point is the publication of the philosopher Judith Butler's *Gender Trouble*. The book became the sign—not cause—of the "linguistic turn" and profound shifts in how gender studies would reconceptualize sex, gender, race, and other identity categories that would form the basis of the discipline in the twenty-first century.

For some time after 2000, we continued to instruct students in feminist theories, but the handwriting was on the wall. The varieties of feminist thought that had enabled some fertile debates among scholars were being superseded by a set of theories and convictions that came to be defined as the appropriate content of academic women's and gender studies.

When our histories are written, scholars may consider other factors that helped to produce the conditions for the transformation of women's studies into gender studies. I'm not a historian, but I'd place two factors at the top of my list.

First, although all the problems that motivated the formation of women's studies weren't solved, the social, economic, and political situation of women improved between the early seventies and the nineties. If we conceptualize women's/gender studies as a social movement seeking to institutionalize itself and expand its influence rather than as primarily an intellectual project, it's inevitable that the locus of the movement would shift to new forms, conceptualizations, and survivors of oppression.

Second, political belief systems were thrown into chaos by the unexpected implosion of the Soviet Union and its satellite states. When Francis Fukuyama declared that the end of history was liberal democracy, there were many skeptics and dissenters, including among academic feminists.[23] Throughout much of the twentieth century, many leftist intellectuals were seduced by the idea of communism, though many eventually rebelled at its reality. Now that the curtain finally appeared to fall on the promise of stateless liberation and egalitarianism, prominent feminist and radical scholars needed a new identity.

Fortunately, the marketplace provided alternatives, including those that could satisfy an appetite for theories that valorized playfulness, indeterminacy, and deadly serious moralizing. If you think: "Wait, aren't playfulness/indeterminacy and deadly serious moralizing incompatible with each other?" you may not be a gender studies professor.

Far removed from plain language and material realities, "increasingly sophisticated" "high theory" won the day over other contenders.[24]

Gender Studies

Although some of us didn't realize it at the time, the next phase of the women's studies project was already underway by the late eighties. As in other cases when social, political, and institutional changes occur, the process by which the gender studies daughter killed the women's studies mother to take her place is complicated and best understood in retrospect.[25]

By the early nineties, the "canon wars" that had been waged in English departments across the country were over. The theorists, many of whom were feminists who wanted to, in a common slogan, "fire that canon," had won. The movement to fire the canon was prosecuted successfully enough that it's a commonplace assumption among students in gender studies today that they won't be subjected to the thinking of dead or living white men. Exceptions, cases of those like Michel Foucault and Jacques Lacan, who are widely understood as progenitors of world-historically correct forms of analysis, prove the rule.

So much for Aristotle, Locke, Machiavelli, Thomas More, Mill, Freud, Hannah Arendt, and a host of other dominant cishet white men (and a few women) in political theory, history, literature, sociology, music, and other traditional disciplines. As well as cis-sometimes-het non-white men.

The theorists didn't accomplish this reversal alone; as the literary scholar Tyler Austin Harper argues, the "identitarian drift" of the humanities is best understood as a material "survival strategy."[26] But progressive scholars pushing hard in the same direction to rid themselves of a masculinist canon didn't hurt. There's an irony here: even as interest in the humanities among students declined, and humanities disciplines commanded less respect in universities, the progressive worldview born in these disciplines spread throughout universities.

During this time, other changes had either occurred or were in the process of occurring. Gender studies inherited institutionalization that included tenure lines, programs, departments, degrees, curricula, organizations, platforms, media, name recognition, and some degree of intellectual respectability from its predecessor. Progressive faculty were hired and students were trained to place particular theories, praxis derived from those theories, and precepts derived from identity-based political activism at the center of their political and intellectual projects.

Along the way, what had been a niche project that most scholars in the sciences, social sciences, and professional schools could ignore if they chose to, became a set of demands and commandments that were impossible to ignore. Or, as the author Michael Lind puts it, "university officials [who] hoped that far-left ideologues would leave the rest of the university alone if they were given their own sandboxes to play in" were "proven wrong."[27]

Some people on the political left ask what the difference is between the "political correctness" of higher ed in the seventies and the situation that came to prevail in recent years. The question is usually more of a challenge; underlying it is the assumption that the only difference is a contemporary moral panic fed by bigots and cynical right-wingers.

But the political scientist Steve Sanders furnishes another answer to this common challenge when he notes that although " 'political correctness" in academe is "nothing new," "what is new is that colleges are now officially pledging allegiance to particular orthodoxies and political projects."[28] For that transformation to occur, progressives either had to attain positions from which they could enact progressive views or scare the daylights out of administrators. They did both.

First, by the 2000s, faculty whose views were aligned with identity progressivism were moving into administrative positions above program director and department chair. At the same time, administrative bureaucracies ballooned with like-minded personnel.[29] Large numbers of the new generation of administrators who were in a position to reorient university policies and practices were women with seniority and institutional experience.

By "experience" here, I mean knowledge of how to use bureaucratic levers to accomplish goals, how to network with similarly-situated allies, and how to present new policies and practices as blandly and disingenuously as possible in public forums.

Second, we've had the scaring part down for some time now. Women's studies was occasionally able to strike the fear of god into administrators and legislators by leveraging the charge that hostility to women's studies was hostility to women. Whenever women's studies and its feminist and gender studies progeny are threatened with retrenchment, faculty and students assert that the field is essential to attract and serve women students.

At some point, we began to shore up this defense by swearing that social justice for all disfavored or underrepresented groups can only be achieved through gender studies' scrupulous scholarship and instruction. According to this frame, gender studies stands in for the university's commitment to disfavored or marginalized groups. Thus, threats to gender studies betray administrators' and legislators' indifference or even hostility to these groups.

I've received many pleas over the years from women's and gender studies programs threatened with termination. Such alarms are calls, if not to arms, at least to barrage administrators at an institution with letters of support for the vulnerable program.

One of these, sent in an email from the National Women's Studies Association in March 2022, was from the Gender and Women's Studies program at SUNY Brockport. The threat facing Gender and Women's Studies was a plan to merge the academic unit with SUNY Brockport's DEI program.

By 2022, DEI offices had come under scrutiny and criticism. Thus, it's possible that gender studies faculty feared their positions might disappear if SUNY Brockport's DEI office were disbanded. The full public letter remains available online; what follows are key excerpts.

> Women and Gender Studies grew directly out of feminist and civil rights movements and continues to be a location for essential intellectual and creative work that dissects and resists dominant power structures including but not limited to cisheteropatriarchy, white supremacism, and racial capitalism. Since the early 1970s, the number of WGS programs have grown nationally and their curriculum has expanded beyond women's rights and histories to include gender theory; LGBT cultures and identities; masculinities; intersectionality; racial justice; class analysis; and global and transnational feminisms. This is the case for Brockport's Women and Gender Studies Department, which adds to **knowledge areas and programming necessary to work toward goals of equity and inclusion, though WGS disciplinary knowledge is distinct and rich and cannot be folded into DEI work.** Additionally, Diversity, Equity and Inclusion (DEI) does not exist as an academic discipline, as informed by a body of scholarly work. To fold WGS into DEI erases it as a distinct knowledge area and blocks important avenues of intellectual production . . . .
>
> The discipline of **Women and Gender Studies is deeply needed and relevant at this historical moment**. In the wake of the #MeToo Movement's collective reminder about the systemic and ongoing nature of sexual assault and violence against women and femmes; the ongoing attacks on civil and human rights of transgender adults and children in the US; the "Don't Say Gay" bill proposal in Florida; and the continuing exploitation of women's labor, particularly queer and trans women, women of color, and women with disabilities; we cannot divest from WGS departments with faculty who study, teach, and advocate against these violences.[30]

We might quibble about certain assertions, for example that, in the United States, the labor of queer and trans women has been "particularly" exploited. But if we're familiar with such rhetoric, we won't be surprised at the foregrounding of the oppression and exploitation of marginalized groups, empirics be damned.

Women's and gender studies units have lost funding or been eliminated at some schools over time, of course. But these kinds of arguments have scared many administrators enough to keep the field intact. If you're concerned, like many programs and departments before it, women's and gender studies at SUNY Brockport was saved. Huzzah?

In the nineties, women's studies scholars began to change the name of the field and its related academic units. In internal discussions, women's studies faculty cited a variety of reasons for the renaming. These included: that faculty were impelled by an institutional growth imperative to make the field appealing to a wider range of students; that curricular transformation would better reflect the diverse research and teaching agendas of faculty; and that a broader framing of what had been women's studies would enable programs and departments to claim intellectual jurisdiction over an archipelago of topics, including—but by no means limited to—feminism, gender, women, sexuality, masculinity, trans/queerness, antiracism, disability, indigeneity, and anticolonialism.

Another reason for the shift from women's to gender studies goes mostly unspoken. This is that a field that centered women could no longer be conceived of as politically and intellectually cutting-edge. Actually, the emphasis on women, and the kinds of research generated by this emphasis, became embarrassing for what gender studies practitioners regarded as its hedonic and theoretical deficiencies.

With regard to the hedonic, one problem with women's studies was that it was too earnest—not fun and sexy enough. We've all heard that feminists have no sense of humor. Maybe progressive scholars believe this too, because the profile of much contemporary progressive scholarship came to feature some combination of rage at injustice and oppression; transgressiveness sold as resistance; and an edgy, camp sensibility.

An example is a peer-reviewed article by the cultural theorists Lauren Berlant and Michael Warner entitled "Sex in Public." The authors aim to challenge heteronormativity by promoting "the radical aspirations of queer culture building." Integrated throughout the piece are various "scenes" that invoke cinema, iconoclastic spectacle, and sexual—especially BDSM—performance. But where is this paean to public sex going?

Or, rather, as Berlant and Warner imagine us wondering, "where is the tweaking, thwacking, thumping, sliming, and rubbing you might have expected—or dreaded—in a paper on sex?" They can hardly wait to tell us. Because their rejoinder to the "sexual purification of New York" via zoning under Mayor Rudy Giuliani is a performance of "erotic vomiting."

"Pork," the live sex show that on the evening of their visit offers erotic vomiting, "typically include[s] spanking, flagellation, shaving, branding, laceration, bondage, humiliation, wrestling—you know, the usual: amateur, everyday practitioners strutting for everyone else's gratification, not unlike an academic conference."

"Transfixed," Berlant and Warner narrate the spectacle from the moment they decide to "stay until it gets messy" until they "cannot leave, cannot even look away." They're not alone.

> People are moaning softly with admiration, then whistling, stomping, screaming encouragements. They have pressed forward in a compact and intimate group. Finally, as the top inserts two, then three fingers in the bottom's throat, insistently offering his own stomach for the repeated climaxes, we realize that we have never seen such a display of trust and violation. We are breathless. But, good academics that we are, we also have some questions to ask.

I'm afraid you'll have to read for yourself to find out what those scholarly questions are, though I'll give you a hint: they involve the "transformation of . . . social norms."[31]

By the time "Pork" featured the round of erotic vomiting Berlant and Warner observed, the theoretical deficiencies of women's studies had become glaring to some who understood themselves as feminist, critical, or decolonial researchers. One scholar who documented the emergence of a mismatch between women's and gender studies was the political theorist Wendy Brown. In a 1997 essay, "The Impossibility of Women's Studies," she pointed out that the infusion of "Critical Race Theory, postcolonial theory, queer theory, and cultural studies" had rendered the discipline "theoretically incoherent."

For Brown, these theories were "destabiliz[ing] the category of woman," "disrupt[ing] the unity or primacy of the category," and "blur[ring] the solidarity of the category."[32] Brown wasn't deploring these disruptions, merely pointing out that they rendered women's studies as it had been conceived in the seventies and eighties a project in need of a gut renovation. Gender studies had been born.

Mainstreaming Illiberal Progressivism

As the transformation from women's to gender studies was underway, the percentage of effort dedicated to addressing women's unheralded lives and contributions, and empirical measures of women's situations began to wane. But these projects also fell out of favor. Such research tends not to be conducted under the auspices of progressive activism or queer, postcolonial, or antiracist theories. Thus, it came to be seen as too atheoretical and retrograde for serious critical scholars.

From the beginning, some scholars and students were drawn primarily by the promise of radical politics. Others were drawn by projects of excavation and measurement. Still others came for the stigmatized knowledge. I may be wrong, but I speculate that the percentage of stigmatized knowledge gender studies offers its acolytes has increased dramatically as interest in excavating the lives of unknown women and meticulously analyzing data on women declined.

What took the place of projects of excavation and measurement were the theories—critical, postcolonial, and queer theories—that Wendy Brown explained had "destabilized" women's studies and made it "theoretically incoherent." The gender studies formation that emerged championed a new set of "sacralized victim groups" or what the political scientist Eric Kaufmann calls "totemic minorities."[33]

These terms seem derogatory, but they signal a useful point. This is that academic progressivism isn't just committed to improving the situation of disfavored groups. Instead, it demands the valorizing of activist claims related to these identities.

If first, women's studies, and, later, gender studies, are best conceptualized as movements rather than as bodies of knowledge, Arthur Koestler's argument that "no movement can exist without a heroic archetype" helps make sense of both the politics of academic progressivism and its "vehement tribal response" to challenges of its claims about victim groups.[34]

In addition to differences between women's and gender studies, there are also many similarities. Both fields borrowed most of their theory from elsewhere. Feminist theories came in many versions of descent from orthodox or "malestream" political philosophies. These philosophies included liberal, radical, Marxist, socialist, postmodern/poststructuralist, and anarchist. For good measure, most texts of the time added other theoretical and epistemological categories, especially psychoanalytic and Black (or women of color) feminisms.

Gender studies narrowed this field of appropriate theoretical sources, building its brand on the explanatory validity of poststructuralist and critical theories. These theories superseded others that were once on the menu. Together with the political activisms deemed sufficiently radical to qualify for the allegiance of cutting-edge progressives, poststructuralist and critical theories emerged as the only alternatives for serious scholars. The homogenous training and hiring of gender and other "studies" PhDs guaranteed that only those candidates who bore the political stamp of approval would be admitted to the discipline.

However, as the number of acceptable theoretical foundations for gender studies research declined, the number of topics over which gender studies and other progressive scholars claimed jurisdiction increased. Even many critics of the progressive academy haven't fully grasped this expansion of intellectual authority over issues that have traditionally been the domain of scholars and clinicians trained in more traditional disciplines.

For example, Francis Fukuyama—no fan of academic progressivism—points out that "the much-feared tyranny of the woke Left exists only in certain limited sectors of U.S. society—universities, Hollywood, and other cultural spaces, and it only touches on certain issues related to race, ethnicity, gender, and sexual identity."[35] Making much the same point, Yascha Mounk describes the remit of academic progressivism as "new ideas and norms about race, gender and sexuality."[36]

Such characterizations of the scope of gender studies' domain are accurate; they just don't go nearly far enough. Indeed, the expertise of progressive academics stretches to encompass vast realms of social, political, economic, moral, and even medical knowledge far beyond the scope of our training and sometimes even our understanding.

Thus, English professors pronounce confidently on US foreign policy. Anthropologists declare, and no doubt teach, that "the US is the greatest predator empire that has ever existed."[37] American Studies scholars vow to "crash the US settler state."[38] The conclusions of such scholars, which are identical to the assumptions they bring to questions about foreign policy, predator empires, and settler states, are, as progressive scholars and students frequently declaim, "not up for debate."

A way to think about this phenomenon is Oliver Traldi's observation that many academics "overextend" the "breadth" of their expertise "for purposes of laundering their personal, non-expert opinions under their expert brand."[39] This tendency was present in women's studies as feminist scholars turned a feminist lens on every social, political, economic, historical, medical, and institutional phenomenon.

It's been supercharged as scholars honed their brands, and the theories, issue positions, and conclusions they marketed were given wider reach by the internet and social media. Being online didn't cause scholars to "overextend" their expertise. But new technology and platforms have made it easier for progressive academics to cultivate audiences and "launder" all the political beliefs downstream from the tenets of progressivism.

An additional explanation for this phenomenon is that progressive scholars aren't overextending their expertise but, rather, practicing activism in the guise of scholarship. I'll get to this explanation in Chapter 3.

Either way, the problem with academia isn't that our narrow training strands us in knowledge silos. It's that a PhD and appropriately progressive politics became a permission slip to exercise expertise on all topics on which we happen to have feelings, opinions, and intuitions. There are a lot of us, and we have a lot of opinions.

Here is only one of many problems with such a mode of knowledge creation. I've often heard a gender studies or other progressive humanities colleague talk about their research project, declaring before a credulous audience that no scholars had ever taken up this problem or question before them. It's tough to find a significant phenomenon that's never been investigated by any scholar. In these cases, I knew that there was, in fact, a body of scholarship on the topic.

The best explanation isn't that my colleagues are incapable of executing a database search. Rather, it's that research on their question hasn't been performed by scholars they trust—that is, scholars like themselves who share their values and commitments. This means that progressive scholars routinely discount scholarship that can be dismissed as patriarchal, cisheteronormative, or insufficiently antiracist.

Such research may be empirical, it may have been produced by unapproved scholars or by way of unapproved methods, or it may have been produced any time before the current configuration of progressive theories and doctrines was solidified. What's left after this culling is anything that's been written on the subject by someone just like them.

If, after you've eliminated all the pernicious scholarship, there's nothing left: Congratulations! You've broken new ground. Colleagues who share a citation circle with you will reward you for not corrupting your scholarship with work that would compromise you politically or inform you in ways you don't wish to be informed.

To understand movements of all kinds, we should try to grasp what participants get from their adherence to and participation in them. Members of movements attest to many benefits and payoffs, including excitement, community, a common worldview that organizes and makes sense of experience, and an ego-enhancing understanding of how the world really works.

I've experienced these payoffs on the left and observed them on both the left and the right. On October 14, 1979, I was thrilled to attend the first March on Washington for gay and lesbian rights. After many years of participant observation at conservative activist events, on January 6, 2021, I stood on the National Mall and watched those who flocked to DC for Trump's "Save America March." With wide smiles, several MAGA marchers posed for my photos.

Many on the left might be surprised that, before the attack on the Capitol, the crowd's vibe was just as convivial as it's been at so many other left- and right-wing events I've attended. In such congenial company, with so many others who think and believe as they do, the happiness at movement meetings is palpable. So, I'm not at all surprised by the commentator David French's insistence that to understand the MAGA movement, we need to consider the joy associated with following Trump.[40] Likewise, women's and gender studies students attest to the satisfactions derived from classes, study, and solidarity with others in the field.[41]

I'm intentional about investigating similarities between movements because I think we can learn a great deal about them, and about ourselves as members of and believers in movements, through such comparisons. For example, movements and activisms often seize moral high ground by borrowing and inhabiting frames, values, strategies, and rhetorical styles from their adversaries. We can see how much progressive academics subordinate scholarship to activism when what they do exhibits a high degree of projection or mirroring of their criticisms of the other side.

Imitating the Other

Regardless of the enthusiasm adherents bring to gender studies, the loose ends, contradictions, logical inconsistencies, and empirical erasures in contemporary gender studies and academic progressivism threaten to come to the surface time and again. If universities functioned as they should, we faculty would introduce alternative theories and empirical evidence that might undermine—and not just support—preferred positions.

We would also help students understand values that point in different directions. Alas, these are the very kinds of activities that have been effectively proscribed in classrooms and research agendas in many fields, including gender studies.

My long experience in women's and gender studies has drawn me back to Richard Hofstadter's quirky analysis of the "paranoid style" in American politics. Recall that when Hofstadter developed his concept of the paranoid style in politics, he wasn't diagnosing a considerable subset of the US population as "certifiable lunatics"—Hofstadter's term, not mine.

Rather, he called attention to a "style" of political thought and expression that shares some features with clinical paranoia while aiming to protect a people or "way of life" from those who endanger it. Who are these enemies? "This enemy seems to be on many counts a projection of the self: both the ideal and the unacceptable aspects of the self are attributed to him. A fundamental paradox of the paranoid style is the imitation of the enemy."[42]

What follows are examples of the genre of mirroring or imitating values and strategies, not an exhaustive list.

First, progressive academics treat and redescribe political points of view and differences as matters of truth and morality. I'll say more about this elision of political perspectives with truth and morality in chapter 3, so let's put a pin in this point for the moment. Just bear in mind how central to the problem of higher ed illiberalism it is that scholars often disappear their politics into morality.

Second, we ban books and ideas. One of our first official acts in women's studies was to vehemently reject the idea of a "canon" that might circumscribe, even tacitly, what should be learned in our classrooms. You might think that, as a result, academic progressives would have created a unique zone of freedom from the hobbling chains of antiquated presumptions of intellectual value. How wrong you would be.

If you pay attention to reporting on book banning, challenging, and suppressing, you'd probably conclude that banning is only a preoccupation of the culture war right. It's more accurate to say that suppressing books and ideas is an equal opportunity problem even if those on the extremes of the political spectrum go about their task in different ways.

Indeed, the writer Kat Rosenfield regards left-wing censorship as "more insidious" than its counterpart on the right precisely because it's often invisible to observers. Rather than "focusing on books that have already been published," Rosenfield points out that progressives use sensitivity readers and pressure campaigns "to suppress 'harmful' ideas," often before books are published or to prevent them from being published. Thus, censorship is "often coming earlier—and from inside the house."[43]

In place of the old canon over which "theory wars" were fought just a few short decades ago is a *de facto* canon that delineates the distinction between good, acceptable authors, texts, ideas, frames, and arguments and those scorned as coming from dominant, cisheteropatriarchal, white supremacist, or colonizing perspectives. Everyone in progressive fields knows there's a line. Some know because they police it. Others learn about the line from students.

Still others, like the author and retired English professor Janet Burroway, learn in the process of publishing. To publish the fifth edition of her popular creative writing text, *Imaginative Writing: The Elements of Craft*, Burroway had to revise her own prose to eliminate newly impermissible words and terms. But the editorial supervision didn't end there; for the first time, her publisher barred her from including pieces of literature that contravened a lengthy list of prohibited words and themes. As a "content creator," Burroway was also "invited" to view and sign off on a "mandatory" diversity, equity, and inclusion (DEI) "orientation module." She declined.[44]

One of the most noxious features of gender studies and its identity studies kin is the curation of an intellectual ecosystem whose hallmark is its boundaries, which are stringently enforced by students and faculty. More challenging is that the line between the canonic and the inadmissible isn't set. Instead, the line moves. Texts, authors, theories, approaches, and ideas that at one time were acceptable or even enlightening to those who banished the canon can quickly become reactionary or offensive.

A diligent faculty member may discern such a shift in a way that allows her to quietly purge anathematized texts from syllabi and bibliographies. If she doesn't, she may suddenly become internet famous, like Phoebe Gloeckner and Erika López Prater. Each was investigated and punished after her students complained that she'd displayed a forbidden image as part of a lesson.

For Gloeckner, the blasphemous text was a page from underground comix artist R. Crumb, which she posted online in her introductory comics course at the University of Michigan.[45] Prater's ordeal began when, after multiple warnings that she intended to show students a fourteenth century image of the prophet Muhammad in the Islamic art module of her world art course at Hamline University, she did so. In return for warning students who might believe they shouldn't view such an image, Prater was rewarded by being denounced as Islamophobic, not only by some students but, officially, by her university.[46]

Third, progressive academics treat emotional and intellectual discomfort as a sign that an objective wrong has been perpetrated. Indeed, we train students to believe that if they feel something, they should say something, preferably to an authority figure and in venues that will encourage crowds to demand that perpetrators be punished. This is the progressive version of an instruction I've seen on the Christian conservative right: when God gives believers certain feelings, they should understand those feelings as signs of some objective reality in the world outside their own minds.

For example, when God gives believers feelings of guilt, they should understand those feelings as indicators that they are guilty of violating divine will and must seek forgiveness. When God gives believers feelings of disgust, they should understand such feelings as divine messages that they are confronting an objectively disgusting object. Objects of disgust include gender and sexual minorities and women who have had an abortion.[47]

Of course, progressives don't believe this *Christian* version of the objectivity of feelings, but they embrace a version of the meaning of feelings that's just as questionable. Fortunately, there's an antidote to such a belief. As long ago as the nineteenth century, John Stuart Mill warned us about making judgments based on "an outrage to our feelings"—our conviction that "things are right . . . because we feel them to be so."[48]

Fourth, higher ed has, in multiple respects, become a therapeutic enterprise. One example is disability diagnoses and accommodations. Writing in *The Chronicle of Higher Education*, religion scholar Alan Levinovitz cites a "widespread sense in disability-services offices that their primary role is provider, not gatekeeper." The result is "surging accommodation requests," often backed by little or no medical validity.[49]

I've analyzed the Christian right's anti-LGBT and antiabortion rights movements as having political and therapeutic dimensions. Long the therapeutic side of antigay politics, the ex-gay movement wasn't just brass-knuckle politics in another guise. It attracted a diverse set of practitioners, including those who believed they'd successfully kicked their same-sex habit. At times, these compassionate former homosexuals even rejected the hard-edged political tactics of those who worked the political side of the movement. Though, for the most part, the goals of the two sides of the movement didn't conflict.[50]

This kind of analysis can be applied to higher ed as well. A prominent example of the university as therapist are statements that academic departments and universities have issued on current events. As Blake Smith points out, these statements often contain "impassioned declarations of supposedly unanimous feeling [and] end with a list of university resources such as counseling programs."[51]

In such a therapeutic milieu, students may be subjected by the university to "compelled introspection."[52] For their part, students assert their need for therapeutic care, for example, reporting themselves to be " 'highly emotional,' 'irrevocably shaken,' 'unwell,' and 'unable to focus' . . . displaying" what the conservative author Heather Mac Donald describes as "all the symptoms of Victorian neurasthenia."[53]

I was reminded of the therapeutic role assigned to faculty every time I recorded grades in my university's course management system. Three emojis were built into the instructor comments field in the system: thumbs up, clapping hands, and smiley face. Whenever I left comments in response to student work, I noted the emojis, which remind me of the stick-on stars that sometimes decorated the elementary school papers I carried home to show my mother. As I recall, those were phased out well before junior high.

Responding to critiques of institutional statements, Len Gutkin argues that, in addition to universities situating students as "political activists [and] paying customers," they also treat students as "subjects of therapeutic concern." Gutkin is even more insightful when he writes that universities' "activist and therapeutic goals have become oddly blended."[54] Although there's some division of labor in the delivery of compassionate therapy and punishment in the academy, in the end, it's difficult to differentiate activism from therapy. Both are predicated on non-negotiable beliefs and assertions about care and harm.

Fifth—and here, academic progressives join arms with followers of Donald Trump—my colleagues take aim at norms of civility and public conduct. Students learn from my colleagues that social norms reflect and perpetuate the power of dominant groups at the same time that they prevent the disempowered from achieving justice and liberation. The alternative is to teach and reward transgression, with extra points awarded for forms of political activism that consist of rubbing our fellow citizens' noses in our counterhegemonic values.

Beginning in 2017, I wondered how my colleagues would process Donald Trump's norm-breaking. Specifically, I wondered whether, in light of the pressure Trump placed on democratic norms and institutions, they might rethink both their opposition to public norms and their warm attachment to transgressiveness. Spoiler alert: believing their politics to be no mirror image of Trump's, they did not.

It's ironic that the progressive academics who teach transgression and applaud liberation from constraining norms and rules are quite comfortable dictating the speech and pedagogy of colleagues. We'll look more closely at such seeming contradictions as we go.

Social movement scholars point out the ways in which movements can firmly fasten on a protective mantle of victimhood. As the columnist David Brooks observes, "left or right, apparently we're all victims now."[55] Thus, the *sixth* similarity of left-wing academic illiberalism and its adversaries is the attachment of academic progressives to victimization.[56]

Not only is "victimhood . . . a status marker," "but we seem to have a tendency to give victimhood actual moral status."[57] More disturbing is evidence that virtuous "victim-signaling" is associated with Dark Triad traits.[58]

Both the political right and the academic left treat with derision the idea that the other side has been victimized and then loudly and insistently claim victim status for themselves as members and allies of sacralized groups. Such a conception of "the people" provides a pathway for getting to many tenets of illiberal left-wing pedagogy that have properly been scrutinized in recent years, including: safe spaces, trigger warnings, microaggressions, and other elements of what has euphemistically been termed "inclusive pedagogy."

A goal of my teaching on social movements was that students come to better understand how fellow citizens who disagree with them think. Because social and political movements in general are so reliant on victimhood, I've sometimes addressed in classes the sense of victimization that's pervasive in the Christian conservative movement.

To help students understand such a sense, I developed a brief PowerPoint timeline of the loss of Christian conservative social authority and policy supremacy. The timeline features decades of losses in civil rights laws and Supreme Court rulings, as well as remarkable shifts in public opinion toward the left on many issues of interest to the Christian right since the sixties, including racial integration, interracial marriage, anti-LGBT discrimination, and same-sex marriage.

Students tended not to buy Christian conservatives' self-conception as victims, pointing out that people aren't being victimized when they lose unearned dominance. But one point of the lesson was that we may be able to understand many movements—even those "we" may see as representing unenlightened reaction—as sharing characteristics that include a desire to reverse historical vulnerabilities and narcissistic injuries.

Rather than providing their members with the latest empirical data on conditions confronting a group, movements service and channel the feelings of their members.

Seventh, As I suggested in the Introduction, groups on both the far left and far right can share a conviction that the only way to build their own utopian world is to burn down the one we currently uneasily share. In fact, this is a popular trope, which I've often heard from students and, as the two vignettes that introduce this book show, from colleagues.

I've found it useful to think about this characteristic of progressive ideology as a function of the maximalist fervor of academic progressivism. A consistent feature of academic illiberalism is the articulation of inflexible, sacrosanct social, political, behavioral, policy, and linguistic demands. Just like their foes on the right, academic progressives don't see compromise as "best possible agreements" but, instead, as "regrettable failures to reach maximal ends."[59]

Colleagues and students alike also evince contempt for the possibility that they might not fully comprehend all aspects of a problem; for incremental approaches to a problem; and for the possibility of compromise—settling for less than they demand.

Finally, social movements almost always speak in the name of the people, and academic progressives do this as well. Generations of scholars of history and politics have noted the irony that some movements dedicated to justice, freedom, and liberation aren't that popular. Indeed, many political views my colleagues insist that everyone must hold are unpopular with Americans.[60]

Sometimes the political views of academic progressives are even unpopular with substantial subsets of groups of Americans for which progressives advocate. One example is a "patriotism gap" that divides progressives from immigrants and racial minorities in the United States.[61] Another is black Americans' "robust" support for policing and police spending in their communities.[62]

As the journalist Josh Barro writes of the Democratic Party, "a mistake we see over and over . . . is the conflation of the interests and preferences of demographic groups with the interests and preferences of . . . insiders from those demographic groups."[63] We can learn much from survey research about the popularity or unpopularity of academic progressives' ideas, demands, and prescriptions with groups and insiders from those groups.

We might, for example, investigate the partisan political identities of Americans to discern how particular packages of political beliefs are distributed across the political spectrum.

The Pew Research Center is "a nonpartisan fact tank that informs the public about the issues, attitudes and trends shaping the world."[64] In 2021, on the basis of its data and analysis, Pew pushed "beyond red and blue" to divide the electorate into nine categories. One of the largest of these is "Democratic Mainstays," the group "with the largest share of Black non-Hispanic adults" and one that holds more "hawkish" views on foreign policy and "less liberal" views on immigration than Democratic factions to its left.[65]

In addition to Pew, an organization that's performed a similar investigation in recent years is More in Common, an "international initiative to build societies and communities that are stronger, more united, and more resilient to the increasing threats of polarization and social division."[66] In 2018, More in Common's "Hidden Tribes: A Study of America's Polarized Landscape" describes "Progressive Activists," its farthest left cohort, as "younger, highly engaged, secular, cosmopolitan, angry."[67]

The farthest left of the nine groups in Pew's political typology, the predominantly young, white, and highly educated "Progressive Left," no doubt overlaps considerably with More in Common's Progressive Activists.[68]

Occasionally, I briefly introduced the findings of surveys like these to students and asked them to guess what percentage of the US electorate falls into a category with which they and their peers might identify. Their responses inevitably overestimated the size of their political cohort, often by many times its size as measured by survey researchers. Progressive Activists and the Progressive Left constitute approximately eight and six percent of the American electorate, respectively. The political scientist and strategist Ruy Teixeira concludes that, in the electoral arena, these progressives are "paper tigers" whose "power derives more from their ability to scare the rest of the [Democratic] party than from their power over actual voters."[69]

Nonetheless, this small faction punches above its weight, especially in higher ed and other epistemic institutions.[70] Universities house a higher percentage of left-progressive activists than does US society at large, an imbalance that no doubt influences perceptions of faculty and students that their favored political views are politically and intellectually unassailable.

Gender studies isn't the only project in which devotees have to work at not exposing the loose ends, internal contradictions, and inconsistencies of their ideology. Political movements and institutions often confront this very dilemma and, when they do, they resolve them in favor of their desired ends. Many in the academy have come to do so too.

I've introduced gender studies and the fact that gender studies' worldview became the worldview of the progressive academy. It's time to address the first characteristic of a populist movement, the unshakeable conviction that "a part of the people *is* the people."[71]

Let's examine the sacralized groups of the progressive academy and the practices by which progressive illiberalism became entrenched in the academy. So entrenched as to be invisible to its practitioners.

2 The People

Sacralized Groups

To ask which groups sit at the heart of a particular political project is to ask who matters. That's a question we might ask of any contender for a normative theory of politics. In fact, to me it's always been one of the compelling questions political theorists investigate. Like many young women political theorists, I gravitated to questions about women's inclusion and exclusion from political thought and practice. And that broad interest brought me to what I still think of today as interesting questions.

In those early academic days, it was exciting to trek through such well-traveled terrain as: what do these theorists—gestures to everyone from Plato and Aristotle to Arendt and Rawls—mean when they address, for example, the rights or responsibilities of people? Subjects? Citizens? Men? Because, in context, sometimes it's clear that they likely mean "all humans" or "all humans who are citizens or under the authority of this state/nation." At other times, it's highly unlikely or actually impossible that, when they refer to these categories, they mean "all humans."

When, for example, "people" or "men" in these great works of political theory are also fathers, sons, soldiers, citizens in the agora, or seducers of women (looking at you, Machiavelli), it strains credulity to believe that we can just pop in the word "women" and go about our business. So, doing as we might be encouraged to do by weary, at that time virtually all male, professors—just read "men" as "people" so we can keep this seminar moving—was an affront to our nascent skills as interpreters of texts.

Like political theories, different places, eras, parties, movements, and coalitions give us different conceptions of the people who matter first or most. Regardless of where you currently stand on something like a left-right political continuum, you can no doubt render a quick and dirty account of who "the people" are for your political kin. I consider rendering these assumptions out loud a useful exercise in coming to terms with what we're up to, in education and politics.

In this chapter, I want to get more specific about the groups that constitute "the people" in the progressive academy. In the face of an emphasis on "belonging" in contemporary universities, not all members of university communities have been able to be "the people." Universities came to advertise their commitment to exercise particular care for students from disfavored, minority, and underrepresented groups. Beneath a commitment to care for members of such groups, another process was at work: reinforcing the ideology about identity that underwrites progressive illiberalism.

This chapter also gets specific about practices that operationalize a worldview of progressive illiberalism. These include, for faculty, the set of policy, practices, and personnel that has comprised Diversity, Equity, and Inclusion. Academics communicate our politics to students through a set of ideas and practices that make up inclusive pedagogy. Taking a close look at DEI and inclusive pedagogy enables a good working understanding of how progressive academia came to define and police "the people."

The People: A List

Perhaps the clearest sign of the identity studiesification of universities is that "the people" of gender studies also became "the people" of universities. Though the categories and conceptualizations of groups sometimes change over time, most of these groups are recognizable from politics of the left.

Academic progressives' scholarship and teaching, and university policies reify and sacralize a collectivity of quite diverse identities. People who identify or are identified with these groups are preemptively considered to be either or all of the following: socially disfavored, politically marginalized, economically exploited, discriminated against, vulnerable to trauma, and disproportionality likely to be or become victims of violence.

The categories are: Black and Indigenous people of color (BIPOC, pronounced BYE-pock); queer; Latinx; Muslims; Asian Americans; persons with a disability; and, most recently, persons oppressed on the basis of caste. I consider caste at greater length than the other categories both because it's a recent addition to the list and because its inclusion has occasioned creative reasoning by those who champion the category.

Obviously, these short précis on identity groups don't contain everything that can, or even should, be said about them. They're just an introduction.

BIPOC. BIPOC is a relatively new umbrella term and acronym that foregrounds people whose ancestors were forcibly brought to the United States and people whose ancestors were original inhabitants of what is now the United States. Perhaps because it is a new appellation, in different contexts it's unpacked in ways that suggest divergences in emphasis and inclusivity. Some who use the term mean "Black and Indigenous people of color," while others mean "Black, Indigenous, and people of color."

For decades, black Americans have been the most loyal Democratic voting bloc. By contrast, while Native Americans lean Democratic, a significant minority vote Republican. The inclusive term "people of color" is no longer considered an appropriate referent for groups under the BIPOC umbrella, who are now more likely to be referred to as "Black and Brown people."

Queer. People of my generational cohort, who became young adults from approximately the late sixties to the eighties, knew "queer" as the most common slur that was once directed at homosexuals and those who engaged in homosexual behavior. Straight people who disaggregated members of this class could use "fag[got]" for men and "dyke" for women. Like many of my generation, I knew about queers before I knew I was one.

The word "queer" has been rescued from the dustbin of history, but it also means something quite different today than it did in those benighted times. Queer is a former slur that became an umbrella term for a set of diverse identities. But not, as some might deduce, just L, G, B, and T, including the "non-binary," who consider themselves to exist outside of a sex or gender binary.

One of the germinal queer theorists, Eve Kosofsky Sedgwick, defines "queer" as "the open mesh of possibilities, gaps, overlaps, dissonances and resonances, lapses and excesses of meaning" related to gender and sexuality.[1] However, this definition is now antiquated. Having come to denote transgressiveness of all kinds, "queer" is democratic; anyone who aspires to join this club can. Indeed, nearly a quarter of Gen Z adults and nearly thirty percent of Gen Z females born after 1996 identify as queer.[2]

Latinx. Latinx is a recent, gender-inclusive term for people of Latin American heritage, including those whose families of origin hail from Mexico, Cuba, Central America, South America, and the Caribbean. The term can substitute for Latino, Latina, Hispanic, Chicano, and Chicana, though "Chicanx" is a newer entrant into the lexicon as a gender-inclusive substitute for Chicano/a. Nearly twenty percent of the US population is of Latin American descent, the second largest portion of the population after non-Hispanic whites.

People of Latin American heritage have been central to the Democratic coalition for many reasons. These include historic anti-Hispanic discrimination in the United States, challenges related to Hispanic immigration, and US government policies on and interventions in Latin America to support US economic and political interests.

The term "Latinx" is quite unpopular with people of Latin American descent. The Pew Research Center reported in 2020 that approximately one in four Latinx people in the United States had heard of the term and that only three percent of them approved and applied it to themselves. One source of disapproval is that the term originated in cultural and intellectual institutions in the United States, not within Spanish-language countries or cultures.[3]

Muslims. Islam is a major world religion, the biggest concentration of whose adherents reside in Africa, the Middle East, and Asia. Fewer than two percent of Americans identify as Muslim. The salience for academic progressives of Muslim Americans as a group increased dramatically after the attacks of September 11, 2001, which were perpetrated by Saudi nationals animated by extremist Islamist ideology.

After September 11, violence and discrimination against Muslims and people perceived as Muslims—for example, Hindus and Sikhs—surged.[4] Post-September 11 violence and threats against Muslims, the US invasions of Afghanistan and Iraq, and passage of the USA Patriot Act combined to stimulate support for Muslims on the political left. Progressives also ally with Palestinians in their long-running conflict with Israel and abhor official US support for Israel as complicity in apartheid, oppression, and genocide.

Asian Americans. The category of Asian Americans is vast, encompassing as it does people with ancestry from countries that make up the largest continent on earth. Most people of Asian descent in the United States have ancestors from China, India, Korea, Japan, the Philippines, or Vietnam. These groups emigrated at different times and have faced different conditions and forms of discrimination.

For some years, however, Americans of Asian descent have presented a stubborn impediment to academic progressive narratives of oppression. The Harvard Graduate School of Education's summary of evidence suggests the challenge to identity narratives buried in good news about this group. "On average, Asian American students obtain higher grades, perform better on standardized tests, and are more likely to finish high school and attend elite colleges than their peers of all other racial backgrounds, regardless of socioeconomic status."[5]

In spite of these high levels of performance, students of Asian descent have often been disadvantaged in university admissions.[6] Although Asian Americans have "mixed views" on affirmative action, 76 percent of Asian American adults "say race or ethnicity should not factor into college admissions decisions."[7]

Persons with a Disability. The language to refer to those who were once known, even on the political left, as handicapped or disabled has shifted to align with the movement in favor of "people first" language. The argument for such language is that it destigmatizes people by emphasizing their humanity apart from the label placed on their identity. The umbrella of disability includes conditions of all kinds, including a range of visible and invisible emotional, cognitive, and physical conditions not limited to those defined as constituting disability in US public policies such as the Americans with Disabilities Act.

Progressive academic teaching and scholarship on disability focuses on systemic barriers to equity, the importance of disabling systems of oppression, and intersectional "disability justice,"

> a broad term to describe approaches to advance access and inclusion for disabled people. A disability justice approach centers the priorities and approaches of those most historically excluded groups, such as women, people of color, immigrants, and people who identify as LGBTQ+."[8]

The critical study of disability incorporates theories of systemic oppression, including anti-colonialism and anti-capitalism.[9]

Survivors of Caste-Based Discrimination. A recent addition to the sacralized groups of gender studies and the progressive academic left are people who suffer oppression because of their caste. The addition came to my attention in August 2021, when the Executive Committee of the National Women's Studies Association circulated a statement condemning "casteism in colleges and universities."[10]

The NWSA statement is a model of passive-voice progressive signaling. If a reader knew nothing about US universities, the statement might convince them of three things: first, that caste discrimination is rampant in American universities; second, that caste discrimination is being committed by official university representatives such as faculty and administrators; and third, that caste discrimination in the United States is not a product of emigration from South Asia. None of these propositions is true. In fact, we can falsify all three by reading carefully and running down the very sources the statement cites on caste discrimination.

The NWSA statement on caste and casteism represents caste discrimination as a world problem that can't be located in any particular region or religion, asserting, for example that casteism "cuts across religions including Hinduism, Christianity, Islam, and Sikhism." I'm not an expert on all Christian faith traditions, but I'm not aware of casteism or caste discrimination as practices in Western Christianity, and the statement relays no evidence for this assertion.

The first and second points are implications that casteism is a persistent presence in US higher education and that it can be found in official acts rather than in social relations. The statement insinuates that these propositions are true by using passive voice to assert that casteism "can be found" in US universities and that "education is one place where we see discrimination based on caste."

Do we see this in the United States? Where's the evidence that discrimination based on caste is preventing lower-caste people from gaining access to a university education *in the United States*? The statement cites no such data. The NWSA Executive Committee also omits specific information about what kinds of acts constitute the discrimination that disturbs the authors and convinces them that universities urgently need to develop a policy response. If NWSA had any such data, I have no doubt they would have produced it. None of the sources the statement cites produce such evidence.

On the third point, that caste isn't a product of migration from South Asia, the sources NWSA cites are very clear, which is to say that those who drafted the NWSA statement didn't innocently obfuscate the prevalence or perpetrators of casteism in the United States because of a lack of clarity in the sources. A report by The Equality Labs, a Dalit civil rights organization cited by NWSA, opens with a 1916 quote attributed to "Statesman, Civil Rights Leader, and Author of India's Constitution Dr. B.R. Ambedkar": "If Hindus migrate to other regions of the earth, Caste would become a world problem."

A bolded subhead in the report proclaims, "Wherever South Asians Go They Take Caste With Them." And in a section that offers "recommendations" for US universities, we find this characterization of the problem that higher ed institutions should understand is a reality for some international students:

> College is a tough place for most people. Doubly so for international students. Given the large populations of South Asian students in American universities, Caste-based jokes and slurs are not uncommon. One respondent says, "I clearly remember my classmates who were upper Caste openly asking me my Caste and then feeling proud to say "I can't even think of dating you because you are from a lower Caste!"[11]

Equality Labs—which, to repeat, is a Dalit advocacy organization—plainly identifies the source and nature of casteism on American university campuses: South Asian peers engaging in social, including dating, discrimination. So why doesn't the NWSA statement just say that, to the extent casteism is a problem on US campuses, it's primarily a social problem perpetuated by upper-caste peers?

To anyone steeped in the worldview of illiberal progressivism, the answer is clear: it will never do to blame members of a sacralized group for a problem when it's possible to blame dominant groups or institutions. Dr. B.R. Ambedkar's representation that casteism might become a "world problem" if "Hindus migrate to other regions on earth" renders the problem with too much clarity for the NWSA Executive Committee.

There have been a small number of legal claims for caste discrimination, and plaintiffs and their advocates cite the cultural persistence of caste in the "Indian diaspora" with responsibility.[12] Increasingly, employment attorneys and law offices recommend as a best practice that employers add caste discrimination to their Equal Employment Opportunity statements and policies. Since 2021, dozens of US universities, including Harvard, Brandeis, and Rutgers, have promulgated policies to ban caste discrimination.

Additional Considerations on "the People"

The economist Glenn Loury has written that "the first lesson Harvard teaches its students appears to be: Market your identity-based oppression."[13] Loury's maxim focuses on sacralized identities, but it also gestures toward the fact that academic progressivism isn't just about particular social groups. It's about the beliefs and prescriptions associated with each identity and each form of group-related oppression. I note here that admission to sacralized groups isn't automatic, and I'll return to this theme later. Because it's received so much attention from critics of academic progressivism, I also address the issue of intersecting identities.

The Price of Admission

A key feature of progressive illiberalism is that even though it ostensibly serves a set of identity groups that constitute "the people," group identity isn't a given. There's a price of admission to these groups that must be paid in the currency of ideology. If you want to either belong to one of these sacralized groups or be recognized as an appropriate ally, you have to talk the talk and walk the walk.

My own conception of "the people" has broadened over time, from women and men of disfavored and underrepresented groups to as close as it may be possible for me, as a person of a particular place and time, to get to "people." In our antagonistic political milieu, some of our fellow citizens intone that "white lives matter" as a provocation. But, shockingly, it's been possible to be fired from an academic position for observing that "everyone's life matters."

This is what happened in 2020 to Leslie Neal-Boylan, dean of the college of nursing at the University of Massachusetts Lowell, when she wrote this phrase in a message of concern and solidarity about the effects of police violence on racial minorities.[14]

Still, people—actual humans who can flourish and suffer—matter. It's possible to worry about discrimination, violence and other threats to members of historically disfavored groups and also worry about violence and other tragedies that befall people who don't belong to these groups.

As in politics, in the academy those who codify who counts as the people and what those people and their allies must believe are elites. The sociologist Musa Al-Gharbi points out that academic progressives who hail from sacralized groups tend to be better off, not only than other members of those groups, but often from members of the groups who are being instructed to confess their privilege and do better.[15]

Indeed, most academics are WEIRD: Western, educated, industrialized, rich, and democratic. And we WEIRD folk are outliers; "people from . . . WEIRD societies . . . are some of the most psychologically unusual people on Earth."[16] Many of us WEIRDos may live in conventional ways, including being married, socializing children to get an education, owning a home, and planning for retirement.[17] What many conservatives refer to contemptuously as "talking left and living right."

Meanwhile, our absolute convictions about what's right and wrong in every domain reveal what outliers we are compared to the non-WEIRDos we share the world with.

Being in the minority doesn't make us wrong. Still, our students would be well served if we acknowledged our elite WEIRDness and really tried to help them understand the diversity of perspectives available within all identity groups, including those with which we most identify.

Intersectionality

A concept related to identity and the sacralized identities of academic progressives is intersectionality. Named by the legal theorist Kimberlé Crenshaw, at its most basic, intersectionality is the practice of taking into account "intersections" of identity or, as Crenshaw, explains, substituting analysis of multiple axes of identity for a "single-axis framework" organized around, for example, race or sex.[18] Some critics of the academy find in intersectionality the intellectual foundation for academic illiberalism. Although I understand why some critics might adopt this perspective, I don't share it, and I'll explain why.

Intersectionality—or an "intersectional lens"—can be an inoffensive mode of research. Indeed, even if it isn't what Crenshaw had in mind when she coined the term, intersectional information gathering and analysis are often helpful for discerning patterns in literature and data and informing policy and other interventions.

What may drive the interpretation of intersectionality as one of the prime villains at the root of progressive illiberalism is that gender scholars tend to use "intersectionality" as a comprehensive term that tautologically refers back to "what we do." So, for example, if a department of gender studies scholars were asked to quickly characterize what binds all the activist, queer, antiracist, and postcolonial scholars together, that group would almost certainly opt to describe themselves as "intersectional."

In a hilarious scene in the Monty Python film, *Life of Brian*, the eponymous Brian, whom the crowd believes is the promised Messiah, tries to induce them to disperse and leave him alone by yelling, "you're all individuals!" In unison, the crowd yells back, "we're all individuals!" My crowd, the gender studies faculty, would yell, "we're all intersectional!"[19]

I think of critics of left-wing academic illiberalism as a "mom" hearing the progressive "kids" upstairs screaming and knocking over furniture. "Mom" yells, "what are you kids doing up there?" Silence. Then the "kids" yell back, "nothing . . . just intersectionality." Some skepticism seems warranted.

By way of testing a quick thought experiment about the use of "intersectionality" as a kind of rhetorical shield, let's imagine a scholar.[20] She collects and analyzes quantitative or qualitative data using categories that enable her to break out preferences, attitudes, behaviors, resources, and effects of all kinds by demographic groups, including "intersecting" dimensions of identity such as black women with advanced degrees and queer-identifying young people.

Depending on the research topic, the demographic categories under consideration might include race, sex, class, religion, age, sexuality, physical ability, and gender identity, if not others. If this hypothetical scholar is situated in the humanities or the social sciences, It's fair to assume she identifies as somewhere to the left of center on the political continuum. Given what we know about her work, she would qualify as an intersectional scholar. But is she an identity progressive with prescriptive beliefs she would use illiberal means to protect?

Some scholars who fit this description don't subscribe to progressive illiberalism, and their research agendas don't lead inexorably to illiberalism. Some are members of minority groups and others aren't. One example is the Harvard economist Roland G. Fryer, Jr., who performed controversial—and, by this, I mean he reached the wrong conclusions for academic progressives—research on police-involved shootings of black men.[21]

Now, imagine that this same scholar has an impressive record of teaching and intersectional research but hasn't in any obvious way affirmed her adherence to the tenets of academic progressivism required by students and colleagues. Knowing her research agenda, but uncertain about whether she shares key beliefs that her colleagues would consider mandatory, would they enthusiastically support her bid for tenure and promotion? If she were being considered for a faculty position, would she be hired?

I've seen just this kind of case, heard faculty colleagues discuss the risk of hiring or promoting such a scholar, and listened while colleagues spelled out the beliefs that she would be expected to share in order to fit into the discipline and department. Can intersectionality be practiced in a way that's illiberal? Sure. But critics of the illiberal university shouldn't think they have a handle on the problem when they repeat the umbrella term provided by academic progressives that can function as a tactic of indirection.

This is why, faced with the terminological dilemma I outlined in the Introduction, I didn't decide to refer to the ideology I criticize as "intersectionality."

So, now that we have a basic understanding of "the people," let's examine the programs, policies and practices that universities have used to center the people. Universities have also used these very programs, policies, and practices to uproot the privilege of those who are not "the" people.

Beginning with Diversity, Equity, and Inclusion (DEI) and moving to "inclusive pedagogy," the rest of this chapter consists of a walk through changes in higher ed that effectively installed gender studies as the tip of the revolutionary spear.

Diversity, Equity, and Inclusion

In what follows, I use the abbreviation DEI for Diversity, Equity, and Inclusion though the term has been supplemented by additional aspirations, including "belonging" (B), "justice" (J), "accessibility" or "antiracism" (A) or "decolonization" (another D).

Oddly for what, under ordinary circumstances, would have been an obscure corner of higher ed and corporate administration, many Americans have heard of DEI offices, programs, initiatives, and professionals. They may recognize this abbreviation from conservative and MAGA political figures and influencers. However, one needn't be conservative or MAGA to have questions about DEI.

As we've come to know it in higher ed, DEI is heralded by its supporters as simply a logical outgrowth of the Civil Rights Movement, the Civil Rights Acts, and even the activism of historical figures such as Rosa Parks. DEI supporters have been careful, especially in public, not to associate it with more recent and controversial figures such as the professor of education Robin DiAngelo and the history professor Ibram X. Kendi. These and other thinkers in the contemporary tradition of antiracism reject "equality" in favor of "equity" and declare the necessity of discriminating against members of oppressor groups to benefit members of oppressed groups.[22]

Given the way that DEI can repudiate and subvert many ideals of the Civil Rights Movement, it's ironic and telling that DEI has consistently been marketed under the Civil Rights Movement brand.

After DEI offices, functions, budgets, and requirements attracted negative attention from skeptics and opponents, proponents in higher ed crafted public defenses. One perplexing defense is that DEI "help[s] ensure that colleges are complying with federal antidiscrimination laws."[23] If DEI functions are essential to universities' compliance with federal law, what did universities do in the decades before 2020?

Two explanations present themselves. One is that universities didn't comply with federal law before about 2015 and only became fully compliant starting in 2020, as the size, scope, and cost of DEI exploded. The other, which I suspect is more accurate, is that, before the advent of DEI, universities were more compliant with federal antidiscrimination law than they would become. If this is so, the defense of DEI as essential to the fulfillment of universities' obligations to federal law is a mendacious rhetorical move by faculty and administrators, many of whom vigorously disapprove of the identity neutrality at the heart of antidiscrimination law.

Other apologia cast DEI functions or requirements in banal and minimizing terms. For example, here's *The Chronicle of Higher Education*'s Adrienne Lu, on requirements for faculty and prospective candidates:

> Diversity statements are intended to allow those applying for faculty jobs or seeking tenure to reflect, typically in one or two pages, on how their teaching, research, and service have helped to advance an institution's diversity goals . . . .
>
> Diversity statements vary across institutions, but they are intended to highlight faculty members' contributions toward diversity goals, such as mentoring students or colleagues from underrepresented groups, designing a curriculum with diverse voices, or conducting research focused on minority groups. They are also used to give recognition to the "invisible labor" that often falls on women and faculty of color.[24]

The heavy service burden that often falls on faculty members of underrepresented groups is a longstanding problem in academia. Because this is so, it would seem churlish to criticize a process that enables job candidates "to reflect" on their "contributions" while "giv[ing] recognition" for disproportionate academic labor.

A related defense of DEI statements is that, while enabling prospective faculty to report information that supports their candidacy, statements only constitute a plus factor in decisions about hiring and promotions. Here, education journalist Megan Zahneis corrects a "misconception" about the uses to which DEI statements are put:

> A common misconception is that diversity statements are used to eliminate candidates, Whitaker says. "It's not something that we use to say, 'This person is racist or classist or sexist,' and we push them out. It's a way to say, 'Show us another part of yourself that traditional academia doesn't often invite.[25]

The most positive thing I can say about this defense of DEI policies and statements is that it would be pretty to think so. But before I turn to what we've learned about the DEI contribution to faculty hiring, let's look at some concerns and arguments of DEI critics.

A variety of serious criticisms have been levied against the DEI bureaucracy and its products, including that some practices associated with DEI aren't supported by empirical evidence; that it's costly for universities, students, and citizens who pay the bills; and that it doesn't produce the kinds of results proponents understand as its justification.[26]

The most visible form taken by the DEI regime in higher ed has been the DEI statement as a mode of determining who should be hired and promoted. Critics charge that DEI statements have been used as "political litmus tests" to enforce ideological homogeneity and exclude members of some groups from faculty positions.[27] Intended or not, such statements have "operate[d] as a selection mechanism for less free-expression-friendly faculty."[28] For those who may disagree with DEI in whole or part, DEI statements require affirmative acts of conformity, or what Harvard Law professor Randall Kennedy calls "ritualized dissembling."[29]

One way to analyze policies is to systematically evaluate their likely or actual unintended consequences. For example, DEI adherents may not reflect on the adverse consequences of hiring, promoting, and evaluating faculty based on "their contributions to improving society" according to a specific progressive vision. Having established such a standard, what happens if future "legislators or voters want to judge them based on how they advance a different understanding of social progress, one that departs more from their own—for example, how they've contributed to a war effort widely regarded as righteous"?[30]

In other words, as I often asked my students, what would you think if people on the other side made this same kind of claim or demand? As this thought experiment suggests, DEI-related efforts to instantiate progressivism have "politicized campus life" in ways that are invisible to progressives only because they agree with its values and goals.[31]

Most recently, some critics have called attention not only to groups that are included within the ambit of DEI but to those excluded from its scope of protection. For example, these critics charge that DEI will "never protect Jews," who tend to be classified in the belief system that underwrites DEI as white settlers flush with "ashkenormativity"—thus, oppressors.[32]

A common accusation against critics of DEI is that they reject the idea that there's group-based discrimination in American life and institutions. Not true, say both former DEI director Tabia Lee and Randall Kennedy, who describes himself as a "scholar on the left committed to struggles for social justice."[33] Indeed, the linguist John McWhorter clarifies explicitly that it's possible to believe that discriminatory beliefs and practices exist and want to remedy them, and still reject DEI. McWhorter argues that

> we can agree that the legacy of racism requires addressing and yet disagree about how best to do it. Of course in the pure sense, to be opposed to "diversity," opposed to "equity" and opposed to "inclusion" would fairly be called racism. But it is coy to pretend these dictionary

> meanings are what D.E.I. refers to in modern practice, which is a more specific philosophy.[34]

I agree with McWhorter when he characterizes DEI as being animated by a "specific philosophy," and I agree that these critics have identified reasons to be concerned. Progressive illiberalism in the academy is the problem of which DEI is only a symptom. Still, what we've come to learn about DEI demonstrates without doubt that DEI defenders such as those I've quoted misrepresent what DEI is and what it has done.

DEI on the Hot Seat

The most prominent practice associated with DEI is the DEI statement, which came to be required of academic job seekers, candidates for promotion, and faculty reporting their professional activities on annual reports. DEI statements are neither voluntary nor nugatory in their impact on careers and the production of knowledge.

Some sources have challenged the public relations depictions of DEI by investigating and publicizing universities' scoring rubrics for DEI statements and interviews. There's no mystery about DEI scoring rubrics in general. Search online for "DEI scoring," and numerous results appear for companies, non-profits, and universities. These documents give the lie to academic progressives' minimizing defenses of DEI programs and criteria.

Academic associations have developed scorecards, one of which is the American Library Association's (ALA) "Diversity, Equity, and Inclusion (DEI) Scorecard for Library and Information Organizations." The ALA's standard of excellence in DEI requires that a "library provides at least twice-yearly mandatory DEI trainings on current and systemic issues that impact equity in the organization."[35] Organizations and faculty who campaign for academic freedom argue that mandatory sessions like these are actually trainings in what McWhorter describes as a "specific philosophy."

Those familiar with the academy would expect to find illiberalism in the humanities and social sciences, not, for example, in schools of engineering. So, it's informative to see the intricacies of academic progressivism in a scoring tool used to sort DEI-compliant from non-compliant engineers at the University of Nebraska Lincoln. Based on DEI statements, faculty and administrators rate candidates as "exceptional," "adequate," "fair," or "poor" in 3 categories and 9 subcategories.

So far, so bureaucratic. The rubric also includes notes in each category to guide raters as they determine how to score candidates' statements; these notes hint at the ideology that underwrites the scoring exercise. Notes include whether and how candidates use "sensitive language" as opposed to "clichés and platitudes," to refer to groups and DEI goals; evince particular kinds and degrees of appreciation of intersectionality; demonstrate correct understandings of concepts of "diversity," "equity," "inclusion," and "belonging" without confusing the concepts for each other; and explain specifically how to "advance" each of these concepts, in and "beyond the university."

I take this last criterion as an indirect expression of the expectation that engineers, like their colleagues across the university, must commit to being activists for academic progressivism.[36] To be fair, not all DEI scoring rubrics have required outside activism. To have their "future DEI goals and plans" judged "exceptional" in DEI in Yale's Department of Molecular Biophysics and Biochemistry (MB&B), a candidate must merely provide a "clear and detailed plan for promoting DEI through teaching, research, and service" and delineate "how these plans fit into existing activities in MB&B and at Yale."

It's worth noting that, in Yale's MB&B department, scorers choose among four point options in each assessment category: "3 (Exceptional)," "2 (Solid)," "1 (Weak)" and, finally, the complete failure denoted only as "0."[37]

To be clear, over the course of my career, I've created diversity programing, taught courses on diversity, integrated underrepresented authors and materials into course syllabi, mentored minority students and colleagues, performed consulting on gender equity in STEM disciplines, and produced scholarship on issues central to diversity. Yet even if DEI scorers lacked knowledge of my unfortunate tendency to incorporate alternative points of view on contentious issues into my teaching, I might not make the grade.

The most effective data on DEI's impact on higher ed comes from public records requests by the National Association of Scholars (NAS) that exposed faculty hiring documents from public universities. Founded in 1987, the NAS is a 501(c)(3) non-profit that currently characterizes its goal as "uphold[ing] the standards of a liberal arts education that fosters intellectual freedom, searches for the truth, and promotes virtuous citizenship."[38] It's safe to say that the NAS is a conservative organization that's attracted support from prominent conservatives.

In 2023, the NAS filed public records requests for documents related to faculty hiring from 2020 to 2023 at public universities in a number of states. When faculty at my university received word of the requests, we were asked to direct any inquiries we might receive about faculty searches in which we'd participated during this period—presumably inquiries from NAS or similar groups—to the Senior Director of Marketing and Communications. This is the same administrator to whom department chairs were instructed to defer on statements they wished to direct to their units, suggesting that "marketing and communications" is one of the locations within a university bureaucracy that can easily become a black hole for academic freedom.

NAS Senior Fellow John Sailer analyzed the documents received through these public records requests.[39] The result was a series of reports across a variety of media and platforms. Sailer may have revised his opinion after he received my and other universities' data, but in early 2023 he'd speculated that my university "might be the worst offender in the nation—surpassing even such progressive bastions as the University of California, Berkeley."[40]

Because Sailer quoted liberally from the diversity reports, it isn't possible to discount his reporting as the disingenuous contortions of a partisan executing a hit job. Nor did he have to read between the lines; faculty search chairs and committees boasted about their values, standards, deliberations, and choices. The DEI apologists weren't vindicated.

Sailer published his first report on my university's faculty searches in the *Wall Street Journal* in November 2023. The article's opening passage teases the revelations to come:

> A search committee seeking a professor of military history rejected one applicant "because his diversity statement demonstrated poor understanding of diversity and inclusion issues." Another committee noted that an applicant to be a professor of nuclear physics could understand the plight of minorities in academia because he was married to "an immigrant in Texas in the Age of Trump."

Surveying the eight hundred pages of diversity reports he received from Flagship State, Sailer documents several patterns in the data, including that finalists for faculty positions were explicitly selected and rejected on the basis of the candidates' identities. Those selected to advance to final rounds of competition include—in direct quotes pulled from the diversity reports—"a person of color and a member of the LGBTQ+ community;" "a first generation, fat, queer scholar of color;" "a queer, neurodivergent Latinx woman in STEM;" and "a disabled scholar and queer woman of color."[41]

A white man received the benefit of the doubt in one search because he had recently published on Critical Race Theory. This information may provide a road map to success for those who lacked the foresight to marry "an immigrant in Texas in the age of Trump."

DEI proponents characterize diversity statements as plus factors in hiring and promotion decisions, but it would be generous to say that this defense doesn't hold up in the face of the data. Departments reported "weighted rubrics" in which the DEI statement was evaluated to be as important as expertise in the discipline. It was possible to receive a score of zero if, instead of mirroring back to the evaluators what they wanted and expected to hear, candidates merely acknowledged that forms of unacceptable bias still exist in the academy.

Just to be clear, while earnest DEI apologists were swearing that candidates for faculty positions were not being excluded from candidate pools based on DEI criteria—indeed, that only bigots would say they were—prospective faculty were consistently being excluded from candidate pools based on DEI criteria.[42] Sailer notes that, at my university, DEI statements judged to be inadequate were "the sole reason for eliminating certain candidates in fields as varied as aquatic ecology, lighting design, military history and music theory."[43]

Document dumps such as those accomplished through academic public records requests raise an important question: how should we treat and process mendacity on the political and academic left? Starting in 2016, many citizens and groups called for news media and political commentators to stop applying euphemisms to Donald Trump's various scams, schemes, ad hominem denunciations, assaults on democracy, and efforts to install his whims as law. To call deliberate falsehoods what they are: lies. I vote to apply this standard to both sides.

Whither DEI?

Given the backlash against DEI bureaucracies and mandatory DEI statements, it was probably unavoidable that DEI rollback and retrenchment would commence.

The most extreme form of rollback has been the banning of DEI offices, functions, and personnel in state universities undertaken in red states such as Texas, Florida, and Utah.[44] Rollback has occurred through advocacy by free speech organizations like FIRE, as at the University of Massachusetts Boston and many others.[45] It's also been imposed by senior university officials at some institutions. After the underlying ideology of DEI policies and practices became public, criticism began to emerge from within the faculty.[46] Finally, some organizations and universities have opted to "go quiet" and rebrand their DEI offices and functions to evade unwanted scrutiny.[47]

Sailer published the first tranche of reporting on my university's faculty hiring in the *Wall Street Journal* on November 20, 2023. It's no coincidence that on November 21, Flagship State updated its "Diversity, Equity, and Inclusion" policy statement and directed members of the community to the revised policy on the Office of Marketing and Communications "Key Issues" webpage. There, my university asserted that

> with regard to hiring, [Flagship] State follows all state and federal employment labor practices and does not make hiring decisions based on race, gender or other protected classifications. While [Flagship] State has never had a university-wide requirement to use diversity statements in hiring, individual colleges and units have used diversity statements as part of their hiring.[48] The university is in the process of developing and implementing a more consistent set of university-wide practices for the hiring of both faculty and staff. These practices will not include the use of diversity statements . . . .
>
> We have an unwavering commitment to free speech and freedom of expression and believe it is crucial that students learn to engage in difficult conversations while maintaining civility and respect. A central part of [Flagship] State's DEI programming creates opportunities for students to engage in productive dialogue and conversation with peers holding different viewpoints from across the political spectrum and from different backgrounds.[49]

This statement, which reads like standard institutional boilerplate, reminds me of the gauntlet thrown down by the novelist and critic Mary McCarthy in her feud with playwright and memoirist Lillian Hellman. McCarthy declared that "every word" Hellman wrote "was a lie—including 'and' and 'the.'"[50]

It's hard to imagine why Flagship State rushed to amend its DEI policy statement if nothing in Sailer's initial report embarrassed the university or was perceived to put it at risk. Wasn't it the case that a robust DEI bureaucracy was necessary to implement federal law? Readers may judge for themselves the extent to which the faculty hiring practices revealed in Sailer's reporting contradict US universities' avowals that they had always followed federal antidiscrimination law.

As materials from public records requests show, many of the practices that universities could do little to defend were enthusiastically perpetrated and amply documented. Yet, for the most part, those responsible for overseeing the practices exposed by the National Association of

Scholars remained in their positions.

One result of reporting on DEI has been a backlash against it. But even if DEI offices were eliminated virtually universally, universities wouldn't be out of the illiberal woods. Many mechanisms remain for training, hiring, and promoting faculty to sustain the progressive belief system and practices that threaten academic freedom.

How to Select "the People" as Faculty

How does the progressive academy ensure that the right people and beliefs are "centered" in faculty hiring? Let's go back some time before the present crisis of academic freedom. When I started out as an academic, most faculty job ads were approximately a paragraph long. They tended to be written in something like this form:

> Department X of the University of Y seeks a [rank] professor who specializes in subfields A, B, and/or C for a tenure-track position. Successful candidates will have completed a PhD in the discipline by [date], and will show evidence of teaching experience and scholarly excellence. Send a letter of application, a c.v., and three letters of recommendation by [date] to: Chair, Department X Search Committee, [address].
>
> The University of Y is an Equal Opportunity/Affirmative Action employer. Qualified women, minorities, Vietnam-era veterans, disabled veterans, and individuals with disabilities are encouraged to apply.

Note that, in this obsolete template, no political beliefs or theoretical commitments are specified. Given the value of a faculty line to a department, specific ideas about the needs of a department would be debated in a spirited fashion in camera. But, before 2000, I never heard a group of political scientists posit that what the department needed was another faculty member who cleaved to a theory or belief system to which all faculty were expected to adhere.

To the contrary, such conversations often took account of what existing faculty already "did" and what other perspectives, theories, or methods might be necessary to contribute to strengthening a subfield or the department as a whole. Verbal jousting and negotiation might ensue.

Now, consider the following job announcement, which I reproduce in its entirety. Not all job announcements in gender studies are this detailed and specific, but this one advertises the radical, queer, decolonizing political and activist commitments of gender studies.

> The Women's, Gender & Queer Studies Department in the College of Liberal Arts at California Polytechnic State University, San Luis Obispo, is seeking an Assistant Professor in Feminist/Queer/Trans* Dis/Ability Studies.
>
> The Women's, Gender & Queer Studies Department at California Polytechnic State University (Cal Poly) in San Luis Obispo, CA seeks applications for a full-time (academic year), tenure-track assistant professor with a specialization in feminist, queer, and/or trans* dis/ability studies, with a particular focus on critical approaches that emphasize dis/ability as a social situation and a political process; consider dis/ability in the context of settler colonialism, cisheteropatriarchy, and racial capitalism; and center the knowledges and experiences of people with dis/abilities, studying cultural and artistic productions, social, cultural, and/or political theories, public laws and policies, professional practices, and/or everyday life.
>
> Applicants must have graduate training in Women's, Gender & Queer Studies and/or Dis/Ability Studies, which can come from a range of disciplinary homes, and should approach scholarship and teaching from interdisciplinary perspectives. Candidates must demonstrate: 1) an ongoing commitment to scholarly inquiry, education, and activism in critical feminist, queer, and/or trans* studies that utilizes an integrative approach, exploring the intersections of gender, sexuality, dis/abilities, race, ethnicity, socioeconomic class, religion, citizenship status, and other social categories within local, regional, national, and transnational networks and contexts; 2) the ability to collaborate with students/faculty/staff both from within the College of Liberal Arts and across the university; and 3) a record of and commitment to working to ensure an equitable and inclusive campus for all. The successful candidate must also have the ability to work effectively with students,

> staff, and faculty from a diversity of racial, ethnic, socioeconomic, and other cultural backgrounds.
>
> Candidates are expected to demonstrate a commitment to, or potential for, teaching excellence and scholarly activity at the university level and will teach WGQS core courses that contribute to the Women's & Gender Studies minor and/or the Queer Studies minor; new and existing courses in Dis/Ability Studies; and courses that contribute to the university's general education curriculum. Candidates should also demonstrate experience with and/or interest in curriculum and program development, especially via collaborations across departments, colleges, and/or additional institutional units.
>
> Cal Poly strongly values diversity, equity, and inclusion (DEI), especially in the classroom and among its areas of study. This position is part of a college-wide cluster of searches designed to increase curricular coverage of areas related to DEI, as well as to promote inclusive and equity-minded teaching strategies across the university. Successful candidates will be expected to contribute to the college's goals in these areas.[51]

See any difference between these two ads? Just kidding—of course you do.

Reading closely, we see that in addition to holding a PhD from an accredited institution, having teaching experience, and demonstrating scholarly potential—long the stuff of faculty searches across disciplines—the successful candidate must meet several conditions. For my purposes, two stand out.

First, the candidate *must* have a particular political perspective on and in the subfield of specialization that is carefully spelled out: "a particular focus on critical approaches that emphasize dis/ability as a social situation and a political process; consider dis/ability in the context of settler colonialism, cisheteropatriarchy, and racial capitalism." Second, the candidate *must* be committed to activism of the particular kind laid out in the description of the field. Indeed, "an ongoing commitment to . . . activism in critical feminist, queer, and/or trans* studies" is the first of three requirements enumerated in the posting.

Now, these criteria for the successful candidate might not have been broadcast so openly. They might just have remained the criteria faculty in the department applied to all applicants behind the scenes, consigning those who didn't advocate their beliefs and activist bona fides vigorously enough to rejection.

So, it's significant that these criteria were publicized. Here's an analogy: In the 2000s, my partner was posted to a two-year position in Sioux Falls, South Dakota and, come the 2004 elections, it was fascinating to see businesses all over the city and state blossom with "Vote Republican" signs. These business owners clearly understood that they would only *gain* business through signaling their political preference. In fact, in that environment, silence on their political preference might be misconstrued as support for Democrats! So, they signaled. Vigorously.

I see these requirements of shared beliefs and activism similarly: as public signaling that lays to rest any suspicion about the commitments of the faculty. But it's also a sign that faculty who searched in this way had nothing to fear from higher administration. I would go farther: at least until free speech organizations, Republican state legislators, and the Trump administration came calling, these faculty knew that administrators would be thrilled.

Remember that, in the early period of women's studies, faculty came out of traditional disciplines. It follows that faculty hiring in women's studies reflected an interest in representation of intellectual fields or subfields: "women and/in" law, health, labor, literature, art, film, public policy, media studies, and so on. Such hires could manifest a degree of intellectual diversity that reflected disciplinary theories and methods.

Since then, political and intellectual homogeneity, both within gender studies and across disciplinary boundaries, has increased. And instead of selecting for *difference*, the most progressive disciplines select for *sameness*. Or, rather, the difference they select for is identity difference. To target and hire members of identity groups, searching for scholars in traditional fields and subfields is out. Searching in fields defined by identity, such as indigenous, black, queer, Latinx, and disability studies is in.

Now that we have a sense of how the progressive academy selects "the people" as faculty, let's examine how progressives organize pedagogy around and for those groups, socializing students about the meaning of diversity, equity, and inclusion as they go.

How to Educate "The People" and the Rest

When John Stuart Mill considered the role of political parties in a two-party system, he noted that there's always "a party of order or stability, and a party of progress or reform." For Mill, "both [are] necessary elements of a healthy state of political life," each "deriv[ing] its utility from the deficiencies of the other."[52]

More recently, journalists, pundits, and some political scientists nicknamed the Democratic Party the "mommy party" and the Republican Party the "daddy party." The linguist George Lakoff explains the distinction as resting on opposing models of family that express political morality. Conservatism expresses "Strict Father" morality and liberalism expresses "Nurturant Parent" morality.[53]

Extending this analysis, we can understand important dimensions of our current crisis in higher ed as consequences of the repudiation of daddy pedagogy by a mommy pedagogy that replaced it, not just in practice but in official university policy.

In general, daddy pedagogy is the retro system characterized by professorial authority, high intellectual standards that some students may fail to meet, the ideal to challenge students without regard for their discomfort, and some less savory aspects we olds recall from our own training.

For example, I'd locate the elderly male professor who announced to an undergraduate class in which I was a student that he didn't like "girls" in his classes and that, in his classes, "girls" earned lower grades than "men" on the daddier edge of daddy pedagogy. A few years later, the faculty member who directed my dissertation employed daddy pedagogy when he left the following comment in the margin of a draft page: "This is stupid. Take it out." Not deterred from dissertationing, I talked with him, saw his point, and took it out.

Mommy Pedagogy, by contrast, is characterized primarily by affirming student feelings and effort, and evincing deep concern with student wellbeing, including or especially students' mental and emotional health. Mommy pedagogy takes as given the emotional fragility that many observers of higher ed have criticized as producing bad outcomes for students themselves.[54] Empirically, mommy pedagogy also means inculcating students with elements of "caring" progressive ideology that faculty regard as irrefutable moral truths.

In women's and gender studies, we've always taken for granted that daddy pedagogy is bad for students and education. Our norms, conventions, instructional standards, teacher training, and faculty evaluations demonstrate and reinforce this conviction.

Bear in mind that mommy and daddy pedagogies are umbrella categories within which there may be a considerable range of goals, behaviors, and outcomes. Just as the daddy party in US politics isn't all male and the mommy party isn't all female, daddy and mommy pedagogies don't match up perfectly with sex. Finally, it's possible, and may even be pedagogically effective, for teachers to use mommy and daddy pedagogical tools to achieve different goals.

But one doesn't have to be male to perceive the liabilities of mommy pedagogy. In recent years, merely believing that policies ought to be applied, and students treated, equally was sufficient to mark one as a proponent of daddy pedagogy. And as someone who might pose a threat to university students.

The perception that young adults are, in fact, emotionally fragile is a driver of mommy pedagogy. Even if we set aside the fraught question of whether young adults are more fragile than they were three decades ago, something significant has clearly shifted since the eighties, when I started teaching. One way to frame this difference is that adults have for many years instructed college students that teachers and university faculty are responsible for monitoring and ameliorating their discomfort.

This explanation also helps to account for the ways in which many students have come to outsource the management of their group-based identities to those around them. By this I mean that it's common for students to believe that faculty should mirror back to them the inevitably progressive language and worldview that conforms to their self-understanding. To the extent that contentious political issues are tied to identity—and virtually all can be—mommy pedagogy requires that students' emotional investments in particular points of view be validated.

Mommy pedagogy was put into action through practices that came to be known collectively as "inclusive pedagogy." These innovations include "microaggressions," "safe spaces," "trigger warnings," "grading for justice," "progressive stacking," "community agreements," and "land acknowledgements." Bias reporting systems aren't an element of classroom practice, but they function to further the goals of inclusive pedagogy.

Microaggressions

Microaggressions aren't a feature of inclusive pedagogy but, rather, a kind of injury that inclusive pedagogy is engineered to preemptively identify and rectify. The University of North Carolina School of Medicine defines "microaggressions" in a way that's now customary: as "everyday slights, insults, putdowns, invalidations, and offensive behaviors that people experience in daily interactions with generally well-intentioned individuals who may be unaware that they have engaged in demeaning ways."[55]

Universities develop and disseminate education, policies and messaging about microaggressions. University personnel share material and best practices across institutions. As a result, discourse, policies and practices with regard to microaggressions are relatively homogenous across universities. Eliminating or lessening "slights, insults, putdowns, invalidations, and offensive behaviors" that might compromise learning and employment environments certainly seems like an admirable goal.

Even as universities share best practices, however, they don't acknowledge the theoretical, philosophical, or activist foundations that dictate the concept and content of microaggressions. For example, expressing a belief that race neutrality is a laudable social goal generally constitutes a microaggression. Different kinds of speech are likely to be classed as microaggressions if they express disagreement with another's lived experience or "stories."[56]

As opposed to what we might now call "macroaggressions"—overt bigotry by people whose conduct is likely to be intentional and may rise to the level of illegal discrimination—microaggressions are virtually always understood as unconscious, unintentional, and even imperceptible to those who commit them. Without the kind of education provided by universities, some microaggressions might even be imperceptible to those who suffer them.

Safe Space(s)

Of all the elements of inclusive pedagogy, perhaps the most notorious is "safe spaces." In conservative quarters, the concept provokes disgust with fragile and privileged college students. It's useful to remember, however, that progressive students and faculty aren't the only people who have come to demand spaces from which all discouraging words have been evacuated. It's become common for groups of believers of all kinds to expect universal affirmation, and even obeisance, from those they interact with, in person or online.

It's more challenging to define the concept of safe space as it has prevailed in higher ed than it is to define some other elements of inclusive pedagogy. This is because, whereas some other elements are defined rather straightforwardly in documents and policies, it's tough to nail down what universities mean when they tacitly or explicitly represent the classroom as a safe space.

One definition of safe classroom space is offered by the executive director of Behavioral Health and Counseling and Psychological Services at Stony Brook University: "By their simplest definition, 'safe spaces' are those places where people feel they can be who they are."[57] Okay, let's test this definition with a simple thought experiment that's also the kind of thing that happened in classes in the time before "safe spaces."

Let's say a student in one of my classes spoke up during a discussion of LGBTQ issues and attested to his belief that homosexuality violates

God's will for human sexuality and intimacy. As the professor, what should I do?

A. Look like a deer in the headlights
B. Point to my class's "community agreement" (don't worry—we'll get to this anon), inform him that he's violated this agreement, and outline the consequences he'll now incur
C. Acknowledge his position and thank him for offering it. Inform the class about the source of this value and provide a pocket history of how contentious debates over the issue have shaped the current political environment
D. Inform the student that he's made the classroom unsafe for LGBTQ+ students. Assure queer students that their peer will be dealt with in a way that ensures both their safety and their freedom not to endure hearing such a viewpoint
E. B and D, if not A

Of course, my response to such a breach in safety was "C." The student in my example is, indeed, being who he is, just as Stony Brook University advises and celebrates. Nevertheless, my colleagues wouldn't consider his intervention to be consistent with what they mean by safe space. We're best off being highly skeptical that safe classrooms are those that enable students—all students—to "be who they are," much less air their ideas.

Many universities have, in recent years, offered safe space "ally trainings." These provide students and faculty with training specific to the putative needs of particular marginalized groups. In the past, I've affirmed the value of voluntary identity-related groups, and I still think these can be fruitful for many people. As we might expect, however, safe space trainings are conducted from didactic, progressive theoretical and activist perspectives that leave little room for productive disagreements among those who share a group identity.

With regard to demands that classrooms be safe spaces, the former college instructor and writer John Warner distinguishes "safety" from "security" and suggests that "everyone actually agrees about safe spaces." I'm very much in favor of probing to see how much agreement might be wrung or rescued from disagreements. Unfortunately, contra Warner, I doubt that "95 percent" of us agree that student "testimonies" of feeling unsafe should be taken as facts.[58]

Trigger Warnings

Nearly as notorious as safe spaces are trigger warnings. These are content alerts generated by instructors, authors, publishers, and platforms intended to provide advance warning of potentially unsettling material. As this brief description suggests, trigger warnings emerged from psychology and, more specifically, from trauma counseling.

Feminists' attention to trauma-related trigger warnings may have been influenced by Judith Lewis Herman's 1992 book, *Trauma and Recovery*, which analyzed similarities between psychological trauma associated with warfare and trauma associated with sexual assault. The connection between these forms of trauma is now so widely accepted that the National Center for PTSD (Post-Traumatic Stress Disorder) of the US Department of Veterans Affairs straightforwardly treats sexual assault as a cause of PTSD and provides information and resources to veterans.[59]

Trigger warnings debuted in feminist media in the late nineties and quickly began to be integrated into feminist classrooms. Their earliest versions identified violent content, especially so that girls and women wouldn't be blindsided—and, as the understanding went, emotionally ambushed and retraumatized—by words or images.

As trigger warnings became more popular and institutionalized in the 2000s, their use to protect students from trauma came to be taken for granted. The subject areas for which such warnings were regarded as appropriate—even required—expanded. Students began to request warnings for a wide range of topics and materials, and express dismay or anger if they didn't receive them. And faculty and students came to believe that students had a right to receive alternative materials that would substitute for texts, videos, lectures, and assignments they self-diagnosed as triggering.

There are a number of reasons to be skeptical of trigger warnings. They can disrupt lesson plans and impose significant costs on instructors and students in the form of foregone instruction time, bespoke lessons, and self-censorship. Many instructors avoid certain topics altogether when they know that students will regard having to read, view, or hear material as threatening their emotional wellbeing.[60]

But the most compelling reason to scale back or reject trigger warnings altogether is, as many clinicians and researchers have put it, "trigger warnings don't work." A comprehensive meta-analysis of trigger warning studies performed by the psychologists Victoria M. E. Bridgland, Payton J. Jones, and Benjamin W. Bellet examined four dimensions of effects associated by proponents with trigger warnings. They concluded that "trigger warnings had no meaningful effect on response affect, avoidance, or educational outcomes (i.e., comprehension). However, trigger warnings reliably increased anticipatory distress before viewing material."[61]

Trigger warnings persist, nonetheless. In the kinds of spaces where instructors deliver warnings and students expect them, anxiety and trauma reactions are understood to express "objective" "experiential reality."[62] Under such circumstances, trigger warnings become a proxy for caring about students and wanting to do everything in one's power to spare them harm. The failure or refusal to provide them is ill advised for those whose teaching will be judged by their peers as well as by students.

Grading for Justice

I want to preface my account of grading for justice with a quick overview of related practices: "equitable grading" and "ungrading." A proponent of equitable grading, author and educator Joe Feldman, explains that the practice was developed with a goal of making "grades more accurate and fair for all students by excluding nonacademic criteria, dampening subjective biases, and reducing the impact of resource disparities."

Feldman acknowledges that some proponents may have "misinterpreted and misapplied" the equitable grading framework in ways that raised concerns from skeptics about rigor and grade inflation. Practices that have been widely associated with equitable grading include awarding a minimum score of fifty percent instead of a zero grade for missed assignments, not grading homework, and attaching no penalty to work turned in after a deadline.

According to the Columbia University Center for Teaching and Learning, "ungrading" "critically views grades as a systemic practice and offers alternative ways to reimagine how student learning can be assessed more equitably."[63]

I introduce equitable grading and ungrading because grading for justice emerged from a similar set of concerns from educators about "ways in which our traditional grading practices disproportionately benefit or harm groups of students," especially "low-income students and children of color."[64]

Grading for justice came to public attention after a white Minneapolis police officer murdered George Floyd in 2020. In 2021, UCLA instructor Gordon Klein was suspended from teaching in the Gordon School for Management for refusing a white student's request to grade black students differently than white students because black students might have suffered trauma from Floyd's killing. FIRE advocated for Klein, he was reinstated, and he subsequently sued UCLA.[65]

Nor is Klein's the only case of pressure on a faculty member to practice grading for justice. Zack De Piero taught writing at Penn State Abington. In 2024, De Piero alleged in a lawsuit that university administrators pressured him "to incorporate race into his grading." As a result, De Piero attested that "he had to discard his own race-neutral grading rubric and instead 'penalize students academically on the basis of their race.'"

De Piero complained about the grading issue and forms of training and instruction he received on race at Penn State Abington before publishing his concerns. He was disciplined by his institution and had his employment evaluation downgraded. He sued, and the lawsuit was permitted to go forward when the court found that he'd "plausibly alleged that he was subjected to a race-based hostile work environment while at Penn State."[66]

Progressive Stacking

"Progressive stacking," or "taking progressive stack," is a classroom technique in which students are called upon "to speak on the basis of race, sex, and other group membership, with preference given to members of groups that are considered the most marginalized."[67] Progressive stacking is a two-step process. First, during discussion the instructor keeps a list of all students who indicate their interest in speaking ("taking stack"). Second, the instructor executes the progressive turn:

> To prevent a class discussion from "reproducing dominant hierarchies of privilege and power," foreground voices that are typically silenced in dominant culture. According to Justine and Zoë, two self-identified transwomen who were active in the movement, progressive stack means that "if you self-identify as trans, queer, a person of color, female, or as a member of any marginalized group you're given priority on the list of people who want to speak—the stack. The most oppressed get to speak first.[68]

And also last. The investigation into my teaching came to include an accusation that, in an undergrad class, I didn't call on students with particular group identities to have the last word in discussions of issues related to those identities. My response to this charge was that, in class discussions, I tried to keep track of who wanted to speak and call on students in the order in which they indicated their interest in speaking. The exception to this approach, I reported, was when it appeared that a student wanted to respond specifically to something a peer had just said, in which case I confirmed that intention and invited the student to respond before returning to the order.

Even as I responded to this accusation, I knew my answer indicted me. By my own admission, I wasn't a progressive stacker. Worse, I clearly didn't believe that any one group of students should always get the first, last, or only word on an issue related to identity.

One empirical problem with progressive stacking is that the process relies on how students self-identify and what instructors perceive about students' identities to suss out how they should be "stacked" to ensure that the oppressed shall be first and the oppressors last.

Even if I were so inclined, I can't imagine collecting enough information about students to cleanly distinguish oppressors from oppressed. If I had perfect information, however, I still wouldn't have engaged in this practice because I cared about treating students as individuals, not as bearers of ascriptive traits.

Skepticism about progressive stacking is dismissed by one blogging progressive professor as emanating from "the fever swamps of right-wing Reddit and warmed-over piles of gamergate droppings."[69] I'm here to attest that one doesn't have to be male, a gamer, or a Redditor to be critical of progressive stacking.

However, the Tattooed Professor does offer a fine example of the view that *only* far right-wingers can possibly take issue with the terms of inclusive pedagogy manufactured by faculty and administrators. Implicit in this explanation is the now familiar belief that critics of academic progressivism can all be safely dismissed as right wing.

Community Agreements

I first learned of "community agreements" when I read a grad student's syllabus for an undergrad class in my gender studies department. I don't recall if the syllabus specified what kinds of acts, including speech acts, would constitute a violation of the class's values. But the consequence for such violation was memorable: transgressors would be asked to leave the room and wait outside while the group deliberated on their punishment.

The grad student's class policy was such a flagrant violation of students' academic freedom that I found it hard to believe it hadn't been flagged for faculty oversight. To my knowledge, it wasn't. The grad student remained in good standing and was praised for outstanding teaching.

So, community agreements are pacts developed by an instructor and her students in a particular class to establish norms and values, as well as procedures for dealing with their violations. The National Equity Project (NEP), a non-profit "social impact organization" that collaborates with schools, education organizations, and teachers, defines community agreements in a way that I recognize from the progressive academy.

For the NEP, community agreements affirm

> a consensus on what every person in our group needs from each other and commits to each other in order to feel safe, supported, open, productive and trusting . . . so that we can do our best work, achieve our common vision, and serve our [students/families/constituents] well.[70]

Women's Studies was born with a yearning for consensus, and here we are.

Let me offer an example, both of the fashion for community agreements and of the impulse to backtrack under scrutiny. In early 2023, Barnard College had this to say about community agreements:

> Perhaps one of the greatest (and most complex) uses of community agreements is in establishing what steps people can take to repair the learning community when the threads that hold them together start to become frayed. This can be handled by developing exercises or explicitly asking students to work together on identifying practices for sticky problems: how they will engage in debate with each other; how students can make their concerns known when they feel harmed by a member of the community; how members can take responsibility for transgressions; and how the community will move forward when a person does take responsibility for their transgression.

No matter how many times I read this passage, I get stuck on the assertion about the "greatest and most complex" uses of community agreements—what could that mean? And the conclusion of the passage makes me queasy because of the clear echoes of the many totalitarian contexts in which people have been forced to confess and "take responsibility for their transgression."

But people, and institutions, live and learn. And they cover tracks. By early 2024, Barnard was emphasizing that community agreements should never be used as "a security measure that preempts and prevents conflict or disagreement between students or between students and you as an instructor." Or as "a disciplinary measure that can be drawn from to stifle dissent and difference within the classroom." If community agreements become either a tool of security or discipline, Barnard wants us to know that "they have become a policing mechanism" and that it's "time to revisit and revise them."[71]

If we learn anything from Barnard's conversion experience, it's that no US university ever suggested that students should be expelled from the classroom to await the community justice pronounced by their professor and peers. Any suggestion to the contrary is fake news.

Land Acknowledgements

Inclusive pedagogy reaches into all aspects of instruction. Suggested elements for inclusive syllabi include a land acknowledgment of a sort that's now familiar to academics. By 2020 or so, land acknowledgements were widely recommended to instructors, and we quickly became accustomed to starting meetings, lectures, and conference panels with some version of an acknowledgement that the land occupied by our workplace had been obtained illicitly or by force from its indigenous inhabitants.[72]

Oddest of all was the experience of hearing these acknowledgements recited when the meeting or conference was taking place in cyberspace and "we" were in many states or countries.

One thing to keep in mind about such "recommended" political statements is that they can be revised to fit different circumstances but only as long as the emendation intensifies the progressive sentiment expressed by the statement. So, for example, when a heterodox academic decided to test his university's appetite for free thought and wrote his own "acknowledgement," the result was instructive.

Confronted with a prefab land acknowledgement as a "best practice" for course syllabi, University of Washington computer science professor

Stuart Reges put a personal spin on his acknowledgement that featured a Lockean labor theory of value. The statement Reges placed on his syllabus read as follows: "I acknowledge that by the labor theory of property the Coast Salish people can claim historical ownership of almost none of the land currently occupied by the University of Washington."[73]

Reges composed his personal land acknowledgement to make the point that faculty were being pressured to post on syllabi a political statement that was superfluous to their courses. This would not do. His university sanctioned him for making an inappropriate and offensive statement. *Inside Higher Ed* reported on University of Washington spokesperson Victor Balta's response to Reges' transgression:

> Commonly utilized land acknowledgements are not politicized statements about land claims or ownership nor expressions of personal viewpoints about land ownership, but are rather statements of fact—the purpose being to acknowledge that the university sits on the historical ancestral lands of the Coast Salish people.

Balta added that "the syllabus for an intro to computer programming course is not the appropriate place or manner for a debate about land acknowledgements."[74]

Kudos to Victor Balta for providing a beautiful example of the common social movement practice of redescribing political positions as unmarked truth or morality claims. A psychoanalyst might also identify projection here: it's not the "best practice" of land acknowledgment that's political but, rather, objecting to and satirizing the best practice. I'm not being political, you are!

Although land acknowledgements differ from each other by listing diverse sets of native tribes and peoples, similarities provide a recognizable template. Here, for example, was the land acknowledgement "approved syllabus template" of the College of Arts and Sciences at my university:

> We would like to acknowledge the land that [Flagship State University] occupies is the ancestral and contemporary territory of the

> Shawnee, Potawatomi, Delaware, Miami, Peoria, Seneca, Wyandotte, Ojibwe and Cherokee peoples. Specifically, the university resides on land ceded in the 1795 Treaty of Greeneville and the forced removal of tribes through the Indian Removal Act of 1830. I/We want to honor the resiliency of these tribal nations and recognize the historical contexts that has and continues to affect the Indigenous peoples of this land.[75]

By contrast, here's the land acknowledgement you deliver when you're among friends—in this case, before some job talks at Flagship State:

> I want to mark that [Flagship State University] is on stolen land. We at [Flagship State University] and we who live in a city named for a brutal colonizer occupy the lands of many indigenous people who were forcibly removed and who continue to demand and deserve reparations for thievery, murder, and cruelty against humans, animals, and non-humans alike. We pay our respects to the Shawnee, Potawatomi, Delaware, Miami, Peoria, Seneca, Wyandotte, Cherokee and Ojibwe/Chippawa peoples, who demand land back. A cluster hire at [Flagship State University] in indigenous studies is but one attempt that the university makes to create relations with those whose land is stolen.

I suspect that many colleagues would volunteer to make the case that this acknowledgement represented a statement of fact and an apolitical best practice. Perhaps senior administrators and university attorneys should talk among themselves.

Collective Responsibility

Another element of inclusive pedagogy is a statement of "Collective Responsibility for Addressing Privilege and Oppression." This one is recommended for course syllabi by the University of Denver Office of Teaching and Learning.

> We acknowledge that racism, classism, ableism, homophobia, trans-

> phobia, sexism, and other forms of oppression exist. Any critical examination of oppression requires us to recognize that we have been systematically taught misinformation about our own group as well as about members of other groups. It also means that, if we are a part of a dominant group (e.g., white, male, upper/middle class, able-bodied, and/or heterosexual), we have unearned privilege that carries into the classroom and for which we are responsible. Being responsible means examining our words and actions and considering how we can be allies to others. *We cannot be blamed for the misinformation that we have learned and for taking unconscious advantage of our privilege, but we will be held responsible for repeating misinformation or engaging in oppressive behavior once we have learned otherwise.*[76]

We will be held responsible. As my brief account of community agreements suggests, this isn't just boilerplate language. Faculty and students stood by to make good on the threat.

Bias Reporting Systems

Bias reporting systems proliferated at American colleges and universities after 2010. Institutions with bias reporting systems invited students and faculty to anonymously report instances of what they regarded as bias to Bias Response Teams. These teams, usually staffed with student conduct administrators, and "armed with open-ended definitions of 'bias'," were explicitly given leeway to, as the Foundation for Individual Rights and Expression put it, "impose sanctions for speech they dislike."

FIRE warned in 2017 that the predictable result of Bias Response Teams functioning as they did, including "without training on freedom of expression," was that they might "expose a wide range of protected speech to punishment." But wait! Supporters of bias response systems noted that in many cases, these systems merely "provide 'education' to the offending speaker instead of formal punitive sanctions."

FIRE responded that when universities provide "education" that contravenes principles of academic freedom, they "create—indeed, they are intended to create—a chilling effect on campus." "Encouraging students and faculty to anonymously report one another to administrators for subversive or offensive views is illiberal, and antithetical to a campus open to the free exchange of ideas."[77]

What do these bias response systems look like on the ground? In 2023, I read the websites of many US colleges and universities to see how higher ed institutions framed the need for such systems. A few examples reveal how easy it's been for universities to ignore the existence of the First Amendment and principles of academic freedom to implement subjective standards for speech that triggers scrutiny and sanctions.

Truman State University in Missouri defines a "bias-related incident" as

> *any act that appears and or is perceived by the targeted person* as motivated, at least in part, by hostility toward the target person or an entire group because of that actual or perceived age, disability/ability status, race, color, gender identity/expression, national origin, religion/spirituality, sexual orientation, socioeconomic class, etc. Not all acts of bias violate University policy or law.[78]

Truman State's definition urges students to be alert for acts, presumably including speech acts, that may "appear" or be "perceived by" a "targeted person" as "motivated . . . in part" by "hostility" toward that person or "an entire group." It seems there's so little chance that someone who perceives herself as a "targeted person" could be mistaken that the possibility doesn't bear mention.

The vagueness and believe-the-victimness that characterizes so many bias response systems is also in evidence at Pittsburgh's Carnegie Mellon University.

> A bias incident occurs when *our culture is disrupted through negative and/or discriminatory conduct, speech or expression* directed toward a group or individual in the Carnegie Mellon community based on perceived or actual race, color, national origin, sex, handicap or disability, age, sexual orientation, gender identity, religion, creed, ancestry, belief, veteran status, genetic information, or any combination of these factors." Bias incidents, whether intentional or unintentional in their

> occurrence, contribute to creating an unwelcoming environment for individuals and groups at the university.[79]

At Carnegie Mellon, it's not necessary that actual discrimination has occurred for students to have a cause of action.

I have no doubt that unwanted political ideas and empirical evidence could constitute a "negative" disruption of "our culture" sufficient to create "an unwelcoming environment."

In 2023, the psychology department at the University of Washington made generous use of the language of trauma when assuring members of its community that reporting bias is courageous, requiring as it does the reliving of difficult experiences. The psychology department vowed to provide support and information about university health resources to bias reporters.[80]

For reference regarding these traumatic experiences, the department posted its Bias Reporting Annual Reports for 2020–21 and 2021–22 online.[81] Fortunately, all those reported for comments, microaggressions and infelicitous terminology professed to see the error of their ways, apologized to the bias reporters, and took action to repair injury to the community.

Even the professor reported in 2021–22 for failing to include asexuals/aromantics in a class discussion of *romantic* relationships "was receptive" to the criticism. Faculty assured community members that promised training on gender and sexuality would make injuries like this one less likely in the future.

Finally, Colorado State University informs students and faculty that its bias reporting system serves three purposes: support, education, and assessment. The Support function consists of providing "critical support" to students "who are *targeted by perceived bias-related incidents*" "as they work through their own process and feelings." The Education function is activated when the bias response team members

> engage in optional conversations with individuals and groups who, whether intentionally or not, may have caused harm to others related to some form of bias. These conversations are rooted in education and

> aim to provide critical context to why an action may be perceived as biased. In order to do better we must know better.[82]

Colorado State provides bias response services to students who are "targeted by perceived . . . incidents," which can only mean that students' perceptions of having been "targeted" are to be treated as unassailable.

This interpretation is strengthened by the university's intention to "engage in optional conversations with" members of the community to educate them about why what they did was "perceived as biased." The university's goal is a variation of the dismissive injunction aimed at those who transgress progressive belief across social media: do better!

As for the idea of "optional conversations," whose option would it be to engage or not engage in these tutorials? Is it the perpetrator who's already being exhorted by their university to do better? Or does the bias response team make this call? The lack of clarity isn't unusual in university policies about bias and may enhance the threat associated with being caught up in the Bias Reporting System.

Bias reporting policies and procedures have varied, so not all demonstrate the same deficiencies. But the deficiencies are glaring. Of those I surveyed, not a single university explicitly instructed students that they, their peers, and their instructors are part of an institution dedicated to free expression and academic freedom as well as the pursuit of truth. Not one.

On some bias reporting policy webpages, I saw something concerning that I hadn't known to look for. This is that, in many cases, instructions for reporting incidents that students perceive as bias-related shared the page with instructions for reporting hate crimes that may involve criminal acts. It should be obvious that students are likely to conflate these situations.

In practice, this might mean, for example, members of university communities believing that a student reading *Mein Kampf* on campus and a student attacking another student because he's Jewish are pretty much the same thing.[83]

How Inclusive is Inclusive Pedagogy?

As is true for social movement ideology and practices generally, inclusive pedagogy can not only violate individual rights and academic freedom but also generate its own internal contradictions. Nor are such violations and contradictions difficult to locate.

Let me offer one example from inclusive teaching at Northwestern University that demonstrates the point. Northwestern's resource on inclusive learning and teaching is organized around eight principles. Principle 5 is: "Cultivate a Welcoming and Inclusive Course Climate." The principle, or rather its failure, is illustrated with a comment pulled from a Northwestern Student Experience Report: "I am especially dissatisfied with students who trivialize Black problems and issues. There have been a number of instances in classes where we were discussing Black culture and students would say incredibly inappropriate comments without being reprimanded."

I call attention to the key phrase, "without being reprimanded," because directly below this quote, we find this laudatory account of inclusive pedagogy:

> The ideal course environment is one in which *all students feel a sense of belonging and that their points of view matter*. To encourage pedagogy that is conducive to belonging, it is essential for instructors to move away from a teacher-centered manner of instruction to a learning-centered manner of instruction, where instructors focus on the perspectives, experiences, interests, capacities, and needs of students . . . . *Instructors should commit to engaging with students in ways that do not exclude, privilege, or center any specific group, identity, or experience.*[84]

A couple of things. First, this statement reeks of mommy pedagogy. What is "teacher-centered" instruction? It certainly sounds bad and uncaring. And who decides what kinds of instruction are best suited to particular subjects and material? A blanket admonition to "focus on the perspectives, experiences, interests, capacities, and needs of students" and avoid "teacher-centered" instruction is bound to preclude some necessary and appropriate forms of teaching and learning.

Second, in light of the pull quote about "inappropriate comments" in class, I'm confused about Northwestern's position that the "ideal course environment" fosters a "sense of belonging." Should we reprimand those who offer perspectives with which some class members don't agree? Or should we strive to create an ideal course environment in which all students feel a sense of belonging and that their points of view matter?

Left unspoken, but well understood, is the resolution to this dilemma: only some students' sense of belonging and points of view matter. Those whose sense of belonging does not matter should expect to be disciplined—at the least, reprimanded, either by their peers, the instructor, or both. At most, they might be reported to a Bias Response Team or effectively expelled from the class for having violated a community agreement.

Echoing Orwell, the psychologist Rob Kurzban's deadpan conclusion that "all students are safe but some are safer than others" is a serviceable coda to an account of inclusive pedagogy.[85]

Now that we have an overview of how higher ed has evolved to foreground "the people" under our belts, the second element of populism is the moralizing of politics in ways that raise the stakes of political differences and foreclose compromise. It's not unusual for social movements to insist that political claims aren't political claims at all but are, instead, just truths and moral mandates. But those of us who've studied social movements didn't expect to be able to find this lens fruitful for analyzing the social, institutional, and employment transformation of higher ed.

3 Moralizing Politics

Morality vs. Academic Freedom

On the political left, a firehose of scorn greets anyone who suggests that the left or any subset thereof threatens free speech or academic freedom. While commenting online on issues related to speech, the academy, and politics, I've been told by lefties that I'm dangerously uninformed about the academy and US politics (maybe!). I've also been told I should be ashamed of myself for, I assume, bolstering right-wing talking points by asking questions and making observations that wouldn't pass progressive scrutiny. (As the existence of this book suggests, I am not).

In the late nineties, a group of disaffected scholars called a conference on "Left Conservatism" that was intended to highlight the adverse and counterrevolutionary elements in "our" progressive midst.[1] "Left conservatism" was coined as a sardonic term of reproach. Nevertheless, it turns out that the signs are clear: compared to gender studies and a modal politics of the humanities, it appears that I'm probably a left conservative. Or perhaps a social democrat,[2] an "enlightened centrist,"[3] a "vital center" liberal,[4] or just a "normie."[5] Given the realities on the ground, if I did venture to identify as progressive, I'd have to accept being a PiNO—a progressive in name only.

As I've become more worried in recent years about the consequences that might occur if the political center cannot hold, I've also become more disposed to identify with a center that some of us hope might anchor our affectively polarized politics. For the sake of parsimony, and to confirm that I don't consider the label a slur, I answer to "liberal."

In the early days of women's studies, we were certain that groups engaged in more wide-ranging deliberations and arrived at better conclusions when they were diverse rather than homogenous. What we didn't think we needed were people who fundamentally disagreed with our theories, premises, or goals.

John Stuart Mill's famous brief supporting free speech is the best-known statement on why we're better off not inhabiting political and intellectual echo chambers. Elaborating on John Locke's insight that "everyone is orthodox to himself," Mill points out that on contentious questions, we should support free speech because "while every one well knows himself to be fallible, few think it necessary to take any precautions against their own fallibility."[6]

Even if it turns out we're right on some issue, we receive a "benefit" from allowing minority opinions to be heard: "the clearer perception and livelier impression of truth, produced by its collision with error." So much is at stake in protecting individuals from the "peculiar evil of silencing the expression of an opinion," that "mankind would be no more justified in silencing" the person who thinks differently "than he, if he had the power, would be justified in silencing mankind."[7]

Mill might even be understood to suggest that suppressing differences in viewpoints, evidence, and judgments can make us stupider. "Structural stupidity" is what Jonathan Haidt and Zach Rausch call the result we get when "dissent is punished and self-censorship increases." "Stupid ideas are not challenged if they fit with the dominant ideology, so before long, a group of very smart individuals start behaving as if they were stupid."[8]

How do we know that the queer, anticolonial, antiracism championed by academic progressives and universities is better—more empirically accurate in its diagnoses and normatively better in its aims—than other alternatives? Especially if those who disagree or show up with contrary data and analyses are systematically deplatformed?

In April 2023, the writer and podcaster Coleman Hughes delivered a TED Talk entitled, "A Case for Color Blindness." Hughes expatiated briefly on the promise of the title, outlining the history of the idea of color blindness, contesting arguments that colorblindness is a conservative idea, and making a case that "class is almost always a better proxy for true disadvantage than race."[9]

After Hughes stood on the TED stage, some interlocuters disputed the case he'd made. One of these was a psychologist who offered evidence from psychological studies against colorblindness whose validity and reliability were then, in turn, disputed. These debates were an intellectually healthy reaction to what Hughes no doubt understood would be a tumultuous TED debut.[10]

Two things make Hughes' talk relevant to the moralizing of political differences: an internal staff revolt inspired by the speech at the TED organization and the organization's response to the revolt. In a bid to satisfy what Jesse Singal refers to as TED's "most hysterical employees," it appears that TED's CEO tried to place conditions on the availability and publicizing of Hughes' talk.

Because no TED talk is extemporaneous, the organization knew the content of Hughes' talk before it was delivered. Thus, it's easy to trace the subsequent altercation to political disagreement at TED.[11] For his part, after months of wrangling with TED over the talk, Hughes insisted that he'd dedicated his "last word" to the controversy.[12]

In Chapter 1, I enumerated ways in which academic progressives and their political adversaries practice many of the same moves. I promised to return to the first example later, and now's the time. Academic progressives redescribe political ideas as matters of truth and morality. They protect the inviolability of the positions they insist that students and colleagues alike must hold by insisting that these positions are moral and epistemic truths.

The sociologist Dawne Moon's ethnographic scholarship on the Christian right is helpful in unpacking this move. Moon analyzes the process by which Christian believers she studied "naturalize" political claims, transforming positions on contentious issues that "feel timeless, natural, [and] unquestionable" into "common sense" "taken-for-granted beliefs." Such a process protects "foundational assumptions" embraced by group members from being "expose[d]" "as 'not universally true.'" In this way, political views are recast as not political views at all. Just irrefutable truths.

Moon suggests that her account of this process of naturalizing political views is widely applicable to "forms of debate in contemporary American society," including "secular political culture."[13] Indeed, for both right and left, the redescribing of what are obviously political demands and viewpoints as truth and morality is a bid to insulate political perspectives and demands from contestation.

The salience of such an analysis is clear. If movement actors can persuasively represent their positions on contested social, political, and economic issues as beyond politics—as solely questions of morality—they can cast those who disagree, and even those to whom disagreement can be imputed, as immoral reprobates.

The consequences of asserting and defending political positions on all contentious issues as mere truth or morality manifest in too many ways to enumerate. The attorney and columnist Jill Filipovic identifies one such context in her reporting on positions taken by students and faculty during campus protests in 2024.

Filipovic observes that many protesters weren't merely advocating for specific victims and policies. Instead, they believed that "non-righteous causes and individuals . . . should not be allowed" and that "content-neutral time-place-manner restrictions on protest should [not] apply to them." She notes that protesters rejected "generally applicable protest rules" as "broadly irrelevant" to them "in light of the stark moral claims" at stake.[14]

I've long known that, on the progressive left, it's considered to be the responsibility of all who oppose the political right not to contradict the claims of the most enlightened among us. It's also our job to care for the outcast and oppressed in exactly the way those who speak for us dictate they must be cared for.

Nonetheless, if members of the feminist academy of the eighties had gone to sleep and awakened in the twenty-first century, at least some would be shocked at how "care" has metastasized. Certainly, other social, political, and economic factors played a role in promoting what some critics have come to call "safetyism."[15] But faculty in the most progressive disciplines and subfields also became subject to explicit instructions about how to make protecting members of marginalized groups from oppression and harm the centerpiece of our pedagogy and scholarship.

The result is damage to the mission and reputation of universities that may prove very difficult to reverse, especially in circumstances of ascendant right-wing illiberalism.[16]

In this chapter, to investigate the moralizing of political views, I provide accounts of the emergence and inflation of harm as central to pedagogy and research; the requirement that scholars function as activists for the proper political perspectives; how to understand the relationship between sacralized groups and the ideas championed by academic progressives; the argument over indoctrination in the contemporary academy; and the efforts of progressives to control language to limit the political choices others can make and express.

But first, a quick primer on the path from care ethics to care illiberalism in the academy.

On Care and the Perversion of Care

Caring is a primary value in the academy, lauded in curricula, teaching evaluations, student affairs practices, and universities' statements of "shared values." We're all exhorted to care, and we're often provided with explicit instructions on how and to whom such caring should be extended.

To understand how we got here, let's go back in time. At the center of the women's studies project of the seventies to the nineties was the problem of sex-based oppression, which encompassed bias, prejudice, stereotyping, marginalization, exploitation, discrimination, and violence. Theorists who hailed from different sectors of feminist theory formulated theories of what constituted oppression, how oppression could be identified, and what kinds of acts represented resistance to oppression.[17]

The flip side of the harms wrought by various forms of oppression was care, whether exercised toward the self, intimate others, one's social or identity group(s), humankind as a whole, non-human living creatures, or the earth itself. To generalize, we feminists didn't exactly welcome the stereotype handed down to us from history that it was our job to perform caring labor. Nevertheless, we usually lauded women's capacity to care and the urgent need to install care at the center of human ethics and practices.

Many prominent feminist scholars of the period contributed to literature on care, caring, and the harms associated with failures and refusals to care. Three of these—in the order in which they published influential works on care—were the psychologist Carol Gilligan (*In a Different Voice: Psychological Theory and Women's Development*),[18] the philosopher Nel Noddings (*Caring: A Feminine Approach to Ethics and Moral Education*),[19] and the political theorist Joan Tronto (*Moral Boundaries: A Political Argument for an Ethic of Care*).[20]

Care ethics informed the thinking of many feminist scholars. To generalize, these scholars challenged the supremacy of theories of moral reasoning that emphasized cognition, universalism, and abstraction from relational contexts, which they associated with male experience, and ideals of masculine individuation and individualism. They emphasized the social and epistemological implications of female practices of caregiving. And they applied care perspectives to domains that weren't typically associated with care, including economics, politics, and public policy.

It's not surprising that as the academy became more female, women scholars and administrators would introduce their political and theoretical considerations into policy and curricula. As women achieved greater parity with men in higher ed, many installed caring as a principal goal of the academy. Not just any caring, though; a very specific, progressive understanding of care became ubiquitous in higher ed.

Nor is a progressive conception of care limited to the elements of inclusive pedagogy and curricula in some disciplines. Illiberal progressives insinuated their philosophy and praxis of care into every function of the university.

If I were on the outside of academia looking in, I might wonder what could possibly go wrong when universities place the value of caring at the center of the functions of teaching, research, and service. In fact, in many of the examples I offer throughout this book I mean to show, not only that the specific ideas that comprise the progressive academic worldview are vulnerable to criticism, but that imposing this worldview has made universities illiberal.

Installing "care" as the prime value of the university and mistaking *a* conception of morality for morality itself, universities injected progressivism into nooks of their functioning where many critics might not know to look. A small example is the funding program my university created on the theme of Care | Culture | Justice. While the theme is prosaic, the description clarifies the specific ideology the theme expresses.

The description begins with a quote: "Care is linked to justice because without care there is no reason to value justice and no possibility of its realization. It is also a way of understanding justice—not as punitive or disciplinary but as a relationship grounded in recognition and reciprocity."[21]

I can imagine using this quote and the statement that follows in a class and asking students to respond to prompts such as the following: What is justice? What does it mean to care for/about something? Are justice and care connected? If so, how? What might it mean to say that justice can or should only be understood in relation to recognition and reciprocity [be sure to explain what you mean by "justice," "recognition" and "reciprocity"]? How would you respond if someone told you they believe justice sometimes requires punishment? What do you think is the political perspective of the authors of this quote? Do you agree or disagree with the view expressed in the quote?

Of course, none of those kinds of questions would be considered appropriate because the quote isn't an attempt to encourage fertile questions. It's intended as a statement of fact. And the set of questions for scholars seeking funding assumes those facts into evidence:

> Who provides care and for whom? Who and what do we care about? How do we cultivate more caring relations across differences? Across borders? Within ourselves? How might we envision a more caring and just politics? How might collective care offer strategies for enduring and thriving in precarious, disabling environments? How do we build agile infrastructures to resource wider forms of care to address global health disparities? What opportunities emerge if care is centralized at every scale of life—including non-human forms? How is care inherent to the arts and humanities? What role can the arts and humanities play in expanding our capacity to care?[22]

I'm not sure about a more caring and just politics, but a more honest and intellectually rigorous fellowship solicitation might acknowledge that there are widely diverging theorizations of and empirical research on caring and justice. Some scholars connect the two and insist that justice normatively should be linked to values of care. Others distinguish them from each other, insisting that in order to achieve other goals, justice may not always maximize "recognition and reciprocity."

Some dreadfully uncaring daddy/Strict Father/heterodox souls might even think that—and hear me out—sometimes justice might be well served by punishment or discipline.

As a final word on Care | Culture | Justice, I'll just point out that the kinds of scholars who might compose such a solicitation tend to believe that, under some circumstances, justice does require punishment. For example, the kinds of people who would argue with the contention that justice can only be grounded in recognition and reciprocity are likely to be good candidates for punitive justice.

Come to think of it, exploring the incongruity between recognition and reciprocity for my friends and punishment for my ideological enemies might be a fruitful prompt for research funding.

How did we get from theories and an ethic of care to the dominance in higher ed and other epistemic institutions of an illiberal regime justified by care?

In recent years, several critics of the academy have noted the ways in which a feminist commitment to caring curdled into illiberal practices of surveillance and punishment turned on those accused of failing to care in the right way for the right groups of oppressed. Such critiques suggest rich avenues for reconsidering care without the limitations imposed by progressive ideology.

One such critic is the author and former political scientist Carol Horton, who holds that "the old feminist promise of a new ethic of care has become twisted, technocratic, and increasingly dystopian." Horton describes a care-based "toxic femininity" at work in repudiations of reason, free speech, and debate.

> The old free speech culture (which, again, used to be part of the liberal left) that valorized open, rational, and often fierce debate over contested political issues has been rejected as harmful and even dangerous. In the name of being kind, caring, and sensitive to the most vulnerable—all traditionally "feminine" traits—progressives are expected to refrain from asking even the most basic, obvious, and logical questions about all sorts of highly consequential issues.[23]

Here, Horton acknowledges the fraught divide that's come to separate liberals—advocates of "the old free speech culture"—from academic progressives, who regard that culture as "harmful and even dangerous."

Rob Kurzban suggests another way to interpret a "dystopian" regimen of caring. For Kurzban, safetyism, the operationalization of progressive care, is typically understood as "a ***defensive*** norm: to *protect* others. However, safetyism might not be actual concern about the safety of students or 'the community at large.'" If claims of safetyism are "moralistic," they might be "better understood as a kind of ***offense***, a pretext to launch moral attacks. Safetyism, in other words, might be a rhetorical and psychological weapon."[24]

In *The Righteous Mind: Why Good People are Divided by Politics and Religion*, his germinal study of moral psychology, Jonathan Haidt offers many astute observations and conclusions about care and harm that can inform debates about care in the academy. There, Haidt identifies 6 moral foundations: care, fairness, loyalty, authority, sanctity, and liberty.

Of these moral foundations, those he identifies as liberals—essentially WEIRDos of the political left—lean heavily on care and its violation, harm, for their moral judgments and also rely on fairness and its violation, cheating. Conservatives and traditionalists rely on all of the moral foundations. A good deal of vigorous moral disagreement between the two sides may be traced to the fact that the two sides use different foundations or interpret the same foundations differently.

For example, whereas Haidt's liberals interpret fairness as mandating equality, conservatives interpret fairness as proportionality: "everyone . . . pulling their own weight" or getting what they deserve. Moral agents operating under a conception of fairness as proportionality might conclude that some people aren't pulling their own weight or even deserve a negative sanction.

But Haidt's liberals are likely to recoil from this kind of balancing of accounts. For them, the retributive side of desert triggers the care/harm foundation and the requirement that we extend compassion to those threatened with harm. Some exceptions may apply.

Finally, Haidt determined that many people in his study who talked about "harm" engaged in moral "reasoning in support of their emotional reactions." By this, he means that subjects "weren't condemning . . . actions *because* they foresaw . . . harms," but, rather, "*inventing* these harms because they had already condemned the actions." The "harm" they reached for was a post-hoc justification for moral judgments they'd already reached.[25]

Anyone who's ended up on the bad end of a dispute over harm might well have difficulty squaring the experience with the discourse of care as it was practiced in the heyday of feminist care ethics. It's a sign of how badly wrong progressives' understanding of care has gone that "caring" can be as prescriptively defined as it is. The injunction to structure scholarship, teaching, and service around the value of "care" has led to defining "harm" as broadly and punitively as we've seen it defined in the academy.

Cathy Young links such broadening of harm to political illiberalism, arguing that "students' self-righteous insistence that they [are] on a mission to prevent 'harm' reflects the illiberalism at the heart of today's social justice movement. It is also a far-reaching rationale for speech suppression—after all, there is almost no issue that cannot be framed as harm prevention by either the left or the right."[26] I agree with Young, though I think it's more accurate to target the big fish. My correction would be: "professors' self-righteous insistence."

The psychologist Nick Haslam provides an explanation for the expansion of harm. For Haslam, "harm inflation" is a consequence of "concept creep," the "semantic broadening" of concepts to reference "a much wider range of phenomena than they did in earlier times." "Harm" isn't merely subject to concept creep but is, rather, "the common thread among the identified creeping concepts" such as bullying, trauma, abuse, hate speech, and many others.

Besides the suppression of what are deemed harmful forms of speech and expression, as concepts creep and harm inflates, Haslam and his colleagues warn about the appearance of new forms of identity that come to rely on being victimized by phenomena newly designated as harmful "to make sense of their experience."

The psychologists also express concern that concept creep constitutes "expansion entrepreneurship by politically or otherwise motivated actors."[27] In other words, this vigilance about harm is a deliberate strategy of the political actors who are also known as our colleagues.

No Quarter

One illustration of harm inflation in higher ed is the case of the University of Toronto psychologist Yoel Inbar. In 2023, Inbar's partner was being considered for a faculty position in the Department of Psychology at the University of California, Los Angeles. Upon being offered the position, she requested that the department consider Inbar as a partner hire. What followed is a process familiar to academics: a campus interview for Inbar complete with a job talk and meetings with faculty and students.

Later, on the *Very Bad Wizards* podcast, Inbar unpacked with fellow psychologists what transpired during and after his UCLA interview. Perceiving that the psychology faculty were "very enthusiastic" about his candidacy and that the interview was more a "recruiting visit" than a typical arms-length evaluation, Inbar relates that he was surprised when the departmental diversity committee questioned him about views on DEI and institutional neutrality that he'd aired years before on his podcast, *Two Psychologists Four Beers*.[28]

In 2018, Inbar had expressed skepticism about both the utility of mandatory DEI statements in faculty hiring and the appropriateness of academic professional associations taking public positions on contentious political issues like abortion rights. On *Very Bad Wizards*, Inbar describes how members of the diversity committee confronted him with his podcast remarks, asking him if he was "prepared to defend" his positions and how he would respond to grad students who were "upset" by the positions he'd staked out.

Inbar declined to defend his 2018 comments on the issue of DEI statements, but he agreed to tell the committee members what he thought about such statements in 2023: "the goals are good, but I don't know if the diversity statements necessarily accomplish the goals. So I'm skeptical." Inbar indicated that he would share his "actual views" with students just as he had with faculty members of the diversity committee. He also met with grad students and, although he believed that meeting "mostly . . . was fine," the students begged to differ.[29]

It wouldn't be hard to guess what came next.

The grad students quickly produced a lengthy denunciation of Inbar and the threat he posed to them, the department, the university, and the profession. Over sixty students signed the letter, which was addressed to the three faculty members of the ad hoc departmental committee assembled for the partner hire: Benjamin Karney, Carolyn Parkinson, and Hal Hershfield.

Excerpts from the students' letter convey a taste of the case the psychology grad students made against Inbar:

> We believe that Dr. Inbar would not enter the Social Area as a member committed to creating a safe, welcoming, and inclusive environment, and that his hiring would threaten ongoing efforts to protect and uplift individuals of marginalized backgrounds.
>
> Most concerning to us as students is Dr. Inbar's opposition to

> institutions endorsing positions on sociopolitical issues he has deemed "contentious" or "controversial."
>
> Dr. Inbar does not understand nor value the need for an inclusive culture of academia either interpersonally or intellectually as a means of broadening and elevating the rigor of our science.
>
> [H]e defends perspectives and positions opposed to values our university system has affirmed as fundamental to fostering a safe and inclusive environment for those most widely and deeply afflicted by ongoing sociopolitical issues.[30]

The aspiring psychologists averred that they "could not set aside the[ir] values for the sake of a partner hire, even if this impact[ed] [partner's name redacted] decision to work" in the UCLA Department of Psychology.

So instructed, the ad hoc hiring committee recommended against hiring Inbar. Annette L. Stanton, the Department chair, delivered the bad news, noting in an email to him that "unusual events occurred surrounding [his] visit" and that she was "disappointed with the outcome."[31]

In the matter of Yoel Inbar, the psychology faculty failed to cover themselves in glory when they bowed to their grad students' "adamant" demand that they reject his candidacy.

An irony of the furor over Inbar's views on DEI is his research agenda: "how intuitions and emotions—particularly disgust—affect our social, political, and moral beliefs" and "the varied ways in which moral intuitions guide beliefs and judgments, especially in social and political domains."[32] Full disclosure: I've cited Inbar's research in my work on conservative political orientations toward LGBTQ people and issues.[33] How useful it might have been for grad students at UCLA to consider the possibility that moral intuitions and emotions guide social and political beliefs and judgments, including their own.

Inbar wasn't investigated by his university. He just wasn't hired and, because nobody has a right to a faculty position, no harm, no foul? Yet the controversy fills in more information about how harm expansion has underwritten the quest for academic homogeneity.

Progressive Harm

In *Sin, Sex, and Democracy*, I used John Stuart Mill's famous harm principle and commentaries on it to analyze Christian conservative arguments about the harm caused by other peoples' sinfulness.[34] The pairing is strange on its face. Christian conservatives want to define as harm—to believers, to the nation—a variety of rights and practices that Mill would exclude as not "occasion[ing] perceptible hurt to any assignable individual except" the individual exercising the right or engaging in the condemned practice.[35]

The Christian right's position on harm makes more sense if the harm principle can be extended to take into account practices of which Christian conservative moral entrepreneurs disapprove. One such extension of the harm principle is "indirect" or "remote" harms, in which an act can be conceptualized as leading to harm at a distance rather than being an immediate effect. Another is the idea of "accumulative" harms, which stipulates that individual acts may accumulate over time to add up to some identifiable harm, perhaps collectively to a group if not to a specific individual.[36]

Like the Christian right invoking harm that requires interdiction, academic progressives find themselves at odds with Mill's harm principle. Just as Christian conservatives redefine moral disagreements and the consequences of unbelievers' sin as harm under their own harm principle, progressives redefine disagreement, discomfort, and offense as *actual* or *literal harm* that justifies intervention and punishment.

The sign that such harm has occurred is the angry, offended, or discomfited reaction it elicits in the moment or even later, upon reflection. People who do or say things that elicit these reactions can also be held responsible for remote harms such as violence against members of minority groups. And such harms are held to accumulate, creating conditions of "unlivability" and challenges to the "existence" of members of these groups.

Narratives of actual and literal harm are the backhanded tribute academic progressives pay to the liberal tradition they despise.

I do think that our job is to care, not about our students' feelings but about their learning. That may sound "masculinist"—a term first applied to me in grad school. In spite of this infirmity, I tried in my own way to be gentle with students who were encountering information they'd rather not hear. But, at least in the before times, I wasn't deterred from offering that information.

I believed that my students had a right and an intellectual interest to know relevant facts, arguments, and academic findings that bore on our topics. I believed my students had a right to be heard, whether I agreed or disagreed with their perspectives. And I believed it was my job to respond to different perspectives in ways that were as informed, measured, careful, and respectful as I could be. I didn't always succeed in these goals, but that was what I was going for.

From the seventies to the nineties, care ethics were irrelevant to the intellectual interests and expertise of most scholars. In the years since, progressives have justified significant aspects of an illiberal agenda with the requirement to exercise care. For them, protecting members of marginalized and disfavored groups requires more than the academic study of care and harm. It requires a commitment to activism that puts all the mandates of progressive morality to work in institutions.

Scholars as Activists

Like academics in other identity studies fields, women's and gender studies scholars have long seen ourselves as activists as well as scholars. From the beginning, we gave ourselves the charge to change the world and not just interpret it.

As time went on, I couldn't help seeing ways in which the ethos of activism can come into conflict with the ethos of scholarship. Unless we're willing to presumptively declare that careful observation and analysis of data will always yield results that serve particular political agendas, how could they not conflict?

When confronted with even the possibility that there may be a conflict between what activism requires of us and what scholarship requires of us, academic progressives deny that there can be such a conflict. And they wonder why anyone would raise the question unless they were harboring right-wing impulses in their heart.

Faculty activism appeals to students and faculty. Tyler Austin Harper notes the attraction to students of, for example, "the high percentage of prison-abolitionist faculty." And some faculty tributes to student activism bear hallmarks of parental pride, as when a faculty member at Columbia, speaking on behalf of her colleagues, used a megaphone to tell students, "We're so proud to be your professors."[37] Google the phrase, "so proud to be your," and the first noun that pops up is "mom." Out of the mouth of autocomplete.

Universities even market their histories of student political activism to attract prospective students, the "radical history" of some Ivies having "become part of the way that Barnard and Columbia sell their $60,000-plus annual tuition."[38] The universities could, of course, advertise their commitment to free speech, academic freedom, and intellectual diversity instead. Educating young adults about the history and significance of these principles and practices for liberal democracy would be a noble mission.

At the end of the day, it doesn't occur to my progressive colleagues to distinguish scholarship from activism because they're convinced that, in both domains, they have right on their side. The British author Helen Pluckrose points out the consequence of this worldview, that "the answer to 'Why did you see so clearly that this behaviour is authoritarian/this reasoning incoherent when they did it but not when you do?' is always 'Because we are right and they are wrong.'"[39]

Whether you're an orthodox Christian or an academic progressive, if you believe that you and those who agree with you have the only answer to every contentious question—that you understand what is at stake morally and politically, and your opponents are dreadfully, even wickedly, wrong—you will embrace, and demand that others embrace, "rigid orthodoxies." You will not consider it a matter of "moral and intellectual courage to take the other side seriously and to report truths and ideas that your own side demonises for fear they will harm its cause."[40]

Inevitably, some progressive academics publicly divulge how to use their positions as scholars to advance political goals, also known as saying the quiet part out loud. One of these is the English professor Julie Stone Peters, whose reflections on how to think about the political goals of instruction couldn't be clearer.

> Not all of our students will be original thinkers, nor should they all be. A world of original thinkers, all thinking wholly inimitable thoughts, could never get anything done. For that we need *un*original thinkers, hordes of them, cloning ideas by the score and broadcasting them to every corner of our virtual world. What better device for idea-cloning than the cliché? . . . . Maybe we should . . . strive to send our students forth — and ourselves too — armed with clichés for political change.

Peters' examples of academic clichés that do "real political work," "chang[ing] how people see, what they think, and, ever-so-slowly, what they do," are "performativity" and "genderqueer."[41] In this startlingly cynical vision of education, we pretend to help students learn to think while they do the grunt work of spreading our political ideas. And they pay us for the privilege. Is this a great country, or what?

In addition to holding the view that there's no conflict between activism and scholarship, my colleagues instruct their students that this is so. Because to acknowledge that such a distinction—even contradiction—might exist is to open the larger enterprise of academic progressivism to criticisms we're unwilling to entertain.

What's the problem with such a way of doing intellectual business? As the psychologist Joe Forgas argues,

> At the most basic level, social activism (presuming that there is certainty about what should be done and no more questions are necessary) is fundamentally incompatible with science and the search for truth that requires an open mind and the acceptance of uncertainty and divergent opinions. Social justice movements, virtue signaling and DEI requirements are fundamentally incompatible with the demands of scientific discovery.[42]

How can we know that the ends of activism and scholarship aren't perfectly aligned? For one thing, we don't expect activist organizations to, for example, sponsor debates on their bedrock principles. And we don't expect them to encourage staff, donors, and volunteer advocates to critically consider moral, empirical, and theoretical dimensions of those principles and the modes of action that follow from them. That's not what activist movements and organizations are for.

We should expect to find these elements in higher ed. If we don't find them, we should take their absence as a sign that we're failing to do our jobs. Resistance to these elements provides one important pathway to understanding the way gender studies and other progressive disciplines work, including our norms, curricula, teaching standards, grad student admissions, faculty hiring, university policies, and the representation of our values and goals to and in the world outside the academy.

When professors deliberate about the best way to operationalize their politics in their teaching, progressive politics don't "escape academia" in "an ideological 'lab leak.'"[43] The "leaking" is the point. We won't be surprised, then, that what happens at university doesn't stay at university.

The strain of illiberalism that's been nurtured in particular sectors of the academy has consequences for a host of cultural and intellectual practices and institutions. These include the natural sciences,[44] news media,[45] non-profits,[46] libraries,[47] K–12 education,[48] publishing,[49] therapy,[50] independent bookstores,[51] and many small corners of civil society.

No matter how many sites of left-wing illiberalism critics identify, apologists will have ready responses. In *The Canceling of the American Mind*, Greg Lukianoff and Rikki Schlott refer to a variety of tactics collectively as The Obstacle Course.[52] One of these is minimization: *That is a fringe case*; or, confronted with a kind of thing that happens too frequently, *that doesn't happen*. Another popular response is whataboutism, which can go something like this: *So, I guess the centuries of enmity and exploitation don't matter when members of dominant groups are getting a little taste of their own medicine?*

My personal favorite is a version of ad hominem questioning of motives. Invariably delivered with a cool yet vaguely menacing tone of appraisal, the question is, *Why do you care?* The riposte is a bid to end conversation on a matter of public concern with just the lightest touch of threat.

Of course, other tactics routinely show up in progressive instruction, talks, and published scholarship. One of these is a barrage of leading, insinuating questions that will never be answered by a speaker or author but that impute guilt or malice to opponents. Although others have copied this affectation, its champion is Judith Butler. Another move is hiding evidence that would bolster an opponent's claims deep in a written work, though I mentally award points when such evidence is disclosed at all. I've already noted the commonplace tactic of conflating disagreement with progressive views or practices with bigotry, antifeminism, or fascism.

I can't help perceiving similarities between the Christian conservative movement and the movement of illiberal progressives that has held sway in higher ed. One of these is following the dictates of trusted sources. Movement elites rely on or produce archives of ideas with which followers are socialized.

Of course, movements aren't content to let nonbelievers go their own way; they want the rest of us to genuflect as well.

The Good Books

The mandate to defer to trusted sources exposes a problem that routinely plagues the political left: from which sources should we take direction? For bible-believing Christians, primary sources include not only a text, the bible, but also exegeses of the text from trusted sources. I don't mean to suggest that meaning and interpretation are invariable. Interpretations of scripture have been revised many times; and different sets of believers interpret their sources in ways that are diverse enough to, at times, be contradictory. Indeed, elites shift interpretive strategies to move followers for political purposes.

However, none of these differences across time or faith traditions alters the infallibility of the Christian conservative movements' trusted sources at any particular moment. In response to Christian conservative claims to merely follow the literal meaning of scripture, the theologian Randall Balmer argues that evangelical Christians employ a "ruse of selective literalism" that enables them to profess the doctrines they want to profess and ignore those they don't.[53] I find Balmer's analysis of Christian conservative biblical literalism helpful in thinking about demands for obedience to progressive mandates, truth claims, and policies in the academy.

While Christian conservatives consult the bible and trusted interpreters to confirm their positions on a wide range of social and political issues, academic progressives insist that the answers to these very questions can only be determined by assessing the will, beliefs, narrated personal experience, and political analyses of sacralized groups.

The problem is that no matter which associational or ascriptive group we point to, there's no consensus on many issues. BIPOC people don't all agree with each other. Neither do all LGBTQ people. It turns out that, whoever "we" are, we contain multitudes.

Given this diversity of perspectives, and given that large demographic groups can't be easily polled, what counts is the will, beliefs, narrated personal experience, and political analyses that elites, representatives, and vocal subsets of sacralized groups share with academic progressives.

And yet diversity of thought persists. For example, over the past several decades, the percentage of black Americans who vote Republican has mostly remained consistent at a little over ten percent, though Trump increased his share of support from African Americans after the 2020 election.[54] When we factor in religion, we find that black Americans are more religious than Americans as a whole and that black Democrats are more religious than whites with whom they share a party identification.[55] These and other kinds of group differences are significant for politics and learning about politics.

Everyone with a passing acquaintance of the progressive academy knows how to resolve the dilemma of the persistence of political and intellectual diversity. Centrist, moderate, conservative, Christian, traditional, skeptical, ecumenical, and heterodox views cannot be appropriate for serious intellectual consideration.

The alternative to ruling these kinds of views out of bounds is always available: actively seeking out diverse sources, evidence, and arguments. Perspectives associated with traditional—that is, non-WEIRD—moral foundations would fit this bill.[56] As would engaging with members of sacralized groups who diverge from their fellows. For example, referring to the conflict between Israel and Hamas, Simon Sebag Montefiore suggests sardonically that "perhaps the West's Hamas apologists should listen to moderate Arab voices instead of a fundamentalist terror sect."[57]

The self-described "Palestinian-American creative" Mo Husseini is one likely candidate to meet Montefiore's challenge.[58] In his essay, "50 Completely True Things," Husseini uses acerbic humor to expose the groupish tendency to attribute virtue to a preferred side in the conflict between Israel and the Palestinians. Although it's hard to choose just one fact to illustrate Husseini's argumentative style, no. 37 provides a taste:

> FACT No. 37.
> No one in the Levant is indigenous. Every fucking empire in history has fucked their way through the Levant. There is no pure indigeneity. And let's be honest: the entire planet has been colonized by hominids from the Great Rift Valley.[59]

Discuss!

For the most part, academic progressives selectively rely on those who share their worldview as representatives of the people. In this, they are like Christian conservative elites. If one were an American evangelical Christian in 2017, to whom should one listen? The Trump-affirming president of the Family Research Council, Tony Perkins, or the editor in chief of *Christianity Today* and Trump critic, Russell Moore? Trump pastor and televangelist, Paula White, or Christian author and Trump critic, Beth Moore (no relation to Russell)?

It's easy. Whether we're Christian conservatives or academic progressives, the people to defer to are those who make the kinds of claims that a group has already installed as building blocks of its worldview and identity. For progressives, this means acknowledging thinkers and activists they recognize as suitably radical and decolonial, even if their claims are at odds with those held by majorities or pluralities of disfavored or underrepresented group members.

Not BIPOC? Your role is to listen to and follow BIPOC people. Which BIPOC people? *Those who support progressive ideology.* Not queer? Your role is to listen to and follow queer people. Which queers? *Those who support progressive ideology.* Repeat as necessary.

I confess that one dimension of my pedagogical practice has long been encouraging students to take seriously the political claims and arguments of those with whom I knew they disagreed. This practice took many forms. Throughout my career, I assigned the work of straight (in some cases, I had to presume, since not all scholars list their sexuality in their work!) white men when I believed they had compelling arguments from which we could benefit *or* ideas we needed to be informed about in order to think through important questions.

I frequently asked students what they thought was the best argument that could be rendered in defense of a position they disagreed with. This isn't rocket science; the writer Caitlin Flanagan recalls that, when she was growing up, her father deflated her pretensions to rectitude on all subjects with a similar question.[60]

When students asked me directly what I thought about a particular issue, and I didn't see any pedagogical harm in answering honestly, I often prefaced my response with this good-humored phrase: "This is an editorial comment, which you are free to disregard." And they were.

The rest of the time, students might attribute to me either views that comported with their own or beliefs that were utterly antithetical to theirs. I didn't concern myself with what was being attributed to me on the principle that what someone thinks of me is none of my business.

Although I abandoned this kind of instruction after I was investigated, my goal was often to explore with students the best cases that could be made against a position they believed was the only one decent people could embrace. Receiving this kind of instruction sets off alarms for students who believe that progressive political positions are mere truth and morality and that professors are obligated to function as apostles for these truths in the classroom.

The principal charge levied against me in my investigation was that when I used an empirically accurate example to illustrate a potential ethical challenge gender studies researchers might confront, I inducted students in my graduate seminar on research methods into a "non-consensual thought experiment."

Because I'd like to think I learn something from experience, I hereby issue a warning: what comes next is a thought experiment.

A Thought Experiment

First, I give what I understand to be the most generous reading of what many of my colleagues have done with regard to moralizing intellectual debate in academic contexts and undermining academic freedom. Then, I follow with a more jaundiced view. Neither is accurate or inaccurate on its face; I'm showing my work.

The Generous Reading

My colleagues see the group-based inequalities that are evident in history and all around us and, over a period of many years, despair that any of these inequalities will be rectified. Like Marx surveying the mass dislocations and suffering that accompanied capitalism and industrialization, they feel the heavy hand of the past pressing on the present. They know that, historically, some groups have been disadvantaged and that some forms of disadvantage have been baked into the status quo of social, political, and economic norms, practices, and institutions.

They are galvanized by moral necessity to challenge unfairness and harm. They passionately hope that people who dispute the wisdom of progressivism will see their error and join the right side of history. They believe in progressivism's righteousness and inevitability.

The Less Generous Reading

Secure in their fiefdoms, with tenure and plenty of institutional support at their backs, my colleagues seize the opportunity to reproduce and coerce a worldview that reflects back to them their intellectual superiority. They're smart enough to know that their worldview may not survive rigorous logical or empirical scrutiny and that their best bet at remaining in privileged positions of influence is to prevent dissenting views from being aired, both in instruction and in scholarship.

They teach declaratively that deviations from correct ideas cause *actual* or *literal harm*. They encourage students to react with rage and contempt for any ideas that don't square with those held by the most radical peers, professors, activists, and influencers. They're not averse to smearing those who disagree; indeed, they get satisfaction and pleasure from seeing their adversaries punished.

Analysis

If you selected the generous reading, it may be because you believe that many scholars work hard and dedicate their lives to improving the world through research, teaching, and service, both to the academy and their community. I see your perspective. I believe that lots of academics feel both a profound sense of responsibility for making the world a better place and possibly even guilt that they have fared so well in a world in which so many have so little.

My favorite passage from Zora Neale Hurston's novel, *Their Eyes Were Watching God*, is apropos: "There is a depth of thought untouched by words, and deeper still a gulf of formless feeling untouched by thought."[61] This is an editorial comment, which you are free to disregard: I suspect that, among left-wing academics, an important element in the "gulf" of "feeling untouched by thought" is a fear that we do not deserve this great gift we've been given—the life of the mind. We may even fear that someone might still come along and take it away.

By demonstrating their resolve to stand up for the oppressed people of sacralized groups, they acknowledge and "check" their privilege. Doing so may require identifying colleagues and students who refuse to abide by the terms of social justice that constitute truth and morality. It may require holding them accountable for their transgressions. Because those who ignore these truths, deviate from them, criticize them, or otherwise side with right-wing forces have to be called out for social justice to prevail and the oppressed to be championed.

If you selected the less generous reading, I see you too. You may be fed up with pious pronouncements about what we should all think and say. You may have seen glimpses of the barely disguised iron fist, virtually always dressed up in the language of care for the vulnerable. You may have also seen what you've interpreted as moments of glee when those with the upper hand flex their institutional authority.

I don't know how you've scored this exercise, but there's no need to turn the page upside down to find the answer. Remember my claim in the Introduction about left-wing authoritarians driving a car filled with progressives? I believe that both of these explanations are true at once. Let me explain.

In 2023, a group of psychologists reported their development of a "Progressive Values Scale" (PVS). In a series of experiments, the psychologists used the PVS both to "assess the ideological schism on the left" between progressives and traditional liberals, and to determine whether progressives and left-wing authoritarians constituted essentially the same group. They concluded that "the PVS did not substantially overlap with measures of left-wing extremism (i.e., LWA)." In other words, although there's overlap in their belief systems, progressives and left-wing authoritarians are best understood as distinct groups.[62]

The conclusion reached using the "Progressive Values Scale" is bolstered by research by an interdisciplinary group of scholars that focuses on the censorship of science by scientists. The study provides an overview of bias in science and science evaluation and finds that "censorship motivated by harm concerns is common," especially by "younger, more left-leaning, and female faculty." The key finding, however, is that censorship of science "is often impelled by prosocial concerns" rather than by authoritarianism of the right or left. Prosocial motives include the desire "to protect vulnerable groups" and concerns about how research might depict "historically disadvantaged groups unfavorably."[63]

That two or more distinct groups might together make up a movement isn't surprising. The Christian conservative movement is made up of many groups whose leaders and members have, for purposes of their collective goals, determined to deemphasize their differences and practice "co-belligerence."[64]

Even smaller sub-movements within the Christian right can be understood as coalitions of groups that converge on some questions and diverge on others. In my work on the anti-abortion movement in the United States, I distinguish between two sides of the movement with distinct histories and sources of motivation. One is a compassionate, therapeutic side centered on the well-being of post-abortive women, and the other side is committed to social and political advocacy organized to prevent the moral abomination of the murder of a child.

Because the anti-abortion movement has abortion abolition as one of its goals, we could treat all antiabortion activism as consistent with abomination discourse. But that would miss important distinctions between the two sides, including differences between female-led organizations and advocacy on the compassionate side of the movement and male political and intellectual leadership on the abomination side.[65]

Left-wing authoritarians and non-authoritarian progressives are distinct groups. Nevertheless, because they work together under the byline of progressivism, I think referring to the group itself as "progressives" or "illiberal progressives" is the best alternative.

My presentation of this taxonomy may suggest that there's a secret decoder ring to distinguish people oriented solely or mostly toward considerations of care and harm from people oriented toward left-wing authoritarianism. Alas, although we may sometimes be certain that we can distinguish these orientations, in everyday interaction there's no guarantee of success.

I thought of this dilemma of sorting academic progressives from left-wing authoritarians when I read the 2022 email conversation among psychologists Jonathan Haidt, Lee Jussim, and Laura King, then president of the Society for Personality and Social Psychology (SPSP). Jussim posted part of the conversation and his commentary on his Substack, *Unsafe Science*.

As background, in 2021, the SPSP received and affirmed the recommendation of its Equity and Anti-Racism Taskforce to ask scholars submitting a scholarly paper proposal for delivery at its meeting to include a Diversity, Equity, Inclusion or Anti-Racism (DEIA) statement. To assist scholars in completing their DEIA statement, the organization helpfully provided prompts and sample responses. According to the SPSP website, reviewers "evaluate the extent to which the submission advances SPSP's goal of promoting diversity, equity, inclusion, or anti-racism"; "after the review process is complete, the decision-makers . . . use these scores to create the program."[66]

The SPSP assured members that "submissions are not required to advance the DEIA goals to be accepted," but it certainly sounds as though the DEIA statement carried weight in final decisions about which scholars would be permitted to present their research. Haidt objected to this plan and conveyed his concerns to Laura King, then president of the SPSP. We don't have the complete email back-and-forth, but Haidt quotes King as pronouncing herself "not super clear on why anti-racism is viewed as problematic."[67]

Having resided in gender studies for many years, when I read that line, I "heard" King's comment in two possible registers. In the progressive register, the speaker is genuinely surprised by a suggestion from a colleague, whom she takes to be a decent, stand-up scholar, that there's any possible ground for rejecting a step of which, after all, *nobody of good will* can possibly disapprove. Can they? In this register, the speaker is befuddled. She may even invite an explanation of her colleague's odd, counterintuitive stance.

But, as is so often true in life, there's another possible interpretation. In the authoritarian register, I hear an undertone of malice. In this version, the speaker isn't perplexed but, instead, issues a warning: you've stepped out of line and challenged a verity you're forbidden to challenge.

Think carefully, because whatever you say in response to what appears to be—but definitely is not—a question may be used against you.

We can have difficulty telling the mere progressives and the left-wing authoritarians apart. I'm not a psychologist with a handy digital file of inventories to administer. My goal here is not to provide a diagnostic tool for distinguishing the two subgroups. Instead, I want to suggest that there are differences within this group of academic progressives and that each of these subgroups needs the other. Without the alliance, it wouldn't be possible to establish the regime of moral pleading and threat paired with occasional actual punishment that can keep incipient dissenters in line.

Such a lack of information can make it difficult to interpret exactly what's happening in particular situations. Are those correcting students and colleagues, pronouncing on the correct interpretation of every phenomenon, and pursuing retribution for disobedience Mark Edmunson's "good people"?[68] Those John McWhorter sees as "nice people" and "just folks?"[69]

Or are they using "social justice as social leverage?" Helen Dale and Lorenzo Warby explain the latter possibility in this way:

> [O]nce something is declared to be a matter of *social justice*, opposition to such a claim becomes illegitimate. This is not a bargaining-to-make-things-better strategy. This is a social dominance strategy. Ostentatious moralizing can make for an effective social dominance strategy. It gives the strategy rhetorical power that can be used to disarm or intimidate others.[70]

On that note, conservative critics of higher ed have long accused academics of indoctrinating students, thereby turning out the left-wing cadres that bedevil conservatives and liberals alike in US politics and society. I managed to get through college and grad school without falling prey to the tenured Marxists so many conservatives warned us about. I'd like to say that there's nothing to the charge of indoctrination today, but I can't.

On Indoctrination

Critics of progressive illiberalism frequently accuse universities and faculty of indoctrination, which can have different meanings. One definition that emphasizes the didactic process students are likely to undergo is that indoctrination is "the process of repeating an idea or belief to someone until they accept it without criticism or question."[71]

My colleagues often say we don't engage in indoctrination, but we're also proud we do, as when the National Women's Studies Association brags about campus protests that "our students are enacting the critical consciousness outlined in our course syllabi and learning objectives."[72]

In discussions of contentious issues, my students often told me they'd learned in other classes why some people hold a viewpoint that the students found erroneous or that in their view compromised the safety of members of a group. Inevitably, I learned that the answer was some form of bigotry, usually racism (or white supremacy), Islamophobia, homophobia, or transphobia. At times, variations on an identitarian theme enabled students to add nuance to this explanation, so that, for example, a position they perceived to harm members of a sacralized group was characterized as an attack on the group's "existence."

In my view, very little of this helps students understand their fellow citizens or reason well on matters of public concern. And, of course, challenging these attributions, even in a careful and conciliatory way, can ignite suspicion about what such a professor is really up to.

Skeptics might ask if there's a difference between the imprinting on impressionable minds that's been a feature of teaching and learning at least since Socrates and what critics of academic illiberalism call indoctrination. There is. On the one hand, students can respond positively to the persuasiveness of individual faculty members or even whole fields of study. Call it the *Dead Poets Society* effect.[73] On the other, there's the unmistakable pressure to conform that can issue simultaneously from peers, faculty, and even the university itself. This pressure communicates the idea that considering certain viewpoints violates a taboo.

Universities have always had norms and rules—for example, those associated with the doctrine of *in loco parentis*. The political theorist Rita Koganzon argues that the situation that came to prevail in higher ed isn't just an extension of *in loco parentis* because of a difference in kind between an "earlier era of paternalism" and a "new paternalism."

> In the earlier era of paternalism, colleges upheld, for a few extra years, the norms of the homes from which students came. In the present era, colleges generate and impose new norms they hope students will absorb and use to transform the rest of the society into the indefinite future.[74]

Critics also accuse illiberal progressives of having installed a secular religion in the academy, with a theology, sacred texts, pastoral care, sermons, and rituals such as confession and public testimonies of faith. These critics include John McWhorter,[75] Len Gutkin,[76] the Pakistani-American writer and activist Sarah Haider,[77] the writer and editor Ian Buruma,[78] the journalist and political satirist Andrew Doyle,[79] and Colette Colfer, a lecturer in world religions.[80]

Other critics see academic illiberalism functioning as a kind of cult.[81] Or as "quasi-religious," that is, having at least some characteristics of a religion. Writing in *Unsafe Science*, the political scientist Wilfred Reilly argues that

> scholars should reject all set quasi-religious frameworks of this kind. Almost all adult citizens have individual honor codes and the like, but to the greatest extent possible—while doing research—we should have no starting/guiding heuristics . . . or at very least try to limit any which we are aware of and may be stuck with. Our only goal should be to follow the data where it leads, seek the pure truth, and find it.[82]

There are antidotes to indoctrination, including teaching students the importance of "follow[ing] the data to where it leads," and being even handed. In practice, on contentious issues this means presenting a robust range of values and perspectives and whatever evidence can be adduced for these values and perspectives.

I was always comfortable teaching students whose worldview differed from mine. I taught students who hailed from a wide range of majors and disciplines. I taught students who could be located at all points on the political spectrum; and I taught students from a wide variety of religious faiths and traditions.

In the classroom, I often presented a range of ideas without definitively affirming one as correct. In the early nineties, I took a group of students to a campus lecture delivered by a colleague in another discipline. During the Q and A, one of my students asked the speaker what she thought was the correct position on an issue she'd raised in the talk. My colleague glanced at me and demurred, suggesting that the student ask his professor. The class laughed when the student responded in mock dismay, "She won't tell us!"

As I became a more skilled instructor, my interest in converting students to a particular belief system declined further. Perhaps because of my personal history with religion, I distrust conversions of all kinds. Or it may be more accurate to say that, because joining ecstatically with a group delivers so many social and biochemical rewards, I think of us humans as conversion prone.

If that's so, converting students to any brand of belief is nothing to be proud of. It's just leveraging the psychology of young adults who are in the process of forming their understanding of the world and their place in it for our own ends. Across much of the academy, such insouciance about reinforcing students' fidelity to the progressive brand polls very badly.

In the absence of a personality-altering head injury, I would never, for example, insist that a student delete a particular phrase that offends my politics from the description of a project or risk receiving a zero grade for the assignment. This is what happened when a student at the University of Cincinnati, writing about controversies over transwomen competing in women's sporting events, used the term, "biological women."

The contretemps followed a predictable pattern: the instructor informed the student that the term, "biological women," was harmful and directed the student to delete it or lose all points for the assignment. The student took the dispute to TikTok. After tempers flared and sides were taken, the university imposed discipline on the instructor before relenting and determining that no university policy had been violated. Though, strangely, the instructor was still required to submit her syllabi for oversight.[83]

Caught in the position of having to rule on whether university instructors could force students to adhere to instructors' political views to pass a course or an assignment, the university punted.

In fact, all instructors who teach contentious issues have to decide how they will respond to the wide range of positions students might profess on those issues. In the 2000s, I regularly instructed Introduction to Women's Studies, a large lecture course that enrolled between one and two hundred students a term. Many students from a variety of majors took the class to satisfy a general education "diversity" requirement.

On each first day of class, I introduced myself and the teaching assistants, gave a five-minute history of the discipline of women's studies, and delivered some version of this promise: If you're worried that we might try to change your beliefs or that you might be judged by your beliefs, I promise you that won't happen in this class. I'm going to ask you to learn material, and I hope you'll learn something here that will be useful to you after the class is over.

Assuring these undergrads that I wouldn't try to indoctrinate them and then living up to my own standard was the easy part. Much harder was keeping the grad teaching assistants I was assigned for each class on the same page. As the years went on, TAs labored with ever-intensifying ardor to undermine my pledge not to impose orthodoxy.

Since they worked more closely with students in small discussion groups than I did as lecturer, the TAs enjoyed many opportunities to thwart my design for the class. For example, they added elements to the part of the class for which they were responsible on the down low. This counter-programming included in-class exercises, readings that were not on the course syllabus, and additional assignments geared to separating, as my intimidating seventh grade Texas history teacher used to intone, the sheeps from the goats.

These backdoor course elements were inevitably intended to instruct students in the tenets of antiracism and queer theory, and to identify oppressed and oppressor identities in students. By the time I taught the introductory class for the last time, the grad teaching assistants were in nearly open revolt. They not only employed the means in their control to push back against the class I'd designed, they took turns instructing me whenever they were dismayed by what I was or wasn't teaching. Which was often.

To entertain myself, I imagined a kind of War Room, in which the TAs met to determine whose turn it was to advance to the front and engage with the adversary: me. After this experience, I decided not to teach any class for which I would receive grad student assistants or graders.

An irony of this experience is that many students from that last large class, with whom, as a voice from the stage, I had little personal contact, stopped after a class to tell me about a conversation they'd had with a friend, romantic partner, or parent about some topic or idea we'd discussed. On the last day of class, several students formed an impromptu line to tell me how much—and how unexpectedly!—they'd enjoyed the class and how much they'd gleaned from it.

I told them what I've always told students in these kinds of conversations: thank you for letting me know you got something from the course; I'm glad you were here. And I was.

I made it my pedagogical business to always, on every subject, hear out students who had an objection to a reading, discussion, or point in my lecture. As these interactions accumulated over time, I had an epiphany of the sort that sometimes causes my friend Jeff to note that I'm *slow that way*. This is that, in my experience, conservative and progressive students responded differently to my pedagogical philosophy of hearing them out.

Let me be clear: *in my experience*, conservative students generally wanted to be heard, and I always tried to do two things: remember to thank them for articulating a point that hadn't been raised up to that time and speak to that point.

If I knew there was empirical support for their position, I'd respond as though operating under the Brady rule. If the point or objection was a matter of social, political, or religious values, I'd explain for the edification of the class how different sets of values might guide us in different ways to these different outcomes and how we could see those diverse sets of values operating in American history and politics. Here's what I wouldn't do: tell such students that they were wrong; talk down to them; and/or denounce them to the class as purveyors of obsolete and bigoted thinking.

By contrast, *in my experience*, progressive students wanted to be validated. What I mean by this is that they wanted to be assured that I shared their views. They also wanted me to present these shared views as correct and as the only ones that would be tolerated in the classroom. This means that, for progressive students, permitting different positions on issues to receive a respectful hearing was a violation of the implicit contract of the course.

Students are alert to the possibility that they're being indoctrinated. Unfortunately, their judgment about what constitutes impermissible indoctrination has been shaped by the progressive ideology they've consumed across disciplines. Thus, when progressive students receive from professors the "correct," progressive answers to social, political, and economic problems, they believe they've been properly informed of the only truthful, moral positions on these issues.

On the other hand, if professors offer a range of different arguments about social, political, and economic issues, and don't definitively affirm that only one is correct, progressive students are likely to believe they're being subjected to indoctrination. Such professors can only be motivated by a malign plan to deflect students' attention away from truth toward falsehood, undermine morality, and harm oppressed people.

This is an important point, so let me slow down and repeat as teachers often must. In progressive classes across many disciplines, a vocal subset of students expect to receive a single correct answer to contentious questions. They will recognize this correct answer when they hear it. Students will assume that professors who don't tender the correct answer have an ulterior motive. Illiberal progressive academics work this system, which can root out colleagues who are insufficiently committed to illiberal indoctrination.

Years of such affirming classroom experience can provide students with a profound sense of belonging that reminds me of an idea that's ubiquitous in American Christianity: that all humans have a "god-shaped hole"—a spiritual void that can only be filled by knowledge of and a relationship with God.

Whether or not we think of academic progressivism as a religion, many professors have been filling up their students' god-shaped hole with its tenets, its rituals, and the bonds of belief they share.

What's So Scary?

What does a progressive commitment to teach politics as morality look like in practice? Here's one example: in 2023, my gender studies department put on an event to promote the field and department to students. The Halloween-themed event, "What's So Scary About Gender Studies?," was held in person before an audience, with a larger audience, of which I was a member, on Zoom. It featured a panel of two gender studies faculty and one PhD student talking about their research.[84]

When panel members finished their presentations, the Q&A commenced, and the first question appeared to be both pre-planned and a response to one speaker's talk. The questioner, whom I couldn't see off camera, noted that he assumed members of the panel disapproved of capitalism; in light of this disapproval, he wanted to know how they would respond to the pharmaceutical industry deriving billions of dollars in worldwide profits from gender-affirming care.

I'd wager that most of my colleagues agree with the speaker I cited in the Introduction and believe that capitalism sucks. But we'll never know that, or how anyone on the faculty might respond to such a question, because nobody replied. The questioner soon left.

After he was gone, people in the room characterized the question as "hostile" and an "attack"; alluded to our shared source of knowledge in "personal experience"; asserted the value of the "love and protection" afforded by gender studies; and framed opposition to gender studies values as originating in fear.

Not long after the event, gender studies faculty processed what had occurred. One faculty member suggested that questions at such events in the future might be moderated, presumably to prevent "hostile" questions from being heard.

Noting the necessity to protect students, a second suggested the possibility of providing participants with de-escalation training. Such training is typically applied to situations that might escalate to violence or in which strong, usually negative, emotions make performing cognitive tasks difficult. Neither scenario occurred in the gender studies event.

A third faculty member referred to the questioner as a "disrupting attendee" and suggested reporting the person to the College of Arts and Sciences.

To recap, instead of responding to the question as a question, my colleagues did the following: refused to respond; brainstormed ways to ensure that dissenting questions wouldn't be heard in future discussions; reiterated the goal of protecting students from what are presumed to be harmful ideas; raised the possibility of treating dissenting questions as potentially violent events and dissenters as disruptive people to be managed; and identified an authority to which such situations—and dissenters—could be referred, I assume for punishment or interdiction.

Wouldn't it have been easier to respond to the question? Isn't that what we're there for? Or are we there to provide caring, love, and protection?

The faculty lost control of the "What's So Scary" event. They'd underestimated what can occur when speakers can't choose their audience and can't impose consequences on dissenters. It's no wonder, then, that—faced with a hostile world of people who don't share their views—progressive faculty and students might reach for more control.

One domain that holds promise for constraining what people think and how they might express those thoughts is language. As Helen Dale and Lorenzo Warby point out,

> the more language is held to structure social outcomes, the more lan-

> guage is held to be the vehicle for creating social outcomes, the more language itself has to be controlled to achieve the transformations demanded by *social justice*. Including by setting what's acceptable to say and how it's to be said.[85]

Universities have led the way.

On Language

Before I turn to discussing the significance of language for academic illiberalism, I beg your patience as I tell a story about my effort to insistently prod someone to adopt a progressive best practice on language in real life. My mom was a Christian conservative and, I, her only daughter, a leftie lesbian PhD. We often disagreed and, as a young adult, I believed it was her job to overcome her beliefs—to see and accept me as I was, regardless of who *she* was.

I was wrong. Fortunately, in the wake of years of silence and struggle, we came to love each other through our differences.

I learned many things about my mom in those later years, including how much she looked forward to our conversations about subjects big and small. She often asked me questions, and her questions made it necessary to do something I did in the classroom: differentiate facts underlying an issue from my analysis of or beliefs about those facts. I admitted when I didn't know something, and we looked for that information together. She would direct me to "look on [my] computer," as though all the world's data resided on my humble laptop.

My mom was alert for any suggestion that some groups of people were inherently superior to others. She would physically recoil from slurs and put-downs aimed at or about any person or group. Although she held uncompromising traditional beliefs about right and wrong, she valued generosity to all of God's children.

And, so, we arrive at the 2000s, when I tried to teach my mom not to use the word "oriental" to refer to everything from Chinese food to people of Asian descent. After decades of referring to Asian-descended people—including the Japanese sister-in-law she loved—as "oriental" without incident, my mom couldn't pivot.

The first time I mentioned that "oriental" was a problem, I just noted that this was a case of what people prefer to be called having changed over time. That was good enough for her, but she couldn't remember to execute the shift. I tried several times before I sat with my discomfort, asking myself why I was tormenting an elderly woman to relieve my anxiety.

The truth was that I feared she would characterize something or someone as "oriental" and that someone—possibly young enough to be her grandchild—would disdainfully correct her. I knew it would hurt her to think she had injured or offended someone. But I also knew from my expertise in the academy that, if you say the wrong words or fail to say the right ones—even if those words have only become right or wrong very recently—your intent doesn't matter. There's even an equation to express the principle: impact > intent.

In failing to teach my mother not to say "oriental," I gained insight into the uncompromising politics of language on the academic left.

The Language is the Message

In 2000, the political scientist James Miller published an essay that I've thought about many times in the years since. Entitled "Is Bad Writing Necessary?," the essay analyzed the debate between those who hold that radical writing must be opaque to subvert dominant modes of power and those who champion "linguistic transparency." The patron saint of the radicals is Theodor Adorno, and the patron saint of the plain speakers is George Orwell.[86]

Rooting for a team is something I'm really bad at. I'm a terrible sports fan—clapping for good plays regardless of the color jersey the player's wearing and reading the news between plays. But if I have to pick between Orwell and Adorno, I'm Team Orwell, in part because of his forceful warnings against politicized efforts to control language.[87]

Recall that the transformation of women's studies into gender studies occurred in the context of a "linguistic turn" in theory. Commentators call attention to the fact that many academics, especially in the humanities, speak, write, and teach students a language that's esoteric and alienating to most in the outside world. One reason I wear the Orwell jersey is my belief that impenetrability isn't necessary. Many excellent scholars speak and write theoretically in ways that are accessible to virtually all readers or listeners.

But progressive scholars use language as they do deliberately. Esoteric language functions as a marker of ingroup membership and adherence to a particular kind of politics.

Such writing is one of the signals progressives send, to students and to each other, that they are in the know and in touch. The style is the message: I have the right set of values; we're on the same side. For academic progressives, lucid writing betrays ideological heterodoxy, ignorance of high theory, and even low intelligence. Lucid writers are assumed to have an agenda: dismantling—a favorite word and concept—radical/critical critiques of "dominant" thought. What would sting even more, I suspect, is if progressive academics discovered that lucid writers and thinkers are mostly indifferent to what issues from progressives.

Students intuit and apply the progressive standard. And, naturally, they mimic the style they associate with stigmatized knowledge and high academic status.

Students quickly come to understand the importance of the politics of language. They also absorb progressive additions to academic and activist language with alacrity. So, for example, most students don't question why new terms for old ideas or identities are essential to avoid perpetrating harm or to create new markers for ingroup membership.

As a result, soon after they've been introduced, terms like BIPOC, folx, misogynoir, cisheteronormativity, transmisogyny, scholasticide, homonationalism, racial capitalism, rainbow capitalism, and Latinx come to be effectively required for all who broach a wide range of social and political issues.

Critics of the progressive academy cite many reasons why those who want to understand academic illiberalism should focus on language. One of these is self-described "old-school" Marxist Freddie deBoer.[88] Correctly calling such language "incomprehensible to ordinary Americans," deBoer explains its proliferation from universities to "left-leaning spaces" in the world outside as logical consequences, both of the desire not to seem "unsophisticated" and of the "mimetic" process by which such language spreads online.

Install such language in the academy, deBoer argues, and "you get people talking about the role of Latinx intersectionality in queering BIPOC spaces in the Global South." You also get "the fashion" of the use of "black bodies" as "an awkward and exclusionary euphemism for *people*, and a term used to show that someone is a savvy, progressive person with the correct attitudes toward race."[89] Simon Sebag Montefiore finds in the "intimidating jargon" that some once thought a sign of physics envy, "a clue to its lack of factual rigor."[90]

It's all well and good to talk about inaccessible, politicized language in the abstract. But it's better to point to examples of attempts to control language and constrain the scope of words that can be used to name particular items and ideas. As we'll see, such efforts aren't about creating a level playing field by extirpating language that would create a hostile learning environment.

Instead, these efforts reflect the moralizing of language and the illiberal project of imposing progressive views on the rest of us.

Compared to many of my colleagues, I'm a free speech absolutist. Of course, I wouldn't tolerate threats in the classroom. Veiled threats—Who will rid me of this meddlesome priest? She's going to go through some things—are also unwelcome. So are name-calling and slurs. But when we turn to universities' efforts to control students' and faculty members' speech, these aren't the language abuses we're talking about. Egregious hate speech is rarely at issue when universities crack down on students and faculty.

Indeed, too much of what universities have worked to proscribe is only "hate" or "bias" because students and faculty who have the upper hand disapprove. Universities defended speech codes and prohibitions by citing the moral necessity to protect students from harm. And prohibitions on words, terms, and ideas proliferated.

Eliminating Harmful Language

Illiberal progressives reject the need to persuade their fellow citizens of the virtues of particular language choices. They reject the idea that it's likely there will be disagreement on these issues. In the absence of agreement, they believe there must be obedience and consequences for disobedience.

I'm going to pick on Stanford University for two reasons. First, the debut of its "Elimination of Harmful Language Initiative" received a great deal of attention from critics of campus progressivism. And second, the initiative was both clumsy and ambitious. Someone who wanted to create a parody of such a project could hardly have done a better job. The Harmful Language Initiative didn't just criticize a wide variety of language choices but was utopian in its aim to *eliminate* them, "a goal to strive for even if it can't be achieved."

And it promised to grow to even more impressive proportions through crowdsourcing. Before Stanford pulled the plug, the initiative's creators conceived it as a "multi-phase, multi-year project" and invited all concerned language users to contribute examples of harmful language. Someone who represented Stanford literally wrote this:

> Do you have a term you'd like added to the list? Please fill out our suggestion form. Your suggestion will be reviewed and added to the list accordingly. If you don't have a SUNetID to access the suggestions form or if you have other suggestions, please contact us.

The preface to the initiative identifies "many forms of harmful language, including racist, violent, and biased (e.g., disability bias, ethnic bias, ethnic slurs, gender bias, implicit bias, sexual bias) language in Stanford websites and code." To prepare the reader for what lies ahead, there's a trigger warning, bolded and indented. It reads:

> **Content Warning: This website contains language that is offensive or harmful. Please engage with this website at your own pace.**

I have a question: without this warning, would readers have felt obligated to consume the contents of the site at one sitting? Yet another thing I'll probably never know.

As for the impermissible words and terms themselves, they are grouped into ten searchable categories: Ableist, Ageism, Colonialism, Culturally Appropriative, Gender-Based, Imprecise Language, Institutionalized Racism, Person First, Violent, and the oddly-titled Additional Considerations (the first alternative that came to mind was "Authoritarian Miscellany").

Each category opens up to a chart that lists a repudiated word or term, the word or term to "consider using" instead, and an explanation of why, to borrow a catchphrase of *Drag Race* impresario RuPaul, the term is "up for elimination."[91]

The initiative recommends against referring to US citizens as "American," heterosexual people as "straight," and Black (always capitalized) people as "African Americans." The phrase "people of color" to refer to members of the category now denoted as BIPOC is embargoed.

However, as interesting as what's on the lists is what's not. Missing are such timeless sex/gender-based epithets as "slut," "bitch," "cunt," and "whore." For homosexuals, "fag(got)" and "dyke"—which a friend's student delicately referred to not long ago as the obviously unspeakable "d-word"—continue to make an appearance in real life from time to time. And the most execrable race-based epithet in US history is also strangely absent.

The omissions clarify the initiative's purpose. If the goal were to weed out slurs that might compromise students' ability to enjoy an education on equal terms with their peers, we'd see more of my additions on the lists. So, it appears that the point is to identify forms of expression that conflict with progressive political beliefs and instruct users in politic forms of expression.

The initiative is also a lesson in what happens when people who overestimate their knowledge are placed or place themselves in charge of policing others' behavior. For example, the proscribing of the word "ghetto" suggests that the person who nominated it isn't aware of its

European origins and how the word came into use in the United States.

Those who browse the initiative may be amused by different items. The one that stands out to me for unintentional humor is "trigger warning," contraindicated because "the phrase can cause stress about what's to follow. Additionally, one can never know what may or may not trigger a particular person."[92] Well, precisely. That psychological responses to stimuli are complex is one reason why instructors might reasonably hesitate to go down Trigger Road.

Such an understanding could encourage skepticism about trigger warnings. Instead, for Stanford, it somehow suggests that the problem is the word "trigger." If only someone could solve the problem of "trigger" being triggering! Or perhaps, the problem of the word "content"—when it's followed by "warning"—coming inevitably over time to "cause stress about what's to follow." If Stanford can't solve this problem, what hope is there for the rest of us?

In response to reactions from critics who were triggered by the Elimination of Harmful Language Initiative, Stanford downplayed the project as merely applying to its information technology sector and not intended as a standard to be imposed across the institution. The university also discontinued the project and removed the webpage, though it remains available online.

Stanford isn't alone in providing guidelines for controlling other people's language choices. It just provided a rich target. In recent years, we've seen progressives in social work, try to purge the word "field," from . . . their field. The School of Social Work at the University of Southern California acknowledges "that changing terminology can be challenging, and a complete transition will take time." They "thank [us] in advance for joining [them] in this effort and for [our] patience as [they] transition."[93]

The word, "master" has also been removed from the lexicon. Henceforth, instead of students acquiring mastery in a field, they can only hope to gain competence in a body of knowledge.

In the course of my job, I learned that many progressive students and faculty have come to consistently refer to the US government as the "colonial state." And that in at least some contexts, progressive decolonial faculty refer to their students as "settler students." Strangely, although the logic of "settler students" also applies to the vast majority of faculty, I've never heard any of my colleagues refer to themselves as "settler faculty." Probably just an oversight.

It's important to point out that some intellectuals from historically marginalized groups take issue with progressive linguistic mandates. Tabia Lee followed most people of Latin American descent in dissenting from the use of the progressive term Latinx.

And Roland G. Fryer Jr. is unequivocal on the move from the proscribed terms, "African American" and "people of color" to "BIPOC." Declaring that he doesn't "tolerate foolishness at all," Fryer warns that "you can't put me on a task force where we're going to spend the semester talking about the new name for black people. I don't want to do it. You go to my neighborhood and call someone BIPOC, they'll punch you in the face. I care about the real issues."[94]

As a final example of the fetishizing of language on the academic left, I direct your attention to Johns Hopkins University's LGBTQ guide defining lesbians as "non-men" attracted to "non-men." The online guide immediately attracted derision. Stanford recommends not using "straight" to denote heterosexually-oriented people, so I'll note that some non-lesbian feminists were also nonplussed. After an outcry and no small amount of mockery at its expense, Hopkins removed the definition.[95]

History is replete with examples of significant shifts in language use. In the United States as elsewhere, terms associated with minority and disfavored groups have often expressed negative stereotyping of and bigotry toward members of these groups. Over time, many slurs came to be socially stigmatized.

In my lifetime, I've seen such linguistic changes, which can be understood as marking processes of greater moral inclusion.[96] Advocating for such changes takes some degree of patience on the part of those who believe that language choices can reinforce or help to diminish prejudice.

Unfortunately, one common word in the academic progressive lexicon is "demand," which observers can find on display in manifestos progressives issue on matters of public concern. Instead of trying to persuade their fellow citizens in as respectful a way as they can muster, those who are impatient with persuasion have gone straight to rulemaking, public displays of anger, and threats of punishment.

On Pronouns

In the twenty teens, LGBTQ activists placed pronouns on their social and political agenda. Universities responded by developing pronoun policies, encouraging students and faculty to add their preferred pronouns to online databases and other functions, directing faculty to use students' pronouns, and deeming it a best practice for faculty to announce their pronouns in classes and other venues. Predictably, some students and faculty refused, often on grounds of free speech or free exercise of religion.

One early non-adopter was Grant Strobl, in 2016 a student at the University of Michigan and chair of the university's chapter of Young Americans for Freedom. Offered the opportunity to select or create his own personal pronoun, Strobl selected "His Highness" and made the rounds of conservative media to explain why he availed himself of the opportunity to make sport of his university's pronoun policy.[97]

Having already enabled students and faculty to identify their pronouns in various university systems, Flagship State announced a pronoun policy in 2023: the "Guidance on Use of Chosen/Preferred Names and Pronouns." The policy directed members of the university community to

> [u]se an individual's stated pronouns (e.g., she/her, he/him, they/them, etc.) whether they are present or not. Best practice is to introduce yourself using your pronouns and invite others to do the same . . . . Note: In broad communications, the pronouns they/their are acceptable to use as singular pronouns.[98]

The word "pronouns" on the Office of Equity website linked to a webpage, "LGBTQ at [Flagship] State," which revealed the source of the policy. This was a position sheet created by the LGBTQ advocacy organization, the Human Rights Campaign, entitled "Pronouns 101."[99] How did an LGBTQ advocacy group end up linked to a policy at Flagship State?

A little background is in order. Business and socially conservative interests have been innovators in the process of crafting policy blueprints. Lobbyists, trade associations, and advocacy organizations often write government rules, public policies, party platforms, and policy templates. These pre-fab model laws and regulations travel easily across jurisdictions and between organizations. They can be adopted or adjusted for local circumstances by advocacy organizations working in concert with policymakers.

One such policy is the "heartbeat" or "fetal heartbeat bill," the purpose of which was to ban abortion after a fetal heartbeat could be detected. The original heartbeat bill was crafted by Ohio pro-life activists who worked closely with state policymakers and advocates nationwide. The model law spread and was passed in several states, though some were ruled unconstitutional before the Supreme Court's 2022 decision in *Dobbs v. Jackson Women's Health Organization*.[100]

Liberals, progressives, and scholars of democracy have lodged objections to such backdoor processes and policies.[101] One lesson to be absorbed from my university's pronoun policy is that the practice of advocacy organizations writing policy for institutions is bipartisan. It's not tendentious to observe that, like political institutions and parties, Flagship State University outsourced its "pronoun policy" to staff members and activists affiliated with an LGBTQ advocacy organization.

Might conservatives identify such a policymaking process as fair game for exposure and criticism? They might.

One last point on pronouns. In an obvious effort to bolster the legitimacy and irrefragability of Flagship State's policy, the university instructed members of the community that its pronoun policy was required to comply with the Supreme Court's 2020 decision in *Bostock v. Clayton*

County, Georgia. Contrary to what the Office of Equity suggested with its invocation of the decision, nothing in *Bostock* prescribed the use of pronouns, including bespoke neopronouns.

Moreover, the Equity Office neglected to mention a court decision closer to home. In 2018, a transgender student of Shawnee State University philosophy professor Nicholas Meriwether informed Meriwether that she should be referred to with female, rather than male, pronouns. Citing his Christian faith as well as knowledge in philosophy and biology, Meriwether declined the request but came to an arrangement with university administrators to use the student's last name.

Not mollified by this compromise, the student lodged a formal complaint, and Shawnee State insisted that Meriwether comply. Meriwether held his position, and he was disciplined. The professor sued, and, in 2021—after the Supreme Court's precedent-setting decision in *Bostock*—the US Court of Appeals for the Sixth Circuit found in his favor, ruling that Shawnee State had violated his rights to free speech and free exercise of religion.[102] The university agreed to pay Meriwether $400,000 in damages and attorney fees.[103]

Was invoking *Bostock* a cynical attempt to preempt disagreement over a policy? Or did Flagship State's attorneys just not understand how to interpret the decision as well as the Sixth Circuit Court of Appeals did? If we weren't in the room, we'll probably never know.

In recent years, many universities have accused faculty of racism, transphobia, Islamophobia, and other bigotries. In case after case, accusations reflect not objective standards of moral truth that command nearly universal agreement but progressive theories, activist claims, and unremitting demands for obedience.

Social movement opinion leaders and religious elites claim to represent morality. Because I am no longer a member of a congregation, I wouldn't have thought their moral strictures would apply to me. Nonetheless, we've been confronted in recent years with academics acting as though they're primarily in the business of enforcing morality.

Most of us are probably no longer surprised that the uncontested leader of one of two political parties in the United States smears those he wishes to undermine as enemies of the people. We should be outraged that academics and universities came to treat so many of their colleagues as enemies, forcing them into silence, conformity, apologies, preemptive obedience, and sometimes punishment.

4 Enemies of the People

On Silence

It's the mid to late nineties, and I'm watching an episode of Pat Robertson's *700 Club* TV show. School prayer is on the agenda in this episode, and Robertson's co-host Ben Kinchlow suggests an instruction for students who don't want to pray: they should bow their heads and shut their mouths.[1]

Kinchlow recognized that if school prayer were constitutional and compulsory, some students would choose not to pray. Anticipating dissent, he revealed the expectation he no doubt shared with many believers of all stripes—that anyone who disagreed would remain silent and quietly pantomime obedience. Or else?

When I saw this exchange, it didn't occur to me that I'd come to see the dynamic in academia. To be left to do their work in relative anonymity, academics who find progressive doctrines unpersuasive or decline to serve them as the only offering on the menu increasingly became obliged to choose whether to pledge allegiance to these ideas or remain silent.

It's hard to imagine a greater violation of the ethics of scholarly institutions than to insist that all ideas outside the ambit of progressivism cause harm and, therefore, must be silenced.[2]

Modern social and political movements have emphasized the imperative for activists and members of disfavored groups to exercise voice. In the early gay and lesbian movement, same-sex attracted people were exhorted to come out of the closet and to be "loud and proud" about their orientation. This at a time when coming out of the closet was likely to be accompanied by extremely negative consequences. When the HIV/AIDS epidemic burst into public consciousness in the eighties, activists declaimed that "silence is violence" and "silence = death."

So, it's ironic that progressive academics who consider themselves the heirs of the last century's most radical liberationists have not only been willing to enforce silence on their peers but have considered it their obligation to do so. As a result, the Foundation for Individual Rights and Expression reported in 2023 that

> a majority of faculty worry about losing their jobs or reputations because someone misrepresents their words. A third self-censor out of concern over the responses of staff, students or administrators. Moreover, a significant portion of faculty support punishing their colleagues in softer ways that can chill expression. These restrictions include formally condemning certain views but not punishing someone for expressing them; investigating colleagues for controversial expression; and applying social and professional pressure to get colleagues to take mandatory training they philosophically oppose.[3]

Some faculty colleagues have expressed the view that if a minority of faculty—in FIRE's study, approximately a third—feared consequences of exercising voice, things aren't as bad as some of us have made them out to be. We should bear in mind that some subset of the others didn't fear such consequences because they held and professed the "right" views. Nor did these right-thinking colleagues have to be a majority to endanger academic freedom.

As many academics have worried about the consequences of engaging in voice, so have many students. According to the results of Heterodox Academy's 2022 Campus Expression Survey, "nearly two-thirds of students report[ed] that they censor their views in the classroom on culturally controversial topics."[4] While faculty self-censored to avoid conflicts with peers and students, students self-censored to avoid conflicts with peers and faculty.

Among the many productive ways to conceptualize silence and silencing is Elisabeth Noelle-Neumann's concept of the "spiral of silence." The spiral of silence takes as its starting point that "every individual is subject to the pressure of public opinion." From her study of trends in support for political parties, Noelle-Neumann concludes that

> individuals have a fear of isolation . . . . This fear induces them constantly to check accepted opinions and modes of behavior and the potential and direction of change. . . . When people feel they are in the minority, they become cautious and silent, thus further reinforcing the impression in public of their side's weakness, until the apparently weaker side disappears completely except for a small hard core that clings to values from the past, or until the opinion becomes taboo.[5]

People fall silent, the spiral of silence explains, because those "who deviate from the consensus are threatened with isolation and ostracism."

The political scientist Pippa Norris applies the "spiral of silence" to higher ed, arguing that the "hegemonic viewpoint" in progressive academia is reinforced when people who believe they are viewpoint minorities self-censor to prevent "social isolation or loss of status." She observes that, in universities, "the spiral of silence is likely to muffle overt dissent in classroom discussions, departmental and faculty meetings; to weaken rigorous intellectual debate in scholarly talks, professional conventions, books and journal articles; as well as reinforcing the paradigmatic consensus guiding normal scientific inquiry."[6]

To some critics, the state of affairs that Norris describes suggests that there are similarities between the academy and authoritarian or totalitarian states and movements outside the United States. Such comparisons can be facile and inapposite. Many scholars might insist that they are even specious and hysterical.

It's significant, then, that some academics and public intellectuals from the former Soviet bloc and communist China have independently attested to worrying parallels between these states and American academia. These include Cathy Young, the Wilson Center scholar Izabella Tabarovsky, the chemistry professor Anna Krylov, the psychologist Joseph Forgas, the mathematician Alexander Barvinok, and Xiao Li, "an academic based in America" who's written about the dangers of academic illiberalism under a pseudonym.

Writing about what troubles them in academia's illiberal turn, these authors point to such similarities as the repudiation of free speech as a value; the vetting of scholarship based on ideological criteria; the pressure to affirm loyalty to particular ideas; the deputizing of young adults as accusers of nonconformists; and the mobbing and cancellation of those accused of holding or expressing the wrong ideas.[7]

Having written extensively about Soviet communism and post-communism, Anne Applebaum compares elements of academic culture and procedures with characteristics of life under communism. In academia, "breaking a social code" can bring severe social, legal, reputational, and employment consequences. University investigations entail secrecy, the withholding of complete information about accusers and accusations, and the demand that targets remain silent about what's happening to them. Accused people can face personally ruinous consequences without due process. As in illiberal regimes, it's common for colleagues to disassociate themselves from an accused person.[8]

Considering how careful people who fear falling into the grip of authorities and mobs might be to avoid such a fate, the philosopher and legal theorist Renata Salecl argues that, in Soviet and Eastern European communist regimes, vague standards about what could precipitate punishment bred great caution. Under such a regime, intellectuals were "silenced precisely because they were forced to guess what the desire of the government was. Self-censorship thus became a prerequisite for intellectuals' survival."

Conditions like these are likely to produce public obedience paired with private resistance, which reinforces the authority of illiberal states and institutions.[9] Just what nonconforming academics too numerous to list warned us about in higher ed.

But privatizing resistance can degrade the environment for truth seeking. Timur Kuran warns about preference falsification, explaining "that people rely on the prevailing climate of opinion in developing the personal belief systems that underlie their private policy preferences." When large numbers of people fear expressing preferences in public, the resulting "climate of opinion" shapes others' private preferences.

Preference falsification matters at the aggregate level because it can result in "a policy that few people support privately . . . command[ing] an overwhelming public endorsement," a process that leads to a diminution of "the degree of private opposition." The perverse consequence of such a cascade isn't only "that societies retain many policies they would rather change." It's that "policies they inherit from the past shape their members' views and wants."[10]

Kuran's concept of preference falsification shows how dissent from dominant ideas is reduced when people who disagree are coerced into silence. The economist Glenn Loury considers what happens to those who continue to deviate.

In an essay entitled "Self-Censorship in Public Discourse," Loury explains the phenomenon of self-censorship as a function of group dynamics: The "need to police group members' beliefs so as to ferret out deviants." Under pressure to falsify and self-censor, those who have acquitted themselves well as upstanding group members ask themselves a question about the apostacy of others. No, not "Does this argument have merit?" Instead, the relevant question is: "What type of person would say such a thing?"

When someone makes a point that is unthinkable by the group, members make an "ad hoc inference"; they "impute undesirable qualities" to the speaker and conclude that such a person is "dangerous . . . if allowed to remain among us undetected."[11] If professors who believe in intellectual diversity know their students and colleagues will attribute personal bigotry to them whenever they raise an alternative perspective, most will do what's expected of them: they'll shut up.

As we know, some instructors will either insist on teaching a diversity of views, or they'll misstep. If the dissenter is lucky, as I was, a prominent colleague will come to her defense and a free speech advocacy organization will assign her an attorney at no expense. If she isn't, her choices are likely to be more circumscribed. She can retire or just leave her job quietly. Or she can apologize.

She should know, however, that even sincere apologies may not staunch the bleeding and stabilize her career.[12] Apologies can misfire and backfire, inciting more demands and denunciations. Naturally, demands for apologies also open up opportunities. Applebaum points out that websites now offer "sample templates" for people who need to apologize, and some universities offer advice, including lists of good words to use in apologies.[13]

As we'll see, some university administrators, like interrogators before them, will even write your apology for you. It's labor saving when all you have to do is sign. The fly in the ointment is that it's always possible that the perpetrator isn't sorry for her transgression against what her colleagues have redefined as the only acceptable way to practice the profession of research and teaching.

The goal is to produce consensus or even "illusions of consensus."[14] Progressive faculty may not care if their colleagues and students are silent about disagreement because they enthusiastically support all elements of progressive doctrine or because they know when it's in their interest to shut up about any possible disagreements. As the longshoreman and social philosopher Eric Hoffer explains, activists have conviction and confidence on their side.

> All active mass movements strive . . . to interpose a fact-proof screen between the faithful and the realities of the world. They do this by claiming that the ultimate and absolute truth is already embodied in their doctrine and that there is no truth nor certitude outside it . . . . To rely on the evidence of senses and of reason is heresy and treason.[15]

The activism in which students and faculty have been steeped demands that students, faculty, and administrators be ever-alert to possible transgressions against its tenets. These tenets are usually articulated as safety, caring, or the mandate to protect human dignity, especially the dignity of members of sacralized groups.

Violations of human rights can certainly include violations of dignity. Just because this is so doesn't mean that the mere invocation of dignity trumps other values. One scholar who's made this case is the evolutionary biologist Carole Hooven, who left Harvard after progressives applied pressure for her to recant her views.

Hooven argues that "if we restrict research on the basis that it may undermine 'dignities,' then we place severe limits on our ability to discover what is true." She raises key questions that complicate the quest to determine what respect for dignity requires, asking

> [T]o whom should we bestow the power to determine our "dignities," and what qualifies as undermining them? Are these judges of dignity deemed to be the most moral among us? Would they represent everyone's views, or just a subset of society? Or would they be elevated to the position by others with power?[16]

A chapter entitled "Enemies of the People" might well detail as many cases as possible from the voluminous case files of academics and students caught engaging in disfavored thought, speech, and practices. It might curate the most shocking cases of students and faculty silenced or penalized for speech. Even if we were limited to cases that have become public, the list would overwhelm.

The Foundation for Individual Rights and Expression maintains a non-comprehensive Scholars Under Fire Database.[17] Key findings from the database include that attempts to sanction scholars increased dramatically after 2015 and that almost two-thirds of the efforts were successful. As we might guess, organizations that mount sanction efforts from inside universities are primarily on the political left, while those outside, such as Turning Point USA and conservative elected officials, do so from the right.[18] We know that these public stories are the tip of an iceberg of intimidation and punishment.

In this chapter, I provide an overview of how scholars can come to be understood as enemies and some dynamics of cancellation, including a crucial distinction between "near" and "far" enemies. To understand what's happened in academia and why it's illiberal, we'll want to examine some cases that have come to public attention. But we also have to examine what happens out of sight and behind the scenes. For example, it will be fruitful to look closely at such banal instruments as universities' statements of "shared values."

Finally, I survey mechanisms for producing the boundary between right- and wrong-thinking students and scholars. And I explain why I'm not optimistic that higher ed can ditch the illiberalism that progressives worked so hard to institutionalize and render invisible.

An Intro to Punishment

In academia and other epistemic institutions, people who transgress progressive doctrines have been canceled—vilified, boycotted, shunned, and sanctioned. As a socio-political phenomenon, cancellation has been interpreted in a variety of ways. Some insist that it's a figment of the febrile right-wing imagination. Others that it's a legitimate reaction to the expression of views that are beyond the pale of civilized discourse. Yet others read cancellation as a troubling expression of political polarization and hostility toward norms of free speech and expression. I choose door number 3.

It should concern us all, even those who have watched episodes of cancellation from afar, that professors, journalists, and many others who contribute to public discourse became accustomed to trimming their responses on issues of interest to democratic citizens in a sometimes vain attempt to avoid being hounded by a mob animated by social justice, branded as a bigot or "phobe," or losing their livelihood.

After presidents of MIT, the University of Pennsylvania, and Harvard were summoned before Congress to testify about campus antisemitism, the political scientist Eric Kaufmann agreed with the presidents on the point that engendered contemptuous scolding from congressional Republicans: the cogency and relevance of the First Amendment as a guide for campus speech.

> [T]hese leaders were correct, under First Amendment jurisprudence, to reject the idea that talk of genocide should automatically lead to punishment. The problem, of course, is that these colleges are extreme-

> ly hypocritical, clamping down on any speech which might offend totemic minorities (BIPOC, LGBTQ) while clinging to a First Amendment justification for tolerating antisemitism.[19]

Referring to universities' pattern of repudiating some forms of contentious political speech while ignoring others, critics charged that for some time "college administrators ha[d] been weaponizing the First Amendment when it suit[ed] them, and blatantly disregarding it when it d[id]n't."[20] Busted.

Kaufmann blames this state of affairs on the loss of "viewpoint diversity," and he's not wrong. Limiting such diversity has been a feature of academic hiring, not a bug. Valuing viewpoint diversity doesn't entail a regime of establishing the conservative bona fides of potential faculty and then developing affirmative action to recruit and hire them.[21] It does, or would if it were still possible in many disciplines, mean welcoming a diversity of viewpoints among undergrad and grad students and not imposing transparent litmus tests on faculty to determine that they share the views of their colleagues.

When progressive identitarian viewpoints dominate in universities and silence other views, there are few faculty left to present principled liberal or conservative perspectives on contentious issues. Even faculty who perform empirical research that points in prohibited directions can find themselves cast as players in stubborn ideological conflicts.

When this system works, students learn that there is only one acceptable—non-bigoted, non-fascist, non-white supremacist—way to see the world and every question in it. And very few are left to talk back.

One of the more curious features of left-wing illiberalism in higher ed has been the demand that authorities punish deviations from left-wing dogma. After all, aren't leftie radicals supposed to repudiate all forms of hierarchy in favor of a levelling equity? The reality is, of course, more complicated. Even contradictory.

On its face, academic progressive theory does dictate rigorous egalitarianism and the forms of discrimination necessary to achieve it. But authoritarianism insists on punishment for deviation, which can be delivered by peers in the form of community justice or by bureaucratic authorities called upon to use what, in other contexts, progressives might believe are reactionary levers of power to punish disbelief or misbehavior.

When Laura Kipnis rhetorically asked why scholars are such snitches, it was to call attention to the "carceral turn" in American higher ed and its incongruity with the putative values of academic progressivism.

> What's not [to be expected] is the so-called campus left failing to notice the degree to which the "carceral turn" in American higher ed — the prosecutorial ethos, the resources reallocated to regulation and punishment — shares a certain cultural logic with the rise of mass incarceration and over-policing in off-campus America .... But what care social-justice types about fostering the carceral university if those with suspect politics can be flattened, even — fingers crossed! — expelled, or left unemployed and penurious?[22]

Kipnis refers to the philosopher Michel Foucault's analysis of the evolution of state punishment over the course of modernity. He argues that the "tortured body" and the "spectacle of physical punishment" that had characterized states' treatment of criminals before the nineteenth century gave way to regimes that target "the secret souls of criminals."

If the end of official state torture seems like a positive development, Foucault clarifies that the technologies of modern punishment actually bring into existence "the soul," which is "produced permanently around, on, within the body by the functioning of a power that is exercised on those punished" and is "born rather out of methods of punishment, supervision and constraint."[23]

Foucault may be relevant to an analysis of what happens when illiberal academics confront critics and non-conformists, though perhaps not in the ways progressives think. If only I'd realized in grad school that some of my colleagues were reading Foucault as a guidebook for producing the appropriately-configured souls of their peers and students!

Enemies of the people must be punished, but not all enemies of the people are the same. Indeed, there are multiple paths to becoming an adversary to progressivism. First, one might be born that way. The philosopher Kathleen Stock calls certain ascriptive identities such as historically dominant race and class "a problem inherited from history."[24] People with one or more such identities might be able to mitigate the problem through processes recognizable from religious faith: confession, expiation, penance, and, if they're lucky, absolution. The profane versions are often summed up as "doing the work," "educating yourself," and "being an ally."

A second pathway to being an oppressor is to reject the apparatus of illiberal progressivism, in whole or in part. Stock herself became such an enemy when she disagreed with progressive doctrine on gender identity and insisted on the material significance of biological sex. Because she stood by these ideas, she was constructively discharged from the University of Sussex amid threats and her institution's recommendation that she hire security guards to protect herself.

It's important to note that many people who haven't personally caused offense do their best not to consort with those who have, fearing being held guilty by association. Dasha Navalnaya, the daughter of the Russian dissident Alexei Navalny, probably never considered distancing herself from her famous dad. When Dasha was invited to speak at the graduation ceremony for Georgetown University's School of Foreign Service in 2023, her father was imprisoned in Russia for daring to lead a movement of opposition against Vladimir Putin.

However, Navalny wasn't a perfect emissary. He had "made comments calling immigrants 'cockroaches,' used gay slurs" and waited too long to say "he believe[d] Crimea . . . should be returned to Ukraine." Having concluded that Dasha should be held responsible for her father's deviations, hundreds of Georgetown faculty and students demanded that she be disinvited as a speaker. Georgetown declined, and some students settled for standing and turning their backs to her as she spoke.[25]

In early 2024, Alexei Navalny died in a remote Arctic penal colony, a victim of Putin and his authoritarian regime.

A third pathway to being an oppressor is the most idiosyncratic and unpredictable because it points to miscellaneous factors that influence who gets caught in machineries of illiberalism. Such factors include status envy, competition for resources, scapegoating, and even personality conflicts. Thus, identity and political ideology aren't the only determinants of who's punished. Once illiberal practices are institutionalized, bad things can happen to all kinds of people.

This includes those Anne Applebaum describes as "for lack of a more precise word, difficult." As Laura Kipnis, puts it, "anyone who's disliked by anyone is a sitting duck."[26] Considering the possibility that some accused and investigated academics are merely difficult, Applebaum warns that "if we drive all of the difficult people, the demanding people, and the eccentric people away from the creative professions where they used to thrive, we will become a flatter, duller, less interesting society, a place where manuscripts sit in drawers for fear of arbitrary judgments."[27]

Early in this book, I noted that many scholars pursued by illiberal progressives in the academy are liberals, not, as is often reported, conservatives. I'd like to look a little more closely at this phenomenon, not as special pleading to leave the liberals alone but to better understand the phenomenon of "cancel culture" and how it has operated in higher ed.

The Spirit of Cancellation

To understand cancel culture in academia, it's fruitful to consider larger contexts for such social aggression and punitiveness. The philosopher Joseph Heath argues that cancel culture isn't just for progressives in cultural institutions—it's both bipartisan and international.

> In the United States, criticism of cancel culture has been deeply interwoven with controversies over "woke" politics, but . . . . Fear of being labelled a RINO or cuck has had a disciplining effect on speech among conservatives that closely resembles the tyranny of speech codes on the left. So there is nothing intrinsically left-wing or woke about cancel culture. Furthermore, it is not a consequence of political polarization in the U.S., since cancellation has become an enormous issue in China as well, in this case with nationalist mobs policing online speech for minor slights, then extracting groveling confessions and apologies from celebrities.

In Heath's analysis, canceling is a form of "relational aggression" and a manifestation of a human impulse to "recruit third parties to conflict." Although the internet has radically altered the "scale of third-party intervention," cancellation isn't a novel phenomenon.[28]

Many liberal academics have been shocked to find themselves being "called out," informed on, or investigated on the basis of an ideological transgression. People who don't agree with progressives on all issues may still consider themselves to be part of a political left or center that aspires to feed the hungry, clothe the naked, welcome the stranger, and remedy abuses of power.

Thus, liberals who disagree with their peers might consider the disagreements annoying familial spats rather than cleavages that can threaten careers and reputations. Izabella Tabarovsky, who grew up in the Soviet Union, recalls her disorientation when she realized that dogmatism and "calls for censorship" weren't just "*over there*, on the other side of the aisle . . . driven by extreme religious, political, and social conservatism," but originating from [her] own side" against all who didn't embrace the "most radical far-left ideas."[29]

It's misleading when critics of progressive illiberalism in the academy frame disputes as occurring between "liberals" and "conservatives" because such a frame misunderstands the stark divide between liberalism and illiberalisms. It's also misleading because, if we're talking about social or cultural conservatism, there just aren't that many conservatives in academia. This is especially true in disciplines that have served as base camps for progressive illiberalism.[30]

One such scholar is the political scientist Carol Swain, a Christian conservative accused of "bigotry, intolerance, and unprofessionalism."[31] Another is the University of Pennsylvania law professor Amy Wax, who has survived multiple efforts to remove her for a "history of disrespectful and dismissive treatment of various groups."[32]

What makes Swain and Wax stand out is that there are relatively few of them. An irony is that there were probably fewer before illiberal progressives set out to cancel academics who dissented from progressive orthodoxy. Some canceled scholars have taken the "route from antiwoke activism to Trump apologism"—one variant of what Yascha Mounk calls the "reactionary trap."[33]

There are many possible concepts to help us understand what appear from the outside to be internecine quarrels. One explanation for progressive enmity to liberals is what Freud called the "narcissism of minor differences." The concept addresses how relations between individuals and groups that appear to be similar from the outside can be "tainted with a degree of aversion and hostility that we find it appropriate to repress." Thus, a "near neighbor" becomes a "target for aggressive feelings" in the service of projecting onto others aspects of ourselves or our group that we disavow.[34]

A consistent theme in psychological and psychodynamic literatures on groups is the observation that groups scrutinize their own for signs of deviation from prescribed ideology. Discussing the moral foundation of loyalty, Jonathan Haidt notes that "the love of loyal teammates is matched by a corresponding hatred of traitors, who are usually considered to be far worse than enemies."[35] Movements make traitors of those who refuse to only bat for the team. This can include not only those who openly disagree but also those who want to carefully weigh evidence that may point in different directions.

Indeed, intragroup scrutiny of those perceived as turncoats from the one true morality often involves "tension *within* the group linked to competition *between* different groups." By this, Haidt means that groups "channel resentments and frictions within the group" in ways that bond group members for conflicts with outsiders.[36] In groups and movements alert for traitors, their presence provides opportunities for groups to enjoy the "bonding function of hostility"[37]

Such dynamics frequently play out in the real world as groups distinguish between "near" and "far" enemies. A wide range of extremist groups and movements, including Islamist and far right-wing groups, rely on this distinction to plot domestic and international political and paramilitary strategies. Frequently, this means attacking those who seem from the outside to be members of the same broad community but who are ecumenical, apostates, or otherwise insufficiently committed to extremist moral warfare.[38]

In a less theoretical vein, the journalist Nellie Bowles illustrates how such dynamics work in her account of why she stopped canceling people.

> The easy criticism of a cancellation is: You went after someone who agrees with you on almost everything except some tiny differences? Some small infraction? It seems bizarre. But that's the point. The bad among us are more dangerous to the group. Mormons don't excommunicate a random drag performer. They excommunicate a bad Mormon
> . . . .
>
> A cancellation isn't about finding a conservative and yelling at them. It's about finding the betrayer in your midst. They look and talk like you. They blend in perfectly. But they're not like you.[39]

To those uninitiated in a progressive worldview, near enemies in the academy may be difficult to distinguish from their colleagues. It's not nearly as hard for illiberal progressives to make these consequential identifications. Data can come from workplace conversations about hiring, curricula, or other issues. It can come from reports by students about what professors do or don't do, say or don't say.

Liberals and progressives share many concerns. But as progressives entrenched illiberal methods of enforcing adherence to their positions, gulfs opened up between the groups. By practicing value neutrality in contentious debates, actively disagreeing (or seeming to disagree) with progressive mandates, or not enthusiastically embracing illiberal tactics and policies, liberals became enemies of the people.

Gender studies professors and their kin throughout the university teach transgression, but this kind of transgression must be punished.

We can learn a great deal about the coercions and punishments in store for the enemies of the people from a variety of sources, including observers from inside and outside the academy. Some observers who help document and make sense of the politics of the academy are scholars who have been accused of violations of social justice.

Academics whose colleagues and universities have turned on them linger on and dissect different elements of the experience. They bring disciplinary tools of their trades to bear on that experience. And they think, write, and speak about the experience in ways that may reflect their personalities. Many such figures share a political positioning somewhere on the political left. Some even narrate the travails that disrupted their careers with humor.

Kathleen Stock didn't expect to become a poster girl for academic cancellation. In the 2022 paperback edition of *Material Girls: Why Reality Matters for Feminism*, Stock wrote of the uproar that followed her work on "sex [and the] mysterious thing known as 'gender,'" that she knew "what was needed . . . was a high-profile case" that would expose illiberal responses to different perspectives on gender identity. The next sentence displays Stock's wry, understated style: "I did not expect that case to involve me."[40]

Laura Kipnis takes sharp aim at "higher ed's overfunded, secretive, ever-expanding punishment operating infrastructure" in which "snitching has become a blood sport." "Want to muzzle your enemies? Accuse them of something. Title IX officers are standing by."

Kipnis notes that criticisms of academic illiberalism are often dismissed by those who observe that "it's generational."[41] Speculating about the generational hypothesis, Xiao Li compares academic illiberalism to Mao's Cultural Revolution. Li suggests that one motivation for US students to participate in illiberal rituals is envy of earlier generations of civil rights activists and the causes they represented.

> [T]oday's revolutionary vanguard is also made up of young, well-educated people, a disproportionate number hailing from elite educational institutions and working within elite professions. They grew up at a time of unprecedented progress in race relations, but it meant the main action was already over when they were coming of age.
>
> Thus, the idea that elite Anglo-American institutions are filled with closeted racists, absurd though it is to anyone who has worked in them, became an article of faith overnight. Whether it is in newsrooms, universities or progressive advocacy groups, the hunt for secret racists gives these would-be Selma marchers a sense of purpose.[42]

John McWhorter agrees. McWhorter likens academic illiberalism to an "eccentric performance from people wishing they hadn't missed the late 1960s, dismayed that so much of the basic work is already done."[43]

This is a question on which I have anecdotal pedagogical evidence. For many years I taught a course on women of color and political activism, and for some of those terms, I posed questions to students on an informal survey I distributed during the first week of class. I regularly asked if there was a social or political movement in US history that students regretted having missed. The most common response was the Black Civil Rights Movement. Students in classes on LGBT politics have often been wistful about the 1969 Stonewall riots and the liberationist HIV/AIDS direct action of the eighties.

For the record, like my students, I also missed out on the activism of the late 1960s, when I was in grade school and junior high. However, I did get in on what was then the gay and lesbian movement before the nineteen seventies closed. Like same-sex attracted people at that time and before, I hid my desires and relationships. I lied. I distanced myself from others for self-protection, losing friends and family members in the bargain. I was threatened with violence on numerous occasions. I marched. I went to bars whose clientele relied on unmarked doors, weapons, peepholes and, in one instance, an aggressive dog named "Queenie" for protection.

That's how I know it's possible for people who were *there* in those eras to mourn losses caused by animus but also to miss the camaraderie of outlaws, the sense of making history, and—in the case of the queer movement—even the illicit sexuality of an earlier time. My guess is that it's also easy for those who *weren't* there to romanticize days of struggle and legal discrimination.

I suspect that Li and McWhorter are right; progressives in the academy cultivated in students a yearning to return to periods in US history they could understand as having featured unambiguous heroes and villains. Deprived of the chance to fight back against homophobic cops and men in KKK robes, some settled for taking on bookish introverts.

Our politics have changed dramatically in recent years, but the appetite of many on both the political left and right for punishing foes is a constant. One thing we learn from a Cato Institute study, "The State of Free Speech and Tolerance in America," is that while majorities of people on the right endorse firing people who kneel for the national anthem and stripping US citizenship from flag burners, majorities of people of the left endorse punching Nazis and criminalizing a refusal to use preferred pronouns.[44]

To understand how perceived enemies of progressivism fare in the academy, it's necessary to consider a number of different kinds of suspects and scenarios. As we saw in hiring processes governed by DEI, one characteristic that joins these diverse scenarios is that every step in the illiberal process came to be performed in a way that minimizes the risk that what the university or its agents were doing would be exposed. That means we have to go behind the scenes.

Behind the Scenes

Social and political movements innovate. For many movements of both the right and left, goals change too. At times, movements' goals change because longtime aspirations have been achieved, and activists—especially those for whom the cause is a meal ticket—are loath to declare success and disband. Instead, activists may get donors to "open their wallets" by staking out unpopular, transgressive positions and accusing opponents of wanting to "roll back" all progress.[45]

Sometimes goals change because they're no longer viable. One example is the Christian right's shift from a full-court press against same-sex marriage in the years before the Supreme Court's 2015 decision in *Obergefell v. Hodges* to the decidedly muted grumbling the movement managed during the debate over 2022's Respect for Marriage Act.

Even when their broad goals remain the same, movement strategies, tactics, and messaging change over time. Often these changes occur in response to challenges posed by innovations within or between movements.[46] In recent years, many faculty members started making different pedagogical choices in response to the changing political environment in higher ed. Many, for example, stopped assigning particular readings and raising particular subjects. One example is rape law, for which trigger—excuse me, *content*—warnings might not be sufficient to protect aspiring lawyers from harm.[47]

Some changes were subterfuges that would allow progressives to continue to do what they wanted to do in a context of right-wing oversight. After the 2023 Supreme Court decision in *Students for Fair Admissions, Inc. (SFFA) v. President & Fellows of Harvard College (Harvard) and SFFA v. University of North Carolina*, *The Washington Free Beacon* reported on law school administrators "huddling" at the annual meeting of the American Association of Law Schools to brainstorm ways to "circumvent" the Court's ban on affirmative action.[48]

Do progressive academics respond to incentives and disincentives to alter their goals, strategies, tactics, and messaging? Indeed, they do. An example of faculty modifying an instructional tool dates from the post-pandemic period, when universities were under scrutiny from both Republicans and free speech organizations. A next set of examples shows students publicizing interrogations by faculty and administrators, thereby obliging their universities to clean up bad press. Two final examples demonstrate how instances of illiberalism can come into or be concealed from public view, depending on the extent to which academics make decisions that align with the expectations of their progressive colleagues.

Course Correction

In addition to my university's required student evaluation of instruction, instructors in my department were strongly encouraged to use the department's "discursive" teaching evaluation in undergrad and grad courses. In early 2023, my colleagues and I were informed that the college was well pleased with our departmental teaching evaluation tool, which was being proffered as a model for other departments in the college.

Nevertheless, my colleagues fretted that some questions on this model teaching evaluation inventory could attract unwanted attention at a time when higher education in the state was under scrutiny and a bill to reform public state universities was in the works. In particular, two questions drew concern. See if you can detect the possible problem:

- Readings on trans*. Did this class include readings by and about people of color, trans* people, people with disabilities, and/or transnational scholars? Which readings stood out to you the most?
- Promotion of trans*. How did your instructor promote issues of race, disability, transnationality, and/or trans* issues in the class?

Of particular concern was the question that asked students if their course properly "promote[d] issues" of race, trans identity, etc. One colleague worried that students might screenshot the phrase, "promote issues," and report us to advocacy organizations or elected officials. Upon reflection, and with a Republican-sponsored bill to clamp down on public institutions in the state then under consideration, my colleagues agreed that "in this particular [political] moment" we should extirpate the word "promote" from our course evaluation form.

A small, ad hoc faculty committee performed a quick revision, and the rest of us soon received two new questions to replace those deemed too dangerous at that "particular moment."

- Did the class readings help you to think in complex ways about the topics discussed? Which readings stood out to you the most and why?
- Did your instructor encourage complex thinking and analysis about the world? What are a few ways that your thinking has become more complex as a result of taking this course?

Recall that not only did the original questions pass muster in gender studies, but the college hailed gender studies for devising a stellar inventory with which to measure teaching excellence. The vast difference between these two sets of questions shows why such a revision matters. Asking students to rate instructors on the way in which they "promote" particular topics and perspectives primes students to believe that centering particular topics and addressing those topics in very specific ways are indispensable elements of good teaching in every course.

Critics of universities might never know that their oversight had triggered such a revision. Even so, only when outside pressure and oversight increased did we relent and decide to communicate to students the value of "complex thinking and analysis" rather than a set of topics and perspectives ideologically aligned with a gender studies perspective.

I don't believe that piecemeal policy revisions are sufficient to alter the fundamentals of progressive illiberalism in American universities. Yet this example demonstrates that faculty and administrators can change course in meaningful ways as a preemptive response to threats and oversight.

Recording Sessions

In all institutions, much takes place that isn't public knowledge. I'm not talking here about personal and medical data, and proprietary information. I noted in the preface that universities don't welcome publicity about investigations of students and faculty for ideological and pedagogical infractions. It shouldn't surprise us, then, that some of the most enlightening revelations about such charges come not from documents but from recordings made by students of their interrogations by university administrators.

Two such students were Lindsay Shepherd, a politically progressive grad student at Canada's Wilfrid Laurier University, and Trent Colbert, a conservative Yale law student.

In the fall of 2017, Shepherd screened a video clip from an Ontario public broadcasting TV show for the students in her first-year grammar tutorial. The program featured a debate about the addition of gender identity and expression as categories of discrimination under the Canadian Human Rights Act. One of the debaters was the University of Toronto psychologist, author, and pugnacious online personality Jordan Peterson, who's known, among other things, for opposing policies mandating the use of preferred pronouns.

Shepherd told her class she wouldn't take a position on the video debate and offered the segment as a prompt for discussion about gendered language. A student in Shepherd's class complained about her use of the video clip to an administrator in the campus LGBTQ support center. Shortly thereafter, Shepherd was called to a meeting with two members of her department's faculty and a university administrator.

We know what transpired at the meeting because Shepherd surreptitiously recorded the conversation. It's obvious that the purpose of the three on one meeting with Shepherd was to push her to admit she made a mistake and harmed her students, first, by playing the debate video, and then, by failing to tell her students that Peterson's views are wrong.

Without the audio evidence, it might be hard for many to believe that, as the grad student cites the value of academic freedom and viewpoint diversity for learning, the faculty members and administrator directly contradict her. They hint that an instructor doing what she'd done might violate Canada's human rights code by exposing students to the ideas of someone like Peterson. They dispute her contention that all ideas and arguments should be able to be heard in a university classroom.

After she was reprimanded, Shepherd released the audio she'd recorded to media outlets. Once the affair went public, one of the faculty members and the president of the university apologized for Shepherd's disciplinary session. However, the chair of her department attended Shepherd's next tutorial, offered her students any "emotional or mental support" they might need under the circumstances, and remained in the room for the discussion.[49]

Compared to Colbert's interrogation, Shepherd's disciplinary meeting was a warm bath. It's obvious that the goal at Wilfrid Laurier was to instruct Shepherd about her error and escort her back into the fold of progressive ideology. No doubt because he was a member of the Federalist Society, Colbert's interlocuters treated him as a bad actor from the jump. He was neither teaching nor representing himself as a proponent of academic freedom at the time he committed his ideological error. Nevertheless, Colbert's experience exposes the apparatus of punishment that has ground behind the scenes of the progressive academy.

The incident at Yale began with an emailed party announcement. Colbert was throwing a party at his apartment, and he invited members of the Native American Law Students Association (NALSA) and the Federalist Society (FedSoc). The invitation read:

> Sup NALSA, Hope you're all still feeling social! This Friday at 7:30, we will be christening our very own (soon to be) world-renowned NALSA Trap House . . . by throwing a Constitution Day bash in collaboration with FedSoc. Planned attractions include Popeye's chicken, basic-bitch-American-themed snacks (like apple pie, etc.) . . . Hope to see you all there.

When the story broke, I had questions, including this one: do student members of NALSA and FedSoc really party together? The image this summons is Edward Hicks' famous painting, *The Peaceable Kingdom* (and good for them!).

That wasn't what caught the attention of those who were offended by the invitation. For them, the sticking point was Colbert's characterization of his apartment as a "trap house." I confess that, at first, I didn't get it. So, I consulted multiple august sources, including the Cambridge Dictionary and Dictionary.com.

FIRE settled on the Urban Dictionary as most likely to yield an answer that would explain what transpired after Colbert posted his invitation: "Originally used to describe a crack house in a shady neighborhood, the word has since been abused by high school students who like to pretend they›re cool by drinking their mom's beer together and saying they're part of a 'traphouse.'"[50]

The trap house affair began, as these things do, with student complaints. Instead of ending there, Colbert was called to a meeting with two administrators for whom the problem consisted of a combination of perceptions of racism in the invitation and his association with the Federalist Society, a recognized conservative student organization. Perhaps sensing he might be in danger, Colbert hit "record."

The struggle sessions to which Colbert was subjected expose the existence of backdoor punishments; they also reveal that bearing a sacralized identity isn't enough. Being part Cherokee and a member of the Native American Law School Association didn't insulate Colbert from the accusation of racism.

Colbert offered to talk with anyone who was offended by the invitation. The administrators who tasked themselves with resolving the incident didn't accept Colbert's offer to meet with his aggrieved peers. Instead, they issued vague threats—of Yale disciplinary action and even of a report to the bar that might compromise Colbert's legal career. These threats were made to bolster the administrators' effort to pressure the law student into making a public apology.

So dedicated were the Yale administrators to eliciting an apology that they offered Colbert a draft they'd written themselves. Throughout the ordeal, Colbert declined to accede both to the administrators' characterization of his email and to their plan for the incident's resolution. Instead, he went public.

Yale responded predictably by affirming its commitment to free speech and free expression. FIRE characterized Colbert's experience as yet another episode of universities affirming values in the abstract while "betray[ing] those commitments in practice."[51]

Academics Behind the Curtain

Now I want to reflect on a couple of quite different circumstances in which the machinery of illiberal progressivism became visible to people outside the ambit of those personally affected. These cases are atypical; they're not stories of individual academics being accused of harming students. Nevertheless, the examples expose behind-the-scenes illiberal decisions that reveal who are "the people" and who can or should be sacrificed for their well-being.

The first case is a routine faculty hiring process that ended up under the bright lights after a search committee's recommendation was overturned on what were determined to be racial grounds. Second is a case of a professional organization deplatforming a conference panel that promised to challenge progressive doctrine on sex and gender identity.

In the 2022–23 academic year, the psychology department at the University of Washington carried out a search for a faculty position. After virtual campus visits from the top three candidates, the search committee created a rank-ordered short list. The determination of rank ordering and the decision to tender an offer to the first-ranked candidate were made with input from the faculty.

The top candidate was described in a subsequent internal report as a candidate "identified as white" and "deemed to be white." The second-ranked candidate was of Asian descent, and the third-ranked candidate was black. Permission to inform the top candidate that a formal job offer would be forthcoming was requested and received by the search committee, and the candidate was so informed.[52]

As revealed in the internal investigation conducted by the University Complaint and Investigative Resolution Office, the search process then entered a new phase. Members of the psychology department's Strategic Planning Committee (SPC), which had no role in the search process, and members of the department's Diversity Advisory Committee (DAC), one member of which had served as a non-voting member of the search committee, disputed the outcome of the search. The SPC asked the search committee to "prepare a paragraph justifying why they selected a white candidate for first offer."

Before making its decision, the search committee had already taken into account the DEI views and experience of the short-listed candidates in a way that was consistent with a Case Study produced by the DAC entitled, "Promising Practices for Increasing Equity in Faculty Searches." However, having arrived at their decision and having informed the top candidate that they would soon receive a formal offer, the search committee received notice that the DAC would endorse neither the final hiring report nor the first-ranked candidate choice.

Ultimately, the search committee "conceded" to those who disapproved, reversed its decision, and agreed to offer the position to the black candidate. As a "BIPOC" person, the Asian candidate remained in second place, and the white candidate was relocated to third place. Faculty members who acceded did so for many reasons, including to avoid a

" 'bloodbath' at a faculty meeting" and because the discord had caused "personal stress." One search committee member wished they could "quit this job" and another stated they couldn't "condone th[e] search."

Investigators determined that faculty members took affirmative steps to "hide hiring actions that [they] knew were impermissible" and provided "different interview processes based on race." In the end, "race was used as a substantial factor in the selection of the final candidate." The investigation concluded that the process violated university policy.[53]

We know the details of the University of Washington search from Institutional Intake Report Case No. EV2023061355 because the National Association of Scholars filed a public records request to gain access to it.[54]

The second case involved a panel at the November 2023 joint annual meeting of the American Anthropological Association and Canadian Anthropological Society entitled, "Let's Talk About Sex, Baby: Why Biological Sex Remains a Necessary Analytic Category in Anthropology." Scholars scheduled to speak in Toronto were Michèle Sirois, Silvia Carrasco, Elizabeth Weiss, Kathleen Richardson, and Kathleen Lowrey.

After the panel was accepted for the 2023 meeting, multiple prospective conferees objected to its subject matter and to the panelists. Citing damage to "scientific integrity" and "caus[ing] harm to trans and LGBTQI [members] of the anthropological community," conference organizers canceled the panel. It was later platformed by Heterodox Academy.[55]

To be fair to anthropologist Elizabeth Weiss, her heresies crossed over from sex to race. Weiss was locked out of San José State University's research collection of human remains research, for which she'd served as curator for 17 years, and disparaged by colleagues because she'd disapproved of and disagreed with progressive perspectives on the repatriation of ancient human remains to indigenous tribes.

As *Inside Higher Ed* reported, Weiss argues in her co-authored book, *Repatriation and Erasing the Past*, that

> returning bones to their ancestral burial grounds instead of keeping them to study now and in the future limits scientific advancement, and

> that the federal Native American Graves Protection and Repatriation Act (NAGPRA) and parallel state laws on repatriation undermine the Constitution's Establishment Clause by favoring religion over science.[56]

It seems Weiss's perspective that laws and policies mandating the repatriation of ancient human remains run afoul of the US Constitution might be a fascinating prompt for class discussion. But one might not risk having that conversation if one knew what had happened to Elizabeth Weiss.

In both cases, critics of campus progressivism knew they were looking at illiberal practices because they could point to a decision that was initially made and then, under pressure from insiders, unmade.[57] In the case of the psychologists, the search committee decided which candidate to hire before the committee's decision was reversed with explicit reference to the race of the candidates. In the case of the anthropologists, a panel was placed on the conference schedule before the acceptance was rescinded.

Academic freedom proponents pointed to the reversals as proof that academic decisions had been corrupted by factors that had nothing to do with the merit of ideas and scholars, and they were right.

Still, I saw these episodes a little differently because I immediately imagined the counterfactual. What if the search committee in the psychology department at the University of Washington had never put forward a ranking of finalists that placed a white candidate first and a black candidate third? What if the "Let's Talk about Sex" panel had never been accepted? In other words, what if the very actions that critics seized on as evidence that academic values were being vitiated had never occurred? How would we know that something inappropriate was afoot?

Unfortunately, the answer is: we wouldn't. Lots of proposed panels don't get accepted. Most job candidates in any particular faculty search aren't hired. Unless those outside the circle of decision-making receive some inside information from participants, insiders can tell any story they please. Any challenge to the decision process is easily dispensed with by professionals citing merit, space on the program, or some other value.

Having been on the inside, here's my take: academic freedom has been under attack from within for many years and, in the background of occasional public spectacles, it's been compromised more than most observers realize. This isn't only because specific people put pressure on us to recite a catechism, though that does occur. Nor is the problem as obvious as "placards or encampments or Twitter mobs." Instead, academic freedom has deteriorated because left-wing illiberalism "has profoundly changed the way that American institutions operate."[58]

As a result, if we want to grasp the banality and ubiquity of academic illiberalism, it pays to examine obscure bureaucratic verbiage such as statements of shared values.

What's Wrong with Shared Values?

When university hiring practices came under scrutiny from outside groups in 2023, my university quietly ended the practice of requiring DEI statements for hiring new faculty. To take their place, the university disseminated an "optional prompt" that departments could use at their discretion in job postings. Instead of requiring the diversity statements that had been required of job seekers in arts and sciences disciplines, this optional prompt would ask faculty job candidates to reflect on Flagship State's Shared Values.

Announcing this policy shift, a top official of Flagship State informed faculty that the university welcomed and valued diversity of ideas, freedom of expression, and open dialogue. And we were referred to the "Shared Values Initiative" that featured details of "[Flagship] State Shared Values" and the results of a "Values and Ethics Survey" carried out in 2019.[59] The initiative and the "shared values" that resulted from it provide fascinating insights into the vacuous ideal of the university as both an activist and therapeutic institution.

Realizing I'd neglected my duty as a faculty member, I set out to acquaint myself with my university's shared values. What Blake Smith writes about university issue statements is also true of shared values: we are "summoned by them as members of an imaginary unanimous body to feel and think in common. But the process by which a statement is produced is nearly always opaque, as is its meaning to readers."[60]

In the case of my university, a "behavior" "we" commit to under the heading of "excellence and impact" is being "bold in our endeavors." I could probably make the case that spending time over many years sitting in Christian conservative meetings, reading Christian conservative literature, and then trying to make sense of what I'd learned is a marker of boldness in my endeavors.

There's a time and place for boldness, however. Bold disagreement with progressive shibboleths is strongly discouraged.

Under the value of "inclusion and equity," we commit to "acknowledge and address individual and systemic effects of bias and discrimination." This sounds suspiciously as though no disagreement about "systemic," "bias," and "discrimination" is anticipated. But if such disagreement were to occur, how would we ensure that we'd land on the right side of the shared values?

Perhaps the value of "care and compassion" offers some direction. Alas, this value merely instructs us to be compassionate, "nurture a community of kindness," and "empower people." It appears there's also no possibility of debate about the meanings of "compassion," "kindness," and "empowerment" in a context of higher ed research and instruction.

In 2024, my university called attention to its shared values by directing members of the university community to Flagship State's "Guidelines to Ensure Equal Opportunity in University Programs, Activities and Resources." There, the university placed its "shared values" at the center of policy on access to "programs, activities and resources."

> The daily interactions and behaviors of all university community members are guided by a set of Shared Values including Diversity and Innovation and Equity and Inclusion. In support of these values, programs, activities and resources are created with a focus on specific social identities, demographics (which include all of the university's protected classes), *or lived experiences*. These programs, activities, and resources are essential to creating an accessible and inclusive envi-

> ronment. However, *based on our shared values and applicable civil rights laws*, these opportunities must be open and available to individuals without regard to their social identities or demographics.[61]

This sounds good. Let's look a little more closely.

First, the statement reports that my university's programs, activities, and resources are crafted to serve "specific social identities, demographics . . . or lived experience." A phrase that points to federal "protected classes" seems to only modify "demographics," but it's easy enough to give the sentence the benefit of the doubt and assume that the content of the first two categories—"specific social identities" and "demographics"—refer to protected classes in federal public policy.

That leaves "lived experience." I can't read the sentence that contains these categories in any way that stretches federal law to denote the content of "lived experience." The conjunction "or" also seems definitive: "lived experience" is outside the domain of actions governed by federal law. The "or" does important work in the sentence and, hence, in the statement. My reading is that, even if what a member of the Flagship State community does or says does *not* violate federal law, it can still be proscribed and punished if some member of or group within the community attests that the act violates some dimension of their "lived experience."

By the way, the popularity of the concept of lived experience being what it is among academic progressives, the phrase may not have made its way into a Shared Values statement by accident. Regardless of whether it was smuggled in to undercut the authority of federal law with regard to protected classes, its presence provides a path to impose progressive ideology on university relations and operations.

Second, the statement asserts that programs, activities, and resources are to be made available to all "without regard to their social identities or demographics" "*based on our shared values and applicable civil rights laws.*" Maybe it bears repeating: if all this statement says is that Flagship State observes civil rights laws and makes all university resources available to everyone, the university wouldn't have any reason to add that it does so "based on our shared values."

What additional information or qualification for access to university resources does this phrase facilitate? Well, the only one I can find is "lived experience." If that's right, "lived experience" does an enormous amount of work, including placing an asterisk on federal civil rights law. What we can know beyond a shadow of a doubt is that Flagship State continues to warn members of its community that it's possible to contravene university policy by somehow transgressing against someone's sense of their lived experience.

I guess we could say that my university demonstrated the salience of our "shared values" when it backtracked on mandatory DEI statements for faculty hiring and shut down the practice of issuing departmental, college, and university statements on social and political issues. After all, "us[ing] our successes and failures to learn and improve with humility" is a behavior we're exhorted to perform under the value of "diversity and innovation."

So, what—if anything—is the problem with quietly ditching mandatory DEI statements for all faculty job seekers and substituting an "optional" statement? There are two, the first of which is a response to the content of the university's "shared values." Whether they're drafted by committees or a product of pricey consultants, initiatives like "shared values" are likely to be deplorable in multiple ways: expensive, internally contradictory, meaninglessly vague and/or wordy, and ignored by their putative constituents—the "we" who it appears are constantly in the process of holding these ideals and performing these behaviors.

The second problem is that this "option" was aimed at departments, not individual scholars. Thus, individual scholars couldn't determine whether they wanted to pitch themselves to prospective colleagues as adept in the philosophy expressed in DEI. But it appears that departments could use the "shared values" option as a back door for promoting a progressive ideology of sacralized groups and punishing those who don't conform to the terms of academic progressivism.

Shared values are only one means of accomplishing these goals.

Neutralizing Internal Enemies

The mechanisms by which illiberal progressives embedded their political preferences in higher ed, centered "the people" (and their allies), and neutralized enemies can be mostly invisible, even to those who are subject to them. This is precisely why it's necessary to examine them and their lamentable effects for teaching and scholarship.

Mechanisms include, but aren't exhausted by, the following:

- definitions of progressive disciplinary boundaries that exclude from consideration texts and ideas instructors might use to broaden their students' conceptions of frames, arguments, conclusions, policies, histories, the universe, and everything. Some students will marvel when we dare to introduce some of these subversive ideas. Other students and colleagues will be alerted to subversion by such departures from disciplinary orthodoxy;
- characterizations of what core courses are supposed to accomplish in a department's curriculum. There's a difference between core knowledge—about, for example, a particular subfield, institution, period, or topic—and ideological ideas that, for progressive faculty, often constitute the appropriate body of knowledge to be conveyed in core courses;
- student orientation programs, courses, and curricula that definitively state what students are expected to believe with regard to diversity, equity, inclusion, belonging, community, allyship, and all adjacent social and political issues;
- speech codes that prohibit and punish forms of speech and expression that colleges and universities hold are demeaning or constitute harassment to members of groups even if such speech is protected by the First Amendment;[62]
- bias reporting systems by which students are encouraged to submit complaints about their peers and professors, often anonymously;
- course evaluations engineered to prime students to apply particular expectations for what constitutes correct knowledge and pedagogical practice;

- General Education requirements that prescribe very specific kinds of diversity content and perspectives derived from academic progressivism;[63]
- Diversity, Equity, and Inclusion (DEI) offices, policies, and statements that prescribe the holding and reciting of specific kinds of views about D, E, and I (and sometimes other letters) in a wide range of academic contexts;
- DEI categories on annual faculty reports that integrate progressive metrics into faculty evaluations;
- student conduct review boards and procedures that investigate violations of university policies and "shared values";
- statements of institutional "shared values" that can be leveraged by students and faculty to prevent the hiring of particular faculty or to suppress expression;
- Institutional Review Board (IRB) practices that slow walk research proposals, insist on changes to research methodologies, or disapprove particular kinds of research for ideological reasons.[64]
- administrative recommendations and "best practices" that pointedly outline what faculty should do to be good instructors. Students don't distinguish between statements of "best practices" and administrative fiats, and I came to believe that faculty are wise to read statements of "values" and "best practices" as precursors of new mandates to come;
- vetting of guest speakers using ideological criteria, including faculty coordination and encouragement of student protests against speakers who fail purity tests; and
- assessment and course design regimes that prescribe course content and learning outcomes, and assess whether students have learned that content in your class. Such assessment and course design regimes apply to anyone who teaches, either particular courses in a curriculum or, as in my gender studies department, all courses in the curriculum.

It's no accident that these mechanisms can institutionalize a progressive worldview, preemptively deciding matters that are the subject of vigorous political and intellectual disagreement in the world outside higher ed. When they all work together, an instructor who diverges from the true path doesn't need to be denounced by anyone. She is simply no longer fulfilling the basic, "neutral" requirements of her job and role as those have been constructed and imposed by her colleagues.

As in any bureaucracy, the heterodox instructor runs afoul of relatively invisible systems, mechanisms, goals, values, templates, recommendations, best practices, and essential learning outcomes (ELOs). Most of these are simultaneous and unremitting. If you're in a university community, you can neither opt out nor put them in the rearview mirror.

In response to such an enervating state of affairs, some faculty hide. Some join communities dedicated to academic freedom such as FIRE, the Academic Freedom Alliance (AFA), the Foundation Against Intolerance and Racism (FAIR), Heterodox Academy (HxA), and the National Association of Scholars (NAS).

I wasn't surprised to discover that others create parallel intellectual communities they hope will evade the gaze of their attentive colleagues. An example of such collective action is "underground" archeology, a "network of counter-research" organized by scholars as an alternative to "the censorious confines of modern academia."[65] Unlike the lone acts of individual faculty, communities are a form of collective action to address a collective problem. But they're a bandage on the larger dilemma. In fact, such communities can unintentionally reinforce the illiberal project by relocating intellectual diversity away from colleagues and students.

The most important goal of academic progressives has been for dissent to be so vanishingly rare that students never hear alternative points of view on contentious issues. Fulfilling this goal required raising the cost of dissent high enough to deter two closely related kinds of behavior. The first is teaching, speaking, or writing in a way that suggests explicit disagreement with a viewpoint that progressives have defined as the only acceptable one to hold. The second is teaching, speaking, or writing about different viewpoints in a way that suggests there are a variety of reasonable ways of conceptualizing contentious issues.

The silent seamlessness of daily academic life reminds me of Michael Cohen's 2019 Congressional testimony about the process by which Trump's henchmen do his bidding. In response to a Congressmember's question, Cohen indicated that Trump never gave specific instructions to his lieutenants to, for example, break the law.

When Michigan Representative Justin Amash was the only Republican member of the House to wonder what Trump did instead of giving such orders, the following exchange occurred:

> Mr. AMASH. All right. You suggested that the President sometimes communicates his wishes indirectly. For example, you said, quote, "Mr. Trump did not directly tell me to lie to Congress, that's not how he operates," end quote. Can you explain how he does this?
> Mr. COHEN. Sure. It would be no different if I said, That's the nicest looking tie I've ever seen, isn't it? What are you going to do, are you going to fight with him? The answer is no. So you say, yes, it's the nicest looking tie I've ever seen. That's how he speaks. He doesn't give you questions. He doesn't give you orders. He speaks in a code, and I understand the code because I've been around him for a decade.
> Mr. AMASH. And it's your impression that others who work for him understand the code as well?
> Mr. COHEN. Most people, yes.[66]

Leave out the maximum leader, and this reflection expresses how things often work in the most progressive redoubts of academia. We don't have to talk about it for everyone to understand how a faculty search or evaluation, course proposal, curricular reform, research project, graduate admissions process, speaker invitation, faculty hiring process, manuscript review, or conference paper/panel evaluation should go.

My only question about the cases of the University of Washington search committee and the anthropologists who organized the 2023 annual meeting is this: how did those who made the initial decisions screw up so badly? Because ideally, nobody should have to be convinced to do the right thing the first time. Everyone knows: that's the nicest looking tie we've ever seen.

One thing we have not yet seen is faculty—especially those who possess some "dominant," therefore undesirable, identity—who are the most indefatigable about circumscribing academic freedom and punishing dissenters offering to relinquish something to fulfill their political goals. Possibilities include fellowships, placement on the conference program, and—depending on their tolerance for sacrifice—even more in the hope that the resources they surrender might be made available to those whom they believe deserve it more than they do. To these colleagues, I offer a modest suggestion.

A Modest Suggestion

Resignations by government officials offer a template. Under particular circumstances, high-ranking officials sometimes publicly resign and give reasons for doing so rooted in disagreement with public policies or government acts. Several officials resigned in this way during Trump's first term in office, though some, like Attorney General William Barr and Education Secretary Betsy DeVos, held out until the last minute, after Trump incited the January 6 attack on the Capitol.

I challenge my progressive colleagues to follow their lead. A public statement of resignation could list solidarity with disfavored or marginalized groups and explain that the dominant group faculty member was resigning in protest of underrepresentation or discrimination. It would pressure the university, calling for the institution to rectify its bias by hiring a faculty member from one (or more) of these groups to replace the resigning academic.

In the years before the 2023 Supreme Court decision in *Students for Fair Admissions*, universities often took into account the identity profiles of faculty job candidates. It was the best of times for members of dominant groups to resign and try to shame their institutions into doing better. Yet, to my knowledge, none of my colleagues availed themselves of the opportunity.

Instead, some colleagues opted for another approach to increasing representation of oppressed groups: becoming "pretendians," a term usually associated with faux indigenous identity but which can be more broadly applied to white people who falsely represent themselves as people of color.[67] Numerous cases of people in faculty and DEI-related positions—most female—posing as people of color have come to light. These include Ward Churchill (U of Colorado), Rachel Dolezal (NAACP and Eastern Washington U), Jessica "La Bombalera" Krug (The George Washington U), Elizabeth Hoover (UC Berkeley), Qwo-Li Driskill (Oregon State U) and many, many more.

Those who've reported on pretendians or commented on cases often stress pretendians' theft of academic resources and opportunities, not their political orientation. It's obvious enough why white academics might want to masquerade as people of color. Pretendians collect status, resources, and recognition. Perhaps just as important, they swap the identity of "oppressor" for the identity of "oppressed."

One benefit of this transformation is acquiring standing to hector white colleagues about bias and dictate the terms by which white academics can redeem themselves. From all appearances, the standing feels good while it lasts.

Observers seem to just take pretendians' politics for granted. However, it's worth calling attention to the fact that pretendians identify with the progressive left. What is it about pretendians as individuals and the academy as an institution that racial masquerade in the academy is virtually always performed by progressives?

Maybe we should be asking more questions about why academic progressivism seems to lend itself to this specific kind of grift.

While we mull this question, I offer one last chapter—this one on critical thinking. If faculty whose views would place them at different points on the political spectrum were asked if they believe that university students should be trained to think critically, most would say they do. But what does that mean? And, besides teaching and research competence, what should we expect of teachers and learners?

5 Critical Thinking

Undermining Academic Freedom to Save It

Let me begin this chapter with a story about one of my forays into the world of the US Christian conservative movement. It's September 2016, and I'm at the Omni Shoreham Hotel in Washington, DC for the Family Research Council's annual Values Voter Summit (now rebranded as Pray Vote Stand). I read the conference program and decide I can't resist a breakout session entitled, "Intellectual Freedom or Ideological Fascism?"

The description reads:

> The American university is imploding with self-refuting duplicity. In our culture, safe zones are anything but safe and people are bullied by those decrying bullying. The banner of tolerance has become a dark flag of tyranny almost overnight. Join Matt Walsh and Everett Piper—two leading voices fighting for intellectual freedom—in a discussion on ideological fascism, the consequences of ideas, and the solution found in the pursuit of Truth.[1]

Not yet as well known as he would become, Matt Walsh was billed as a "blogger and cultural commentator." Everett Piper was president of Oklahoma Wesleyan University and the author of two books on higher ed. The panel did not disappoint. Walsh and Piper discussed examples that were then circulating among conservatives of universities coddling and propagandizing students.

But the money shot of the panel came when Piper, the university president, asked Walsh whether college students should be taught *how* to think rather than *what* to think. Walsh's response was an unequivocal "no." He explained that students should be taught what to think, specifically, truths revealed by God or nature. Piper concurred, noting that "without truth, there's chaos."[2]

Now, Walsh and Piper believed they were talking to like-minded believers, not a note-taking outsider, but let's give them credit for refreshing honesty. If only we in the academy would be so honest. Instead, too many of us practice something we do too well: rationalize what we do as critical thinking and dare those with less practice, inside knowledge, or verbal acuity to challenge us.[3]

Authoritarians of both the left and right oppose value pluralism and academic freedom. It benefits illiberal progressives to depict all those who disagree with them as fascists, bigots, or right-wingers; to incite fear that these adversaries would impose *right-wing* illiberalism in universities if they could. Better left- than right-wing illiberalism? We shouldn't have to choose between these two unappealing alternatives.

Perhaps we don't have to make this choice. That is, perhaps conservatives don't all oppose value pluralism and academic freedom. In 2024, FIRE, College Pulse, and RealClearEducation released the results of a survey that suggests conservative students (and institutions, such as Hillsdale College) profess more support for academic freedom and free inquiry than do "liberals"—I prefer "progressives"—and progressive institutions.[4]

Professing and doing are two different things, but such a result gives us a reason to see if we can find evidence to support or falsify the proposition that some conservatives value academic freedom. After all, academic freedom benefits conservatives, including Christian conservatives, in primarily progressive institutions.

One conservative who makes a case for free inquiry and value pluralism is Tyler J. VanderWeele, a professor of epidemiology in Harvard's School of Public Health. In 2023, some public health academics tweeted about the fact that, in 2015, VanderWeele had signed an amicus brief in *Obergefell v. Hodges*, the Supreme Court case that ruled that a right to marry is guaranteed by the Constitution. The problem was that VanderWeele had signed onto the wrong side of that decision.

In case tweeting about VanderWeele's defection on same-sex marriage wasn't sufficient to ensure whatever result the tweeters hoped to accomplish, VanderWeele's colleagues received emails about him that highlighted views he'd expressed in other writings. "Within a short timeframe," and right on schedule, students in the School of Public Health called for the professor to be fired over what VanderWeele characterized as "perceived threats to identity." Even if students hadn't been aware of VanderWeele's views, they believed those views constituted a "threat to human rights."

In the case of faculty and students v. Tyler J. VanderWeele, here's what Harvard did. Administrators emailed students and department chairs, acknowledging "that some students were feeling harm and betrayal." A number of "circle dialogue listening sessions" were held to allow "students, staff, and faculty" to air their concerns about VanderWeele as part of a restorative practices process. Faculty and administrators denounced VanderWeele for his views.

More telling is what Harvard didn't do. Harvard administrators didn't affirm the university's support for academic freedom. They didn't apprise Harvard faculty, staff, and students that VanderWeele's writings were protected by the principle of academic freedom. And they didn't communicate that signing an amicus brief and writing as a scholar don't constitute academic misconduct just because majorities of faculty or students don't agree with the views expressed.

VanderWeele sustained costs from the ordeal, including lost research time and reputational damage. In its aftermath, he decried the "lack of respect for the intellectual diversity within our public health community." He spoke up for the academic freedom necessary "to create a respect for viewpoint diversity."[5] And he patiently explained that "scholars with different perspectives" can contribute to "find[ing] some common ground on divisive issues" as well as "improv[ing] the quality of argument and scholarship."[6]

An irony of VanderWeele's ordeal is that it's been absolutely okay to oppose same-sex marriage from the left. During the period in which states were passing laws prohibiting same-sex marriage, including "Super-DOMA" state constitutional amendments, many academic progressives wrote, taught, and lectured against same-sex marriage, which they held to be heteronormatively normalizing and racist.

If anyone filed a complaint based on arguments against same-sex marriage from the queer left, I never heard of it. So, if Tyler VanderWeele had taught his students that same-sex marriage advocacy was racist activism by conservative gays using the currency of whiteness to shore up their heteronormative privilege, he would have been in the clear.

It matters whether we perceive individual incidents of canceling, investigating, mobbing on social media as unique, anecdotal, nothing-to-see-here one-offs or as elements in a consistent pattern. If they acknowledge them at all, academic progressives see them as one-offs. The only patterns my progressive colleagues see are right-wing attacks on the academy and policy interventions intended to bring universities to heel.

Meanwhile, some of us had been trying to foster free speech in conditions where much speech is regarded as harm that's not to be tolerated. One lesson of VanderWeele's ordeal is that professors can't successfully affirm free speech as individuals. I told students at the beginning of terms that I welcomed all questions, comments, and viewpoints. If a student had complained to me about Tyler VanderWeele, I would have told them what I'd told students in the past: take advantage of this opportunity to study for a few weeks with someone who thinks differently than you do. Ask questions, and learn as much as you can from them. It'll be over before you know it!

But I couldn't change the larger social and institutional dynamics that determine expectations for student and faculty conduct. I couldn't change the social and institutional consequences for transgressing norms and policies.

This is how I know a piecemeal, guerrilla warfare approach to respect for free speech and debate is bound to fail. Free inquiry requires institutional infrastructure. It must be modeled across the board by faculty and administrators, and it must be written into policies that are explained to students and then followed.

Unfortunately, many faculty and administrators are opposed to modeling such respect. Indeed, we know by now that respect for free speech and debate is widely perceived as incompatible with queer, decolonial antiracism. But are these values incompatible with critical thinking? It depends on what we mean by critical thinking.

On "Critical Thinking"

While my progressive colleagues and higher education traditionalists both use the phrase "critical thinking," the two sides mean quite different things by that term. If this is so, and we assume we're all talking about the same object but just disagreeing on whether or not it's desirable, we'll be wrong.

When progressive scholars laud critical thinking as their goal, they may be affirming the Frankfurt School philosopher Max Horkheimer's dictum that critical theory "never aims simply at an increase of knowledge as such. Its goal is man's emancipation from slavery."[7] Such a "critical" perspective can be applied to all topics and questions that arise in university classrooms as well as out there in society and politics.

Critical race theory has gotten the lion's share of attention from the political right and Republican elected officials but, essentially, there's a critical theory alternative for every traditional (sub)field. The list includes critical legal theory, critical information literacy, critical pedagogy, critical ecology, critical educational studies, and critical social theory, but there are many others.

A parallel critical field of study is believed to be necessary because the field as originally conceived is so irreparably corrupted by dominant beliefs and values that its collusions with systemic forms of bigotry must be subjected to scrutiny. As a riposte to scholars like me who have written about human rights, there's *critical* human rights. Here again, language use is key. During the years I was writing about international LGBTI human rights, if I discussed my research agenda and I *didn't* describe the field as "critical human rights"—I didn't—the omission would be noted.

So, how do gender studies professors understand what their field delivers to students? In our own ingroup settings, my colleagues celebrate victories in the struggle against dominant forms of power and systemic biases. My colleagues credit themselves and each other with the ability to broach challenging subjects and have difficult conversations with students.

This sounds good, but a translation would be that good professors consistently introduce queer, antiracist, anti-neoliberal, and decolonial answers to every question. When they encounter students who haven't yet heard what the appropriate queer, antiracist, anti-neoliberal, decolonial answer is to a particular question, good professors will correct these students' ignorance.

In our minds and ingroup spaces, and just like adherents of other movements, we are the heroes of our own story. It doesn't matter that many universities or portions thereof became fortresses of progressive doctrine in which curricula reinforced lessons of queer, anti-neoliberal, decolonial antiracism. Even though many of our academic spaces became strikingly politically homogeneous, we were always struggling valiantly against the forces of darkness. The racist, imperialist, Islamophobic, anti-queer empire of hegemonic thought never stopped striking back.

This mindset is clear in the reaction of progressive Yale faculty to Faculty for Yale, a group founded in 2023 whose signatories "insist on the primacy of teaching, learning, and research as distinct from advocacy and activism" and "confirm Yale's commitment to robust free expression."[8]

Faculty who disapprove of such goals and suspect a secret right-wing agenda at work in them called on Yale's president to "reject calls to 'Make Yale Great Again.'"[9] Get it? Only MAGA sympathizers would advertise such an agenda.

In contrast to such ideas, I approve of a traditional ideal of critical thinking, one simple definition of which is "careful thinking directed to a goal."[10] This definition belies the complexity of the concept, to say nothing of how it might be operationalized in academic research and teaching. Among the elements that scholars have identified as integral to critical thinking are a willingness and ability to do the following: evaluate arguments, weigh evidence, keep an open mind, and recognize logical fallacies and cognitive distortions, including our own.

I wager that most university professors don't often reflect directly on the meaning and operationalizing of critical thinking as we propose or choose courses to instruct, construct assignments, and determine modes of student assessment. Rather, training and long practice can contribute to habits of mind that enhance the likelihood we'll conduct research and teach courses in ways that are consistent with that ideal.

That we'll reach the ideal is far from a lead pipe cinch. But if we don't respect and pursue this version of critical thinking, the probability that we'll approach it is very low.

In pedagogical practice, this may mean teaching students about logical fallacies and cognitive distortions, and assigning texts that take different positions or perspectives on topics or questions. It can also include instructing students about research methods and explicitly distinguishing between questions that can be answered more or less definitively with appropriate evidence—the easy ones!—and questions that groups or individuals may respond to differently based on their methods, values or worldviews.

I enjoyed curating such authors, texts, methods, evidence, and accounts of values for my students. I wanted to do right by students. I also wanted to do right by these diverse sources of knowledge—presenting them in the most accurate light I was capable of, all the while considering what students might find intriguing.

Here's a quirky example of what I mean: a couple of times, I taught work by the Russian-American novelist and self-described philosopher Ayn Rand. Knowing that Rand has been embraced by generations of teenaged intellectuals and grownup libertarians, during those terms I joked to friends that I hoped students wouldn't leave my class as Objectivists. Was it possible that they would? Sure. To ensure that wouldn't happen, I could have kept Rand off the syllabi or told students exactly what to think of her. But, if I'd done either of these things, I wouldn't have been able to invite students to think with her and see the world through her and her devotees' eyes.

For those of us who aren't pledged to critical and poststructuralist theories and activist demands and perspectives, thinking critically requires both dispositions and practices. The dispositions that can be cultivated in educational institutions include curiosity and humility. The ability to tolerate doubt, ambiguity, and disagreement. These dispositions don't come easily or naturally; I still struggle to achieve them.

Many scholars testify to the importance of such intellectual values for learning. Patrick J. Casey argues that the "purpose of education" is "conversion to the philosophical way of life" that consists of "becom[ing] an active, lifelong inquirer." Casey contrasts the idea that a university education leads students to "the one true view" with the aspiration for students to learn "the joy of inquiry." The alternative to "*compliance* with a fixed, prescribed outlook" is curiosity and humility about knowledge and knowledge seeking.[11]

The journalist and author Frank Bruni fills in a reason why we need these dispositions in education and life when he says he wants to "teach [students] how much they have to learn—and how much they will always have to learn." There could not be more distance between such an orientation toward knowledge and the conviction that we already know the answers on all important issues. "I'm standing before them," Bruni writes, "not as an ambassador of certainty or a font of unassailable verities but as an emissary of doubt. I want to give them intelligent questions, not final answers."[12]

Cultivating the dispositions of critical thinking requires modeling, effort, patience, and an infrastructure of support from educational institutions. In addition to these habits of mind, critical thinking also requires practices. We learn the value of doubt, curiosity, and intellectual humility by seeing others engaging in practices such as patiently collecting data; recognizing and acknowledging their biases and preferences; listening to the perspectives of those with whom they disagree; and, ultimately, learning to share a world with those who think very differently than they do about matters of public concern.

One intriguing conception of critical thinking about such matters is the eminent political philosopher Hannah Arendt's "representative thinking." Arendt draws on Kant for her account of how, to understand others and the world they inhabit, "one trains one's imagination to go visiting."[13] Representative thinking describes the process by which we can collect and consider as much information as possible about the positioning of others and imagine ourselves in their shoes in order to reason as citizens.

A distinctive characteristic of representative thinking sets Arendt directly at odds with the recent ethos of the academy. This is her skepticism about compassion as a mode of entering into the experience of others. Across her voluminous writings, she offered many reasons for this skepticism, and I'll mention only two.

First, we tend to be morally partial. Arendt points out that "our compassion is guided by our own identifications and sentiments and excludes some even as it recognizes and validates the suffering of others."[14] And second, our membership in social and identity groups generates expectations, including from fellow members, that we'll prefer our own groups to others and adapt our moral standards accordingly.[15] Arendt encountered just this expectation when she wrote as she did about Jewish community leaders in Europe during the Holocaust.[16]

Years ago, after I spent some time reading and thinking about Arendt and her model of critical thinking, I found myself persuaded by her arguments on the pitfalls of basing judgments about contentious issues on our own compassion and our perceptions of others' feelings. We can't think well if we believe we already know the answer to every question. Neither can we think well if we're not willing to question our own interpretations and intuitions. Even really strong intuitions.

The historian Richard Hofstadter called the university "a community devoted to inquiry" that "exists so that its members may inquire into truths of all sorts." What distinguishes universities from other kinds of institutions is that they are spaces where "anything can be studied or questioned—not merely safe and established things but difficult and inflammatory things, the most troublesome questions of politics and war, of sex and morals, of property and national loyalty."[17]

Progressives in the academy strongly contest their critics' characterizations of what they do as indoctrination, but as pejorative as that term is, it fits. If we teach young adults that what we and they believe about every contentious issue is correct and that anyone who disagrees is misguided, immoral, or phobic, we've already surrendered the possibility of learning.

Too often, the critic and essayist William Deresiewicz's description of what's wrong with journalism fits illiberal progressives. "They think they're thinking, but they're wrong. They think that thinking means applying ideas, in the sense that you'd apply an ointment. What it actually means is examining them, reworking them, without fear, without cease." Deresiewicz also gets an implication of academic progressivism that may not be immediately obvious, even to many critics. This is that although "they believe that they are skeptical," "they're alternately cynical and gullible: cynical toward the other side and gullible toward their own."[18]

Academics who are committed to a traditional understanding of critical thinking have increasingly clashed with students and faculty committed to practices derived from activism and critical theories. For example, many students have internalized the view that welcoming all points of view both reveals an instructor's true nature and constitutes a covert invitation to racists and other "phobes." This means that pursuing critical thinking in the classroom can involve some risk for professors.

Two Classes

As universities leaned toward illiberalism, my favorite students were often those who responded to some of my unorthodox overtures with bemused curiosity. Others crossed their arms across their chests—an undeniable signal of resistance. Acting as though I didn't see these warning signs, I weighed students' contributions and objections, expanding on the positions they took so that these were fully explained to the group. At times, I asked clarifying questions.

Sometimes this pedagogical strategy worked, and sometimes it didn't. There were times when students explained to me what I and everyone should think about a particular issue, and I treated that explanation as one possibility, declining the invitation to affirm the position and curtail additional conversation. I was pretty sure that one day such a delinquency on my part would be reported to the authorities, and it was.

And yet, I still loved to teach, and a couple of stories explain why.

The Capstone

Several times over many years, I instructed the capstone course for graduating gender studies students in my department. For one of those terms, before I was investigated by my university, the course I created enabled us to take up a set of topics and questions I knew were integral to the undergraduate curriculum in my department. The innovation of the course was to offer students authors, texts, and perspectives on these topics that I guessed would be unfamiliar—perhaps even disconcerting—to them.

On the first day of class, I introduced the course by noting that, having received the best education we could offer, students were about to leave the university and move into a world where they would find considerable heterogeneity of thought and belief. I wanted to assist that transition out of the university by curating a set of perspectives they might not have encountered.

They were free to agree or disagree with all or part of what they would find in the course, but I invited them to approach the experience with as much intellectual curiosity as they could muster. Although a few responded to this invitation and the content that followed with scowls and arms crossed on their chests, others were game.

Several students said or wrote something about the experience of the course, and I want to paraphrase some students' thoughts. Before reading my paraphrases, keep in mind that I didn't pose a question that would have encouraged them to address me directly and share their thoughts on what they had gained from the course. Neither did I invite them to comment on the field of gender studies or their relationship to it.

Instead, I assigned a final course paper that invited students to choose a particular claim or argument from one of our course texts, explain the claim/argument, explain what they thought about this claim/argument at the end of the course, and then reflect on the process by which they'd arrived at their conclusion. I was surprised that many of the papers were as personal and vulnerable as they were.

In their papers, many students reflected on the class as well as the text and argument they chose to complete the assignment. Commenting on what a particular reading, class discussion, or the structure of the course as a whole had done for them, these students described benefits from participation in the course. The benefits included: greater clarity in their thinking about social problems; an appreciation for tolerance toward those with whom they disagreed; a willingness to consider the ideas of white men; enhanced perspective on themselves, their own beliefs and the beliefs of those around them; a greater openness and willingness to learn from and about others; the value of building resilience; and even an appreciation for what could be gained from experiencing discomfort while learning.

Several students noted that, as a result of the course, they'd become skeptical about things they hadn't been skeptical of before, including: the idea of safe spaces; demands for ideological purity; policing of views among progressives; the ways in which classrooms reinforce rather than challenge students' perspectives; the ways they'd been trained to forebear from triggering their peers' negative emotions through disagreement; and implicit pressure to conform in many classrooms.

Finally, two students broke the fourth wall and thanked me directly for challenging their thinking and for maintaining a classroom in which students were free to express ideas that weren't acceptable in other gender studies spaces.

Honestly, I was blown away by the intellectual and personal vulnerability many of the students displayed, not only in final papers, but throughout the course. Learning to disagree productively and exhibit genuine interest in the views of others is hard work. Several students came to me at some time during the term to tell me that they'd been reflecting on something we'd talked about in class and wanted to chat one-on-one.

I also heard from a few about things they believed they couldn't say in class out of fear that some of their peers might report their apostasy outside the classroom. I just told them I understood their choice.

Banned Books

Now, let me tell you about another class—this one, a post-investigation roll of the dice. Toward the end of my career, I had an opportunity to instruct a one-off undergrad course on a topic of my choice. I tried on several innocuous themes before settling on a topic borrowed from the headlines of the day: banned books. Over the next few months, I researched and read diligently. Finally, I decided on a set of readings I believed would enable me and my students to gain political and psychological insight on phenomena of book banning, challenging, and suppressing.

We would start the course with chapters from Jonathan Haidt's *The Righteous Mind*, which I hoped would provide students with a basis for understanding diverse moral foundations and values. *Why do people with different values and morals want to ban different books? Or the same books for different reasons? LET'S FIND OUT TOGETHER*! Then, we would read several texts that people on the political right have banned or tried to ban. Critical race theory? Check. So far, so good.

After books banned or challenged only by conservatives, we took a break for the piquant humor of a real case that led both *The Onion* and its Christian conservative counterpart, *The Babylon Bee*, to submit amicus briefs to the US Supreme Court.[19] Then we moved on to a book that's attracted the ire of both right and left: *To Kill a Mockingbird*.[20] I considered this book the "hinge" of the class, after which things might continue to succeed or go decidedly sideways.

The final text had been my toughest decision. I knew the last book we read together should be one that only those on the academic and political left wanted to ban or suppress. There were several candidates, and I weighed a number of factors, including what topics and literary genres we'd already sampled. A couple of possibilities I initially considered were, for Islamophobia, Ayaan Hirsi Ali, *The Caged Virgin: An Emancipation Proclamation for Women and Islam* and, for cultural appropriation, Jeanine Cummins, *American Dirt*.[21]

Then I discovered a crucial piece of information. In 2021, an attorney for the American Civil Liberties Union—*the American Civil Liberties Union*—had called for the banning of a book, tweeting, "Stopping the circulation of this book . . . is 100% a hill I will die on."[21] Note: he neither stopped the circulation of the book nor died on that hill. No doubt trading on Abbie Hoffman's *Steal this Book*, a professor had also suggested that her Twitter followers steal and burn the book.[23]

I had a winner: Abigail Shrier's, *Irreversible Damage: The Transgender Craze Seducing Our Daughters*.[24] Shrier, a journalist and author, researched the phenomenon of teenaged girls without discernible histories of gender dysphoria coming out as trans. I knew I was taking a risk by assigning such a book because, however I taught it, assigning it and requiring students to read it might well be adjudged as bigotry and violence.

Although I didn't ask students whether they believed any of the books we read together should be banned, each time we read a book, students volunteered in class and in online discussion posts that they wouldn't support banning it. Until Shrier. Frankly, I was surprised that even though students knew I'd selected *Irreversible Damage*, they didn't seem to hold the choice against me. Nonetheless, virtually every student in the class allowed that they believed this book was harmful and should be banned.

But that's not all there is to be said about this experiment. Together, we had interesting conversations about the book, including a discussion of how Haidt's model of moral foundations, especially a reliance on care and harm, might inform our response. Students were discomfited by Shrier's arguments and tended to believe that, far from being motivated by the care she espoused, she was really motivated by bias against transgender people. But they talked, responding thoughtfully to me and each other without boycotting discussions.

Here is one student's final discussion post on the book:

> Knowing that *Irreversible Damage* has faced the bulk of its opposition from the left, I would expect that most arguments stem from the care/harm principle of morality. It could easily be argued that this book is harmful to the transgender community, invalidating their experiences and fueling skepticism from families, teachers, doctors, and peers. Shrier argues that many adolescents that come to identify as transgender are merely swept up in a craze, seeking nothing more than reprieve from the discomfort of female puberty. Centering the stories of concerned parents, desisters, and detransitioners, she builds a compelling case against gender affirming care and physical/hormonal intervention at such a young age.
>
> This book could easily be discounted as entirely trans-phobic and ripped from the shelves in an attempt to care for transgender individuals of all ages and identities. At the same time however, I believe that Shrier wrote it in an attempt to care for these individuals and their parents in an entirely different way. She implores regretful adolescents to consider detransitioning as an option regardless of how much work they have done to transition thus far and to reach out to familial support systems eager to walk this path with them. She also encourages parents to stay in close contact with their children while allowing for a healthy level of rebellion as they navigate new seasons of life.
>
> I think there is tremendous value in recognizing both of these perceptions. When we villainize the other side and assume that they want nothing more than to harm children and bring evil to our world, we eliminate any chance of respectful dialogue. Reading this book made me realize just how insulated I am in my own media. If someone was to learn about the world solely through my news feed and TikTok For You Page, they would easily come to believe this story of good and evil. While I do not agree with many of Shrier's conclusions, I appreciated the chance to look at this issue from her vantage point. There is nuance and reason to her claims, and I see no utility in assuming ill intentions of her. If we hope to change people's minds, we have to hear them out first, and I can honestly say that this was one of the first times I have truly done so.[25]

And this, ladies and gentlemen, is why I loved to teach.

Those of us who teach could tell so many stories about moments in the classroom when something has "clicked"—when the energy is positive, and many students seem buoyed by the pleasure of learning even if they disagree among themselves. To remind me what teaching and learning can do, I keep a file of cards, letters, and emails I've received from students who tell me what something about a class meant to them.

There's no good reason why this experience of learning so often turns into nightmares of triggered panics and angry denunciations. When faculty credibly fear the consequences of young adults becoming " 'highly emotional,' 'irrevocably shaken,' 'unwell,' and 'unable to focus' " because of something they've read or heard in class, something's gone terribly wrong.[26]

Something has gone terribly wrong.

Parting Thoughts

When universities succumb to illiberalism, sometimes it's necessary to just say no. One professor who said no is JPE Harper-Scott, a musicologist and former professor of music history and theory at Royal Holloway, University of London. Harper-Scott's essay, "Why I Left Academia," is a melancholy love letter to an ideal of what it means to be a scholar.

Harper-Scott discloses that he grew up as a working-class "outsider" and was the first member of his family to go to college. Without much experience to guide him, he believed that scholars were "always committed to the pursuit of truth, never trusting in a commonplace 'fact' without subjecting it to the most serious sceptical scrutiny." He concludes sadly that "this did not turn out to be true." Instead of being "*critical* places," universities had become "increasingly *dogmatic*."

The occasion of Harper-Scott's disillusionment with the academy was pressure from within the academic study of music to "decolonise" "the classical musical canon." Not explore the significance of the fact that many "musical works were written during the period of empire," but, rather, "stop teaching music by Beethoven, Wagner, and co., in the (frankly insane) belief that doing so will somehow materially improve current living conditions for the economically, socially, sexually, religiously, or racially underprivileged."

He acknowledges that, of course, music can be "imbued with the history of its own time" even as it can "offer a form of critique of existing social conditions." Even music created during the "period of empire" "is also, very often, an almost incomprehensibly brilliant expression of human creativity and ingenuity." I identify with Harper-Scott when he explains what classical music means to him. And it's easy for me to extend his reverie to literature and political thought.

> When it entered into my life in a community that was centred on coal mining . . . and manufacturing industry, into a world where novels, poetry, art, theatre, good food, broadsheet newspapers, political awareness, higher education, or classical music had absolutely no purchase, and were in fact broadly considered the luxurious excesses of a monolithic, Thatcherite, uncomprehending South, it opened up stunning new vistas. I discovered, largely through this music, that the world was far bigger than I thought, fuller of beauty and majesty and possibilities for fulfilment.

So, why did Harper-Scott feel as though he had to go? He seems to have reached a tipping point that convinced him that a "dogmatic mode of thinking . . . enforced by mechanisms involving public humiliation, no-platforming, and attempts to have scholars fired" had become "endemic." Harper-Scott had passed the point of no return.[27]

A second professor who said no is the political scientist Morgan Marietta. For a short time, Marietta was the chair of his department at the University of Texas at Arlington. In October 2023, his department hosted an event, "The Hamas-Israel War: Student/Faculty Q&A with Professor Brent Sasley," for students who might have questions about the history and politics of the region.

It did not proceed smoothly. Before the event, progressive students demanded that a "pro-Palestinian" speaker be added. Marietta declined.

During the discussion, students "interrupt[ed], shout[ed] . . . curs[ed]" and, in at least one instance, refused to return a microphone circulated in the room for those who wished to ask questions.

In the aftermath, Marietta's dean pronounced herself "concerned" about his leadership and issued the following set of requirements for future events in his department:

> No events should be scheduled without prior notice. For each such event, please provide the following at least 7 working days in advance: a written management plan, including a risk assessment, risk mitigation plan, and a copy of any comments you plan to give by way of introduction to the event.[28]

Marietta refused and stepped down. He told *The Chronicle of Higher Education* that the policy demanded by the dean "is the death of what universities are meant to do."[29]

Marietta is right: this—all of it—*is* the death of what universities are meant to do.

* * *

This book has given me a precious opportunity to do what I've been fortunate to be able to do for decades: think through questions that fascinate me and try to make sense of a complicated world in which there are conflicts among rights, citizens, and groups.

I conceive of teaching as asking: what might we be missing? What might we have overlooked as we're thinking through this question? To pursue new information; better, more nuanced, perspectives; and insight into the reasons why people disagree, we could do much worse than embracing cellist Yo-Yo Ma's conception of a "beginner's mind."[30] There's vulnerability in this process because it suggests that we can augment our understanding of the world and even change our minds.

Augmenting or changing our thinking about an issue or phenomenon can be thrilling. As a psychologist I worked with in grad school explained, however, having our beliefs challenged can also be ego threatening. Illiberal actors can always leverage this step in the learning process for their own purposes.

Whenever we shut down speech or foreclose alternative views, we do something dreadful in the context of delivering education: we repudiate intellectual curiosity and humility, communicating to students that such ideals are a cynical hoax.

The academic colleagues who want to have their points of view protected by rules, policies, and threats of punishment want to ensure that students never hear alternatives to their ideas. And they want to ensure that they don't have to defend their ideas. Maybe some fear the ideas they propagate can't be defended. Or they believe that the act of defending views betrays that the ideas are perspectives—some among many and, therefore, not indubitably correct.

The most common defense for this intellectually stultifying state of affairs is that it's necessary to prevent harm to members of vulnerable groups. I'm sure that many of my colleagues absolutely believe that this is so. Others may not. Either way, ever-evolving convictions of political factions about what's necessary to prevent harm don't obligate non-believers.

Whether or not Donald Trump truly believes he won the 2020 election, none of us is compelled by the force of either his conviction or his will to behave as though he did. What if we applied this same principle to ourselves? What if, acknowledging wryly that we're all orthodox to ourselves, we decided not to expect and demand obedience from colleagues and students?

Instead of just denouncing right-wing efforts to control what others research and teach while trying to exert control on behalf of progressive dogma, I invite my progressive colleagues to desist. We won't have any standing to condemn right-wing illiberalism until we do. As a bonus, we might even resuscitate the reputation of higher ed. Think about it.

NOTES

Introduction: Tribing Times

1. Wikipedia describes the incident as the "*Hypatia* 'Transracialism Controversy,'" *Wikipedia*, no date, https://en.wikipedia.org/wiki/Hypatia_transracialism_controversy. See also Jesse Singal, "This is What a Modern-Day Witch Hunt Looks Like," *New York Magazine*, May 2, 2017, https://nymag.com/intelligencer/2017/05/transracialism-article-controversy.html.

2. Note: I'm not suggesting that people outside the United States are incapable of coming up with bad ideas. To do so would be to sign onto the idea that all reprehensible motives, policies, and acts in the world originate with the United States, a position I don't hold.

3. Throughout the eighties and nineties, feminist scholars produced many texts intended to introduce students to the diverse approaches to feminist theory. My favorite of these was Chris Beasley, *What is Feminism? An Introduction to Feminist Theory* (London & Thousand Oaks, California: Sage, 1999). From such texts, students learned that feminist scholars could disagree with each other on contentious issues.

4. Steven Pinker, "Rescuing Universities from Themselves: A Five-Point Plan," *Boston Globe*, December 11, 2023, https://www.bostonglobe.com/2023/12/11/opinion/steven-pinker-how-to-save-universities-harvard-claudine-gay/?event=event25.

5. Tara Henley, "Transcending Toxic Femininity: Women, Cancel Culture, and an Appeal to Our Higher Selves," *Fairer Disputations*, November 10, 2023, https://fairerdisputations.org/transcending-toxic-femininity-women-cancel-culture-and-an-appeal-to-our-higher-selves/. See also Amy Wax in Richard Hanania, "Does Immigration Threaten Western Civilization? A Conversation with Amy Wax," *Substack: Richard Hanania's Newsletter*, August 29, 2022, https://www.richardhanania.com/p/does-immigration-threaten-western.

6. Cory Clark and Bo Winegard, "Sex and the Academy," *Quillette*, October 8, 2022, https://quillette.com/2022/10/08/sex-and-the-academy/. Emphasis in the original.

7. Evidence for different male and female preferences and priorities can be found in Noah Carl, "Did Women in Academia Cause Wokeness?" *Noah's Newsletter*, November 21, 2021, (19) https://noahcarl.substack.com/p/did-women-in-academia-cause-wokeness.

8. John Bitzan, "2024 American College Student Freedom, Progress and Flourishing Survey," *Sheila and Robert Challey Institute for Global Innovation and Growth*, 2024, 2024_American_College_Student_Freedom_Progress_and_Flourishing_Survey.pdf (ndsu.edu).

9. Steven Brint, "The UC's Corner-Office Revolutionary," *Quillette*, April 9, 2024, https://quillette.com/2024/04/09/the-ucs-corner-office-revolutionary/.

10. See Jonathan Haidt, *The Anxious Generation: How the Great Rewiring of Childhood is Causing an Epidemic of Mental Illness* (New York: Penguin Press, 2024); David G. Blanchflower, Alex Bryson, Anthony Lepinteur, and Alan Piper, "Further Evidence on the Global Decline in the Mental Health of the Young," *National Bureau of Economic Research*, May 2024, https://www.nber.org/papers/w32500.

11. See Ilana Redstone, *The Certainty Trap: Why We Need to Question Ourselves More—and How We Can Judge Others Less* (Durham, North Carolina: Pitchstone, 2024).

12. C. Fred Alford extends the group psychodynamic thought of Wilfred Bion on groupishness in Alford, *Group Psychology and Political Theory* (New Haven, Connecticut: Yale University Press, 1994).

13. See Eric Kaufmann, "The Mental Health Crisis Does Not Explain Wokeness," *Unherd*, March 18, 2024, https://unherd.com/newsroom/the-mental-health-crisis-does-not-explain-wokeness.

14. Lee Jussim, "The Threat to Academic Freedom . . . From Academics," *Medium*, December 27, 2019, https://psychrabble.medium.com/the-threat-to-academic-freedom-from-academics-4685b1705794.

15. Laura Kipnis, "Why are Scholars Such Snitches?" *The Chronicle of Higher Education*, March 17, 2022, https://laurakipnis.com/wp-content/uploads/2022/03/Chronicle.pdf.

16. Nikolas Lanum, "Hundreds of Silent Masked Students Surround Stanford Law Dean for Apology to Heckled Federal Judge: 'Eerie,'" *Fox News*, March 14, 2023, https://www.foxnews.com/media/hundreds-silent-masked-students-surround-stanford-law-dean-apology-heckled-federal-judge-eerie.

17. Scholars at Risk Network, "Frequently Asked Questions about the Academic Freedom Monitoring Project," 2023, https://www.scholarsatrisk.org/frequently-asked-questions-about-the-academic-freedom-monitoring-project.

18. See, for example, Keith E. Whittington, *You Can't Teach That: The Battle Over University Classrooms* (Cambridge: Polity Press, 2024).

19. See Garrett Shanley, "A Firestorm Against the AAUP," *The Chronicle of Higher Education*, December 5, 2024, https://www.chronicle.com/article/a-firestorm-against-the-aaup.

20. American Association of University Professors, "1915 Declaration of Principles on Academic Freedom and Academic Tenure," no date, https://www.aaup.org/NR/rdonlyres/A6520A9D-0A9A-47B3-B550-C006B5B224E7/0/1915Declaration.pdf.

21. American Association of University Professors, "1940 Statement of Principles on Academic Freedom and Tenure," no date, https://www.aaup.org/sites/default/files/1940%20Statement.pdf.

22. See Charles Tilly and Sidney Tarrow, *Contentious Politics*, 2nd edition (Oxford: Oxford University Press, 2015).

23. University of Chicago, "Report of the Committee on Freedom of Expression," 2014, https://provost.uchicago.edu/sites/default/files/documents/reports/FOECommitteeReport.pdf.

24. Foundation for Individual Rights and Expression, "Chicago Statement: University and Faculty Body Support," 2024, https://www.thefire.org/research-learn/chicago-statement-university-and-faculty-body-support.

25. James Madison Program in American Ideals and Institutions, "Princeton Principles for a Campus Culture of Free Inquiry," *Princeton University*, 2024, https://jmp.princeton.edu/princeton-principles-campus-culture-free-inquiry. Emphasis is in the original.

26. University of Chicago, "Kalven Committee: Report on the University's Role in Political and Social Action," no date, https://provost.uchicago.edu/sites/default/files/documents/reports/KalvenRprt_0.pdf.

27. Len Gutkin, "The Review: Barnard's New and Confused Speech Policy," *The Chronicle of Higher Education*, January 29, 2024, https://www.chronicle.com/newsletter/the-review/2024-01-29.

28. The phrase is drawn from Esther 4:14 (KJV). A good deal of Christian conservative political discourse since the election of George W. Bush has used the phrase to signal the concord of Christian interests with profane conservative—and now MAGA—politics.

29. Core Faculty Members of the Women's, Gender, and Sexuality Studies

Department at Barnard College, "Our Statement," no date, https://archive.ph/XkgMF.

30. John K. Wilson, "What the Champions of Neutrality Get Wrong," *The Chronicle of Higher Education*, March 18, 2024, https://www.chronicle.com/article/what-the-champions-of-neutrality-get-wrong.

31. Ohio State News, "Ohio State Board of Trustees Adopts Campus Free Speech Policy," *The Ohio State University*, May 18, 2023, https://news.osu.edu/ohio-state-board-of-trustees-adopts-campus-free-speech-policy/.

32. The Ohio State University, "Vision, Mission and Values: Ohio State's Shared Values," 2024, https://www.osu.edu/shared-values.

33. Office of Marketing and Communications, "Key Issues: Ohio State Philosophy on Institution and Leadership Statements," *The Ohio State University*, 2023, https://communications.osu.edu/public-affairs/key-issues.

34. Michael Bailey, "Kalvenizing Northwestern University," *Heterodox STEM*, October 22, 2023, https://hxstem.substack.com/p/kalvenizing-northwestern-university/comments; Stanley Fish, "Do Nothing Until You Hear From Me," *The Chronicle of Higher Education*, November 30, 2023, https://www.chronicle.com/article/everyone-just-shut-up-already.

35. Marc Zvi Brettler and Michael B. Poliakoff, "Why Was It So Hard for Elite Universities to Condemn Hamas Terrorism?" *Real Clear Education*, October 20, 2023, https://www.realcleareducation.com/articles/2023/10/20/why_was_it_so_hard_for_elite_universities_to_condemn_hamas_terrorism_987428.html.

36. Michael Ignatieff, "Why the Populist Right Hates Universities," *The Atlantic*, August 6, 2023, https://www.theatlantic.com/ideas/archive/2023/08/viktor-orban-illiberalism-ron-desantis-universities/674915/.

37. Helen Dale, "The Fourfold Attack on Democracy," *Not On Your Team, But Always Fair*, August 27, 2023, https://www.notonyourteam.co.uk/p/the-fourfold-attack-on-democracy.

38. Nate Moore, "The Deepening Diploma Divide," The Liberal Patriot, April 19, 2024, https://www.liberalpatriot.com/p/the-deepening-diploma-divide.

39. Jesse Singal, quoted in Jerry Coyne, "Jesse Singal on Coleman Hughes vs. TED," *Why Evolution is True*, September 30, 2023, https://whyevolutionistrue.com/2023/09/30/jesse-singal-on-coleman-hughes-vs-ted/.

40. Richard Dawkins, "How Can We Have a Proper Debate When We No Longer Speak the Same Language?" *Evening Standard*, August 15, 2023, https://www.standard.co.uk/comment/comment/freedom-speech-debate-language-trans-differing-richard-dawkins-b1100729.html.

41. Cynthia Burack, *Sin, Sex, and Democracy: Antigay Rhetoric and the Christian Right* (Albany, New York: State University of New York Press, 2008).

42. I use the term praxis to refer to my progressive colleagues' understanding that, as scholars, we operate under a mandate to put our theory into practice.

43. See, for example, American Library Association, "Resolution to Condemn White Supremacy and Fascism as Antithetical to Library Work," 2021, https://www.ala.org/sites/default/files/aboutala/content/Resolution%20to%20Condemn%20White%20Supremacy%20and%20Fascism%20as%20Antithetical%20to%20Library%20Work%20FINAL.pdf.

44. In 2018, after Gerson broadcast his criticisms of Christian conservative fealty to Trump across numerous media, the Family Research Council published an article casting Gerson as a liberal. The article, "A Gerson of Interest," attributed to FRC president Tony Perkins, was no longer available online by 2020.

45. The concept is from Ludwik Fleck, *Genesis and Development of a Scientific Fact* (Chicago: University of Chicago Press, 1979), pp. 99–103.

46. Cynthia Burack, *Because We Are Human: Contesting US Support for Gender and Sexuality Human Rights Abroad* (Albany, New York: State University of New York Press, 2018).

47. Pamela Paul, "Progressives Aren't Liberal," *New York Times*, November 16, 2023, https://www.nytimes.com/2023/11/16/opinion/liberals-and-progressives.html.

48. Helen Pluckrose and James Lindsay, *Cynical Theories: How Activist Scholarship Made Everything about Race, Gender, and Identity* (Durham, North Carolina: Pitchstone Publishing), p. 12. Emphasis is added.

49. Sean Speer and Robert Boyers, "Hub Dialogue: Robert Boyers on Why Liberal Professors are Running Scared," *The Hub*, July 30, 2021, https://thehub.ca/podcast/audio/hub-dialogue-robert-boyers-on-why-liberal-professors-are-running-scared/.

50. Alana Newhouse, "Brokenism," *Tablet*, November 21, 2022, https://www.tabletmag.com/sections/news/articles/brokenism-alana-newhouse; Perry Bacon Jr. "CNN's Chris Licht Showed the Problem with Anti-Woke Centrism," *Washington Post*, June 7, 2023, https://www.washingtonpost.com/opinions/2023/06/06/anti-woke-centrism-cnn-chris-licht-atlantic-profile/.

51. Revelation 3:16 (KJV): "So then because thou art lukewarm, and neither cold nor hot, I will spue thee out of my mouth."

52. Joseph J. Siev, Aviva Philipp-Muller, Geoffrey R.O. Durso, and Duane T. Wegener, "Endorsing Both Sides, Pleasing Neither: Ambivalent Individuals

Face Unexpected Social Costs in Political Conflicts," *Journal of Experimental Social Psychology* 114 (2024): 1–11.

53. Gerry Baker and Wesley Yang, "The Successor Ideology and the Threat to Our Freedoms," *Wall Street Journal*, Free Expression podcast, June 13, 2022, https://www.wsj.com/podcasts/opinion-free-expression/the-successor-ideology-and-the-threat-to-our-freedoms/af093a5e-4f8e-4697-a406-ac06673f09b2; Yascha Mounk, *The Identity Trap: A Story of Ideas and Power in Our Time* (New York: Penguin Press, 2023).

54. See Carol Horton, "Why Liberal Confessions?" *Liberal Confessions*, 2024, https://carolhorton.substack.com/about; Lorenzo Warby and Helen Dale, "Self-Deceptive Rationalising Moralisers," *Not On Your Team but Always Fair*, February 23, 2023, https://www.notonyourteam.co.uk/p/self-deceptive-rationalising-moralisers. It's useful to note that there's also a post-liberal right; that's just not what I'm talking about right now.

55. See Susan Neiman, *Left is Not Woke* (Cambridge, UK: Polity Press, 2023).

56. The literature on this repudiation is prodigious. For one example of the diagnosis, see David Kaiser, "Ibram Kendi's Crusade Against the Enlightenment," *Glenn Loury Substack*, October 15, 2023, https://glennloury.substack.com/p/ibram-kendis-crusade-against-the.

57. I borrow the concept of a "privileged position" from Charles Lindblom, *Politics and Markets: The World's Political-Economic Systems* (New York: Basic Books, 1977).

58. Vincent Lloyd, "A Black Professor Trapped in Anti-Racist Hell," *Compact*, February 10, 2023, https://compactmag.com/article/a-black-professor-trapped-in-anti-racist-hell.

59. Wikipedia, "Clastic Rock," September 23, 2023, https://en.wikipedia.org/wiki/Clastic_rock#.

60. Simon Sebag Montefiore, "The Decolonization Narrative is Dangerous and False," *The Atlantic*, October 27, 2023, https://www.theatlantic.com/ideas/archive/2023/10/decolonization-narrative-dangerous-and-false/675799/.

61. See, for example, Alan Sokal, "Preface to the French translation of Helen Pluckrose and James Lindsay, *Cynical Theories*," May 11, 2021, https://physics.nyu.edu/faculty/sokal/preface_to_cynical_theories_ENGLISH.pdf#page=3.

62. Jeff Bloodworth, "Reading Orwell in Tirana," *The Liberal Patriot*, July 5, 2023, https://www.liberalpatriot.com/p/reading-orwell-in-tirana.

63. Although this period has been cited by many commentators, others trace the lineages and symptoms from earlier manifestations. See, for example, Carol

Tavris, "The Ghost of Joe McCarthy: Why Universities have Surrendered on Free Speech Again," TLS, February 9, 2024, https://www.the-tls.com/politics-society/social-cultural-studies/the-canceling-of-the-american-mind-greg-lukianoff-rikki-schlott-triggered-literature-john-sutherland-book-review-carol-tavris.

64. Jan-Werner Müller, *What Is Populism?* (Philadelphia, Pennsylvania: University of Pennsylvania Press, 2016), pp. 22; 19; 4.

65. Benjamin de Cleen and Antonis Galanopoulos, "Populism, Nationalism, and Transnationalism," *Open Democracy*, October 25, 2016, https://www.opendemocracy.net/can-europe-make-it/antonis-galanopoulos-benjamin-de-cleen/you-can-use-populism-to-send-migrants-back.

66. Margaret Canovan, "'Trust the People!' Populism and the Two Faces of Democracy," *Political Studies* 47, 1 (1999): 2–16; Jake Anthony Scott, "There is No Alternative? The Role of Depoliticisation in the Emergence of Populism," *Politics* 42, 3 (2022), p. 326.

67. Theodor W. Adorno, Else Frenkel-Brunswik, Daniel J. Levinson, and R. Nevitt Sanford, *The Authoritarian Personality* (New York: Verso, 1950/2019).

68. John Levi Martin, "The Authoritarian Personality, 50 Years Later: What Questions are There for Political Psychology," *Political Psychology* 22,1 (2002): 1–26.

69. Open Source Psychometrics Project, "This is an Interactive Version of the Right-Wing Authoritarianism Scale," no date, https://openpsychometrics.org/tests/RWAS/.

70. Bob Altemeyer, *The Authoritarians*, 2024, https://theauthoritarians.org/; John W. Dean and Bob Altemeyer, *Authoritarian Nightmare: Trump and His Followers* (Brooklyn, New York: Melville House, 2020). To complicate this very brief account of authoritarianism and the RWA scale, see Karen Stenner, *The Authoritarian Dynamic* (New York: Cambridge University Press, 2005).

71. Thomas H. Costello, Shauna M. Bowes, Irwin D. Waldman, Arber Tasimi, Sean T. Stevens, and Scott O. Lilienfeld, "Clarifying the Structure and Nature of Left-Wing Authoritarianism," *Journal of Personality and Social Psychology* 122, 1 (2022):135–170. Emphasis is added.

72. Bob Altemeyer, *The Authoritarians*, p. 9.

73. Luke Conway, *Liberal Bullies: What Psychology Teaches Us about the Left's Authoritarian Problem—and How to Fix It* (Durham, North Carolina: Pitchstone Press, 2024).

74. PRRI, "Threats to American Democracy Ahead of an Unprecedented Presidential Election," October 25, 2023, https://www.prri.org/research/threats-to-american-democracy-ahead-of-an-unprecedented-presidential-election/.

75. For a libertarian's take on the threats from left and right, see Ilya Somin, "Wokeness is Awful. Nationalism is Far Worse," *The Dispatch*, July 1, 2024, https://thedispatch.com/article/wokeness-is-awful-nationalism-is-far-worse/.

76. Cathy Young, "Our Nasty, Stupid, Frivolous Cancel Culture Fights (That We're Lucky Enough to Have)," *The Bulwark*, March 22, 2022, https://www.thebulwark.com/p/our-nasty-stupid-frivolous-cancel-culture-fights-that-were-lucky-enough-to-have.

77. Charlie Sykes, "Morning Shots with Charlie Sykes: Six Reasons to be Alarmed," *The Bulwark*, October 11, 2021, https://www.thebulwark.com/p/six-reasons-to-be-alarmed.

78. Dawkins, "How Can We Have a Proper Debate When We No Longer Speak the Same Language?"

79. Susie Linfield, "The Return of the Progressive Atrocity," *Quillette*, November 18, 2023, https://quillette.com/2023/11/18/the-return-of-the-progressive-atrocity/?ref=quillette-weekly-newsletter; See also Judith Shulevitz, "Listen to What They're Chanting," *The Atlantic*, May 8, 2024, https://www.theatlantic.com/books/archive/2024/05/pro-palestinian-protests-columbia-chants/678321.

80. The United Nations disagrees. See Office of the Special Representative of the Secretary-General on Sexual Violence in Conflict, "Mission Report Official Visit of the Office of the SRSG-SVC to Israel and the Occupied West Bank, 29 January–4 February 2024," *United Nations*, March 4, 2024, https://news.un.org/en/sites/news.un.org.en/files/atoms/files/Mission_report_of_SRSG_SVC_to_Israel-oWB_29Jan_14_feb_2024.pdf.

81. Chris Freiman, *X*, October 11, 2023, https://x.com/cafreiman/status/1712158045537497376.

82. Michael Powell, "The Curious Rise of 'Settler Colonialism' and 'Turtle Island,'" *The Atlantic*, January 5, 2024, Thttps://www.theatlantic.com/ideas/archive/2024/01/curious-rise-settler-colonialism-and-turtle-island/677005/.

83. Conor Friedersdorf, "Students for Pogroms in Israel," *The Atlantic*, October 14, 2023, https://www.theatlantic.com/ideas/archive/2023/10/college-students-justice-for-palestine-chapters-hamas/675640/.

84. Ben Sasse, "The Moral Decline of Elite Universities," *The Atlantic*, December 14, 2023, https://www.theatlantic.com/ideas/archive/2023/12/interesectionality-american-college/676350/.

85. Jason Blakely, "Where Identity Politics Actually Comes From," *The Chronicle of Higher Education*, October 3, 2023, https://www.chronicle.com/article/where-identity-politics-actually-comes-from.

86. Christopher F. Rufo, *America's Cultural Revolution: How the Radical*

Left Conquered Everything (New York: Broadside Books, 2023).

87. Walter Benn Michaels, *The Trouble with Diversity: How We Learned to Love Identity and Ignore Inequality* (New York: Henry Holt and Company, 2006).

88. Greg Lukianoff and Jonathan Haidt, *The Coddling of the American Mind: How Good Intentions and Bad Ideas are Setting Up a Generation for Failure* (New York: Penguin Press, 2018); Sasse, "The Moral Decline of Elite Universities."

89. Douglas Kruger, *Political Correctness Does More Harm Than Good: How to Identify, Debunk, and Dismantle Dangerous Ideas* (Leeds, UK: Emerald House Group, 2020).

90. Paul R. Gross and Norman Levitt, Higher Superstition: The Academic Left and its Quarrels with Science (Baltimore, Maryland: Johns Hopkins University Press, 1998).

91. Richard Hanania, *The Origins of Woke: Civil Rights Law, Corporate America, and the Triumph of Identity Politics* (New York: HarperCollins, 2023).

92. Alan Sokal and Jean Bricmont, *Fashionable Nonsense: Postmodern Intellectuals' Abuse of Science* (London: Picador, 1999).

93. John McWhorter, *Woke Racism: How a New Religion Has Betrayed Black America* (New York: Portfolio/Penguin, 2021).

94. Jason Blakely, *Lost in Ideology: Interpreting Modern Political Life* (Newcastle, UK: Agenda, 2024).

95. Pluckrose and Lindsay, *Cynical Theories*; Mounk, *The Identity Trap*; Umut Özkırımlı, *Cancelled: The Left Way Back from Woke* (Hoboken, New Jersey: John Wiley & Sons, 2023).

96. Richard Hofstadter, *The Paranoid Style in American Politics and Other Essays* (New York: Alfred A. Knopf, 1965), p. 4.

97. Tracy L. Dumas, Sarah P. Doyle, and Robert B. Lount, Jr., "Self Disclosure and Respect: Understanding the Engagement of Value Minorities," *Organization Science* 35, 3 (2023): 769–1202.

98. Foundation for Individual Rights and Expression, "The Academic Mind in 2022: What Faculty Think about Free Expression and Academic Freedom on Campus," 2024, https://www.fire.org/research-learn/academic-mind-2022-what-faculty-think-about-free-expression-and-academic-freedom.

99. Ryan Quinn, "A DEI Director Ousted for Questioning DEI?" *Inside Higher Education*, March 9, 2023, https://www.insidehighered.com/news/2023/03/10/equity-director-targeted-she-says-questioning-antiracist-orthodoxy.

100. Margaret Atwood, *The Handmaid's Tale* (Boston: Houghton Mifflin Company, 1986), p. 117.

1 Mea Culpa

1. Cynthia Burack, "What Can 'We' Do? Reflections on Politics After January 6," In Khadijah Costley White, Daniel Kreiss, Shannon C. McGregor, and Rebekah Tromble, editors, *Media and January 6th* (Oxford: Oxford University Press, 2024), pp.128–35.

2. James Davison Hunter, *Culture Wars: The Struggle to Define America* (New York: Basic Books, 1991); Carol Mason, *Reading Appalachia from Left to Right: Conservatives and the 1974 Kanawha County Textbook Controversy* (Ithaca, New York: Cornell University Press, 2009).

3. Women's Studies, "The Birth of the Department," *San Diego State University*, 2024, https://womensstudies.sdsu.edu/about-us#:~:text=By%20the%20Fall%20of%201970,as%20a%20truly%20academic%20department.

4. WMST-L, "What is WMST-L?" no date, https://userpages.umbc.edu/~korenman/wmst/wmst-l.html.

5. JSTOR, "off our backs," no date, https://www.jstor.org/journal/offourbacks.

6. National Women's Studies Association, "PhD Program List," no date, https://www.nwsa.org/page/PhDProgramList.

7. Martha C. Nussbaum, *Cultivating Humanity: A Classical Defense of Reform in Liberal Education* (Cambridge, Massachusetts: Harvard University Press, 1997), p. 194.

8. For these and other descriptors of women's studies' "founding mothers," see Florence Howe and Mari Jo Buhle, editors, *The Politics of Women's Studies: Testimony from 30 Founding Mothers* (New York: The Feminist Press, 2000).

9. Michael Barkun, "Conspiracy Theories as Stigmatized Knowledge," *Diogenes* 62, 3–4 (2015): p. 114. See also Michael Barkun, *A Culture of Conspiracy: Apocalyptic Visions in Contemporary America* (Berkeley, CA: University of California Press, 2013).

10. Arthur Koestler, "Arthur Koestler," in Richard H. Crossman, editor, *The God That Failed* (New York: Columbia University Press, 2001), p. 23. Emphasis is in the original.

11. It may not go without saying that by "women" I mean all women as a group at particular times in particular places or particular groups of women

defined by, among other differences, race, class, age, etc. "Minority" and "disfavored" groups can also be delineated in too many ways to generalize about and may or may not include women.

12. Cynthia Burack, *The Problem of the Passions: Feminism, Psychoanalysis, and Social Theory* (New York: New York University Press, 1995).

13. Susan Ostrov Weisser and Jennifer Fleischner, editors, *Feminist Nightmares: Women at Odds* (New York: New York University Press, 1994).

14. Daphne Patai and Noretta Koertge, *Professing Feminism: Cautionary Tales from the Strange World of Women's Studies* (New York: Basic Books, 1994), p. xxiii.

15. Sandra Harding, "Rethinking Standpoint Epistemology: What is 'Strong Objectivity'?" in Linda Alcoff and Elizabeth Potter, editors, *Feminist Epistemologies* (New York: Routledge, 1993), pp. 49–82.

16. Patrick J. Casey, "What is 'Lived Experience'?" *Aeon*, April 18, 2024, https://aeon.co/essays/on-lived-experience-from-the-romantics-to-identity-politics.

17. With the latter, I refer to "the Bell debate," which focused on the Australian anthropologist Diane Bell's ethnographic research. Bell addressed the controversy in Diane Bell, "White Women Can't Speak?" in Sue Wilkinson and Celia Kitzinger, editors, *Representing the Other: A Feminism and Psychology Reader* (Thousand Oaks, California: Sage Publications, 1996).

18. Jonathan Haidt, *The Righteous Mind: Why Good People are Divided by Politics and Religion* (New York: Vintage, 2012), p. 345.

19. Patai and Koertge, *Professing Feminism*, p. xxv.

20. Aldous Huxley, "Democratic Art," in Huxley, *Complete Essays*, I, Robert S. Baker and James Sexton, editors (Chicago: Ivan R. Dee, 2000–2002]), p. 361.

21. Eboo Patel, "How Colleges Can Prepare for a Chaotic Fall," *The Chronicle of Higher Education*, June 21, 2024, https://www.chronicle.com/article/how-colleges-can-prepare-for-a-chaotic-fall.

22. Karla Jay, *Tales of the Lavender Menace: A Memoir of Liberation* (New York: Basic Books, 2000), p. 76.

23. Fukuyama first published his thesis in "The End of History?" *The National Interest* 16 (Summer 1989): 3–18. He followed up with Francis Fukuyama, *The End of History and the Last Man* (New York: The Free Press, 1992).

24. Pluckrose and Lindsay quote the sociologist Judith Lorber in *Cynical Theories*, p. 138.

25. See Susan Faludi, "American Electra: Feminism's Ritual Matricide," *Harper's Magazine*, October 2010, https://susanfaludi.com/americanelectra.pdf.

26. Tyler Austin Harper, "The Humanities Have Sown the Seeds of Their Own Destruction," *The Atlantic*, December 19, 2023, https://www.theatlantic.com/ideas/archive/2023/12/humanities-university-conservative-critics/676890/.

27. Michael Lind, "The Left's Campus Protest Scam," *Tablet*, May 15, 2024, https://www.tabletmag.com/sections/news/articles/left-campus-protest-scam.

28. Steve Sanders, "Judges Have Long Been Deferential to Academe. That's Changing," *The Chronicle of Higher Education*, November 6, 2023, https://www.chronicle.com/article/judges-have-long-been-deferential-to-academe-thats-changing.

29. For the expansion of the higher ed administrative class, see Paul Weinstein, Jr., "Administrative Bloat at U.S. Colleges is Skyrocketing," *Forbes*, August 28, 2023, https://www.forbes.com/sites/paulweinstein/2023/08/28/administrative-bloat-at-us-colleges-is-skyrocketing/.

30. Brockport WGS Support Letter for Signatures, Google Doc, no date, https://docs.google.com/document/d/1N992xwDCr9D_bsOn8UnfCQWcvgjasArgAqwV41Ko4rY. Emphasis is in the original.

31. Lauren Berlant and Michael Warner, "Sex in Public," *Critical Inquiry*, 24 (2) (1998): 547–66.

32. Wendy Brown, "The Impossibility of Women's Studies," *Differences* 9 (3) (1997): 83.

33. Eric Kaufmann, "'Left-Liberal Extremism' has Turned Canada into an International Anomaly," *The Hub*, May 22, 2024, https://thehub.ca/2024/05/22/eric-kaufmann-left-liberal-extremism-has-turned-canada-into-an-anomaly/.

34. Koestler, "Arthur Koestler," p. 49; Haidt, *The Righteous Mind*, p. 345.

35. Francis Fukuyama, "The New Right Loves the State," *Persuasion*, May 10, 2023, https://www.persuasion.community/p/the-new-right-loves-the-state.

36. Yascha Mounk, "How to Argue Against Identity Politics Without Turning into a Reactionary," *New York Times*, September 22, 2023, https://www.nytimes.com/2023/09/22/opinion/identity-politics.html.

37. Mythinformed, *X*, December 21, 2023, https://twitter.com/MythinformedMKE/status/1737993499390144617.

38. The Jefferson Council, *X*, April 19, 2024, https://x.com/TheJeffersonC/status/1781309375929319624.

39. Oliver Traldi, "With All Due Respect to the Experts," *American Compass*, May 20, 2022, https://americancompass.org/with-all-due-respect-to-the-experts/.

40. David French, "The Rage and Joy of MAGA America," *New York Times*, July 6, 2023, https://www.nytimes.com/2023/07/06/opinion/maga-america-trump.html.

41. Jean O'Barr and Mary Wyer, *Engaging Feminism: Students Speak Up & Speak Out* (Charlottsville, Virginia: University Press of Virginia, 1992).

42. Richard Hofstadter, *The Paranoid Style in American Politics and Other Essays* (New York: Alfred A. Knopf, 1965), p. 32.

43. Kat Rosenfield, "The Many Faces of Literary Censorship," *Persuasion*, March 28, 2022, https://www.persuasion.community/p/literary-censorships-evolving-landscape.

44. Janet Burroway, *Imaginative Writing: The Elements of Craft*, 5th Edition (New York: Pearson, 2023); Janet Burroway, "Slouching Toward Sensitivity," *The Chronicle of Higher Education*, November 28, 2023, https://www.chronicle.com/article/slouching-toward-sensitivity.

45. Phoebe Gloeckner, "My Cartoonish Cancellation," *The Chronicle of Higher Education*, November 10, 2022, https://www.chronicle.com/article/my-cartoonish-cancellation.

46. Cole Premo, "Settlement Reached Between Hamline, Former Professor Dismissed after Showing Prophet Muhammad Images," *CBS News*, July 23, 2024, https://www.cbsnews.com/minnesota/news/settlement-reached-between-hamline-former-professor-dismissed-over-showing-islamic-art/.

47. Cynthia Burack, *Tough Love: Sexuality, Compassion, and the Christian Right* (Albany, New York: State University of New York Press, 2014), pp. 22–24; 38–39.

48. John Stuart Mill, *On Liberty and Other Writings* (Cambridge: Cambridge University Press, 1994), p. 84.

49. Alan Levinovitz, "Are Colleges Getting Disability Accommodations All Wrong?" *The Chronicle of Higher Education*, September 25, 2024, https://www.chronicle.com/article/do-colleges-provide-too-many-disability-accommodations.

50. Burack, *Tough Love*.

51. Blake Smith, "Do Administrators Think They're Spiritual Healers?" *The Chronicle of Higher Education*, October 12, 2022, https://www.chronicle.com/article/do-administrators-think-theyre-spiritual-healers.

52. Len Gutkin, "The Review: NYU's Coercive Therapeutics," *The Chronicle of Higher Education*, https://www.chronicle.com/newsletter/the-review/2024-05-20.

53. Heather Mac Donald, "Hysterics for Hamas," *City Journal*, May 9, 2024,

https://www.city-journal.org/article/hysterics-for-hamas?utm_source=Twitter&utm_medium=Organic_Social&utm_campaign=hmd.

54. Len Gutkin, "Are Presidents Finally Quitting the Pulpit?" *The Chronicle of Higher Education*, October 23, 2023, https://www.chronicle.com/newsletter/the-review/2023-10-23.

55. David Brooks, "Therapy Culture Has Undermined Our Maturity," *New York Times*, August 10, 2023, https://www.nytimes.com/2023/08/10/opinion/trauma-mental-health-culture-war.html.

56. See, for example, Bradley Campbell and Jason Manning, *The Rise of Victimhood Culture: Microaggressions, Safe Spaces, and the New Culture Wars* (London, UK: Palgrave Macmillan, 2018).

57. Christopher J. Ferguson, "Cyberbullying and Its Relation to Right and Left Authoritarianism, Trait Victimhood, and Mental Illness," *Psychology of Popular Media*, 13, 3 (2024): 472–480.

58. Timothy C. Bates, Ciara Grant, Leila Hobbs, Claire Johnston, Shahrzad Moghaddam, Kate Sinclair, "Virtuous Victimhood as a Dark Triad Resource Transfer Strategy," *Personality and Individual Differences* 234 (2025): 1–11.

59. Clifford Bob, *The Global Right Wing and the Clash of World Politics* (Cambridge: Cambridge University Press, 2012), p. 17.

60. Gonzalo Schwarz, "American Dream 2021 Snapshot: How Americans View the American Dream and Economic Mobility," *Archbridge Institute*, 2021, https://www.archbridgeinstitute.org/wp-content/uploads/2021/07/2021-American-Dream-Snapshot.pdf.

61. Stephen Hawkins and Taran Raghuram, "American Fabric: Identity and Belonging," *More in Common*, December 2020, moreincommon_americanfabricreport.pdf, p. 14.

62. Linda Balcarová, Justin T. Pickett, Amanda Graham, Sean Patrick Roche, and Francis T. Cullen, "On the Robustness of Black Americans' Support for the Police: Evidence From a National Experiment," *Journal of Criminal Justice* 92 (2024): 1–11.

63. Josh Barro, "Does the House Need a Speaker?" *Very Serious*, October 23, 2023, https://www.joshbarro.com/p/does-the-house-need-a-speaker.

64. Pew Research Center, "About," 2023, https://www.pewresearch.org/about/.

65. Pew Research Center, "Beyond Red vs. Blue: The Political Typology," November 9, 2021, https://www.pewresearch.org/politics/2021/11/09/beyond-red-vs-blue-the-political-typology/, p. 81.

66. Stephen Hawkins, Daniel Yudkin, Míriam Juan-Torres, and Tim Dixon, "Hidden Tribes: A Study of America's Polarized Landscape," *More in Common*, 2018, https://hiddentribes.us/media/qfpekz4g/hidden_tribes_report.pdf, p. 2.

67. Hawkins, Yudkin, Juan-Torres, and Dixon, "Hidden Tribes," pp. 4; 7; 11.

68. Pew Research Center, "Beyond Red vs. Blue: The Political Typology," pp. 94–100.

69. Ruy Teixeira, "The Progressive Left is a Paper Tiger," *The Liberal Patriot*, November 2, 2023, https://www.liberalpatriot.com/p/the-progressive-left-is-a-paper-tiger.

70. Seumas Mill, "Epistemic Institutions: A Joint Epistemic Action-Based Account," *Philosophical Issues* 32 (2022): 398–416.

71. Jan-Werner Müller, *What Is Populism?* (Philadelphia, Pennsylvania: University of Pennsylvania Press, 2016), p. 22.

2 The People

1. Eve Kosofsky Sedgwick, *Epistemology of the Closet* (University of California Press, 1990), p. 8.

2. Joseph Knutson, "Survey: Almost a Quarter of Gen Z Adults Identify as LGBTQ+," *Axios*, March 13, 2024, https://www.axios.com/2024/03/13/lgbtq-identity-us-adults-gallup-survey; Matt Lavietes, "Nearly 30% of Gen Z Adults Identify as LGBTQ, National Survey Finds," *NBC News*, January 24, 2024, https://www.nbcnews.com/nbc-out/out-news/nearly-30-gen-z-adults-identify-lgbtq-national-survey-finds-rcna135510.

3. Luis Noe-Bustamante, Lauren Mora, and Mark Hugo Lopez, "About One-in-Four U.S. Hispanics Have Heard of Latinx, but Just 3% Use It," *Pew Research Center*, August 11, 2020, https://www.pewresearch.org/hispanic/wp-content/uploads/sites/5/2020/08/PHGMD_2020.08.11_Latinx_FINAL.pdf.

4. Civil Rights Division, "Combating Post-9/11 Discriminatory Backlash," *US Department of Justice*, August 6, 2015, https://www.justice.gov/crt/combating-post-911-discriminatory-backlash-6.

5. Leah Shafer, "The Other Achievement Gap," *Harvard Graduate School of Education*, April 27, 2017, https://www.gse.harvard.edu/ideas/usable-knowledge/17/04/other-achievement-gap.

6. Delano R. Franklin, and Samuel W. Zwickel, "Internal Harvard Review Showed Disadvantage for Asian Applicants," *The Harvard Crimson*, June 15, 2018, https://www.thecrimson.com/article/2018/6/15/admissions-internal-report/.

7. Neil G. Ruiz, Ziyao Tian, and Jens Manuel Krogstad, "Asian Americans Hold 'Mixed Views' Around Affirmative Action," *Pew Research Center*, June 8, 2023, https://www.pewresearch.org/race-and-ethnicity/2023/06/08/asian-americans-hold-mixed-views-around-affirmative-action/.

8. Disability and Philanthropy Forum, "What is Disability Justice?" no date, https://disabilityphilanthropy.org/resource/what-is-disability-justice/.

9. Sins Invalid, "10 Principles of Disability Justice," September 17, 2015, https://static1.squarespace.com/static/5bed3674f8370ad8c02efd9a/t/5f1f0783916d8a179c46126d/1595869064521/10_Principles_of_DJ-2ndEd.pdf.

10. National Women's Studies Association, "NWSA Statement on Caste as a Protected Category," August 2021, https://higherlogicdownload.s3.amazonaws.com/NWSA/7a8ba6a5-3bb1-4957-937f-39be8a6ac88f/UploadedImages/Statements/2021/caste_protected_category.pdf.

11. Maari Zwick-Maitreyi, Thenmozhi Soundararajan, Natasha Dar, RF Bheel, and Paari Balakrishnan, "Caste in the United States. A Survey of Caste among South Asian Americans," *Equality Labs*, 2018, https://static1.squarespace.com/static/58347d04bebafbb1e66df84c/t/603ae9f4cfad7f515281e9bf/1614473732034/Caste_report_2018.pdf.

12. Dana Difilippo, "Calls to Ban Caste Discrimination Grow as New Jersey's South Asian Population Swells," *New Jersey Monitor*, October 24, 2023, https://newjerseymonitor.com/2023/10/24/calls-to-ban-caste-discrimination-grow-as-new-jerseys-south-asian-population-swells/.

13. Glenn Loury, "The First Thing You Learn at Harvard," *Glenn Loury Substack*, August 1, 2023, https://glennloury.substack.com/p/the-first-thing-you-learn-at-harvard.

14. Madison Dibble, "Dean of Massachusetts Nursing School Fired after Saying 'Everyone's Life Matters,'" *Washington Examiner*, July 2, 2020, https://www.washingtonexaminer.com/news/dean-of-massachusetts-nursing-school-fired-after-saying-everyones-life-matters.

15. See Musa Al-Gharbi, *We Have Never Been Woke: The Cultural Contradictions of a New Elite* (Princeton University Press, 2024).

16. Joseph Henrich, Steven J. Heine, and Ara Norenzayan, "Most People are not WEIRD," *Nature* 466 (2010): 29.

17. See Naomi Cahn and June Carbone, *Red Families v. Blue Families: Legal Polarization and the Creation of Culture* (Oxford: Oxford University Press, 2010).

18. Kimberlé Crenshaw, "Demarginalizing the Intersection of Race and Sex: A Black Feminist Critique of Antidiscrimination Doctrine, Feminist Theory, and Antiracist Politics," in Katharine T. Bartlett and Rosanne Kennedy, editors, *Feminist Legal Theory: Readings in Law and Gender* (Boulder, Colorado: Westview Press, 1991), pp. 57–80.

19. Terry Jones, director, *Life of Brian* (HandMade Films, 1979). The film is also referred to as *Monty Python's Life of Brian*.

20. It's not me.

21. Roland G. Fryer, Jr., "An Empirical Analysis of Racial Differences in Police Use of Force," *Journal of Political Economy* 127, 3 (2019): 1210–1261.

22. Ibram X. Kendi, *How To Be an Antiracist* (New York: One World, 2019), p. 19.

23. Katherine Mangan, "Under Siege, DEI Officers Strategize to Fight Back," *The Chronicle of Higher Education*, March 20, 2024, https://www.chronicle.com/article/under-siege-dei-officers-strategize-to-fight-back.

24. Adrienne Lu, "Diversity Statements are Being Banned. Here's What Might Replace Them," *The Chronicle of Higher Education*, October 6, 2023, https://www.chronicle.com/article/diversity-statements-are-being-banned-heres-what-might-replace-them.

25. Megan Zahneis, "Diversity Statements Are Under Fire. Here's What They Are and How They're Used," *The Chronicle of Higher Education*, March 7, 2023, https://www.chronicle.com/article/diversity-statements-are-under-fire-heres-what-they-are-and-how-theyre-used?sra=true.

26. Jennifer Kabbany, "UMich Now Has More Than 500 Jobs Dedicated to DEI, Payroll Costs Exceed $30 Million," *The College Fix*, January 9, 2024, https://www.thecollegefix.com/umich-now-has-more-than-500-jobs-dedicated-to-dei-payroll-costs-exceed-30-million/, accessed April 4, 2024; Ari Blaff, "DEI 'Not Supported by the Empirical Evidence,' Canadian Researcher Says," *National Post*, February 13, 2024, https://nationalpost.com/news/canada/dei-initiatives-not-supported-by-the-empirical-evidence-canadian-researcher-says; David Miller Haskell, "What DEI Research Concludes about Diversity Training: It is Divisive, Counter-Productive, and Unnecessary," *Aristotle Foundation*, February 12, 2024, https://aristotlefoundation.org/reality-check/what-dei-research-concludes-about-diversity-training-it-is-divisive-counter-productive-and-unnecessary; Ankita Jagdeep, Simon Lazarus, Mendel Zecher, Ohad Fedida, Gidi Fihrer, Joel Finkelstein, Danit Sarah Finkelstein, Sonia Yanovsky, Lee Jussim, and Pamela Paresky, "Instructing Animosity: How DEI Pedagogy Produces the Hostile Attribution Bias," *Network Contagion Research Institute* (2024): 1–23.

27. Komi Frey, "We Know Diversity Statements are Political Litmus

Tests," *The Chronicle of Higher Education*, January 4, 2024, https://www.chronicle.com/article/we-know-diversity-statements-are-political-litmus-tests.

28. Cathy Young, "Diversity, Equity and . . . Conformity?" *The Bulwark*, July 11, 2023, https://www.thebulwark.com/p/diversity-equity-and-conformity.

29. Randall L. Kennedy, "Mandatory DEI Statements are Ideological Pledges of Allegiance. Time to Abandon Them," *Harvard Crimson*, April 2, 2024, https://www.thecrimson.com/column/council-on-academic-freedom-at-harvard/article/2024/4/2/kennedy-abandon-dei-statements/.

30. Conor Friedersdorf, "The Hypocrisy of Mandatory Diversity Statements," *The Atlantic*, July 3, 2023, https://www.theatlantic.com/ideas/archive/2023/07/hypocrisy-mandatory-diversity-statements/674611/.

31. Samuel J. Abrams, "Hardly Inclusive, Diversity Mandates Have Politicized Campus Life," *American Enterprise Institute*, October 27, 2023, https://www.aei.org/op-eds/hardly-inclusive-diversity-mandates-have-politicized-campus-life/.

32. Armin Rosin: "The DEI Complex Will Never Protect Jews," *Tablet*, October 24, 2023, https://www.tabletmag.com/sections/news/articles/the-dei-complex-will-never-protect-jews; Tabia Lee, "I Was a DEI Director—DEI Drives Campus Antisemitism," *New York Post*, October 3, 2023, https://nypost.com/2023/10/18/i-was-a-dei-director-dei-drives-campus-antisemitism/.

33. Kennedy, "Mandatory DEI Statements are Ideological Pledges of Allegiance."

34. John McWhorter, "Claudine Gay Was Not Driven Out Because She's Black," *New York Times*, January 8, 2024, https://www.nytimes.com/2024/01/08/opinion/claudine-gay-resignation-racism.html.

35. American Library Association, "Diversity, Equity, and Inclusion (DEI) Scorecard for Library and Information Organizations," April 2021, https://www.ala.org/sites/default/files/aboutala/content/2021%20EQUITY%20SCORECARD%20FOR%20LIBRARY%20AND%20INFORMATION%20ORGANIZATIONS.pdf.

36. College of Engineering, "COE UNL Diversity and Inclusion Statement Extended Review Form," *University of Nebraska Lincoln*, no date, https://drive.google.com/file/d/1z_e5jgPEvQvCPPw_YQrRs91OXa9bAION/view?pli=1.

37. Department of Molecular Biophysics and Biochemistry, "Criteria for Scoring Anonymized Statements from Faculty Candidates Diversity, Equity, and Inclusion," *Yale University*, Fall 2020, https://mbb.yale.edu/sites/default/files/files/DEI_Statment_Rubric-SrLecturer2022.pdf.

38. The National Association of Scholars, "About Us," 2024, https://www.nas.org/about-us.

39. Jennifer Graham, "Meet the Man Changing the Conversation about DEI," *Deseret News*, February 29, 2024, https://www.deseret.com/2024/02/28/john-sailer-dei-universities-equity/.

40. John Sailer, "Faculty-Packing at Ohio State," *Minding the Campus*, February 2, 2023, https://www.mindingthecampus.org/2023/02/02/faculty-packing-at-ohio-state/.

41. The latter descriptor is found in John Sailer, "The Ohio State Reports: DEI Contributions in Practice," *National Association of Scholars*, November 27, 2023, https://www.nas.org/blogs/article/the-ohio-state-reports-dei-contributions-in-practice.

42. See also John D. Sailer, "Diversity Statement, Then Dossier: The Rise of Cluster Hiring in Higher Education," *National Association of Scholars*, September 15, 2023, https://www.nas.org/reports/diversity-statement-then-dossier/full-report.

43. John D. Sailer, "Inside Ohio State's DEI Factory," *Wall Street Journal*, November 20, 2023, https://www.wsj.com/opinion/inside-ohio-states-dei-factory-faculty-report-diversity-hiring-cefd804d.

44. John Sailer, "The DEI Rollback," *The Free Press*, January 16, 2024, https://www.thefp.com/p/john-sailer-the-dei-rollback).

45. Haley Gluhanich, "VICTORY: UMass Boston Quietly Removes DEI Requirements from Faculty Applications," *Foundation for Individual Rights and Expression*, November 30, 2023, https://www.fire.org/news/victory-umass-boston-quietly-removes-dei-requirements-faculty-applications.

46. Subcommittee on Antisemitism and Anti-Israeli Bias of the Jewish Advisory Committee, "'It's in the Air': Antisemitism and Anti-Israeli Bias at Stanford, and How to Address It," *Stanford University*, May 31, 2024, https://news.stanford.edu/__data/assets/pdf_file/0033/156588/ASAIB-final-report.pdf.

47. Sarah Kessler, "D.E.I. Goes Quiet," *New York Times*, January 15, 2024, https://www.nytimes.com/2024/01/13/business/dealbook/dei-goes-quiet.html.

48. As Sailer points out in the *Wall Street Journal*, the College of Arts and Sciences did require candidates for positions in the college to complete diversity statements.

49. Office of Marketing and Communications, "Key Issues," *The Ohio State University*, November 21, 2023, https://omc.osu.edu/key-issues.

50. See Katie Roiphe, "Imagining Enemies," *Slate*, December 10, 2002, https://slate.com/culture/2002/12/nora-ephron-s-theory-of-mary-mccar-

thy-vs-lillian-hellman.html.

51. National Women's Studies Association, "Assistant Professor in Feminist/Queer/Trans* Dis/Ability Studies," https://www.nwsa.org/networking/apply_now.aspx?view=2&id=673964.

52. Mill, *On Liberty and Other Writings*, p. 48.

53. George Lakoff, *Moral Politics: What Conservatives Know that Liberals Don't* (Chicago: University of Chicago Press, 1996), p. 12.

54. Greg Lukianoff, "The Empowering of the American Mind," *Persuasion*, June 7, 2021, https://www.persuasion.community/p/the-empowering-of-the-american-mind.

55. "Office of Inclusive Excellence and Community Engagement," *University of North Carolina*, 2024, https://www.med.unc.edu/inclusion/justice-equity-diversity-and-inclusion-j-e-d-i-toolkit/microaggressions-microaffirmations/.

56. Academic Affairs, "Tool: Recognizing Microaggressions and the Messages they Send," *University of California Santa Cruz*, no date, https://academicaffairs.ucsc.edu/events/documents/Microaggressions_Examples_Arial_2014_11_12.pdf.

57. Catherine Marrone, "Safe Spaces: What They Look Like, Professors Who Help Create Them," *Stoney Brook University News*, May 15, 2023, https://news.stonybrook.edu/university/safe-spaces-what-they-look-like-professors-who-help-create-them/.

58. John Warner, "What if Everyone Actually Agrees about Safe Spaces?" *Inside Higher Ed*, September 6, 2021, https://www.insidehighered.com/blogs/just-visiting/what-if-everyone-actually-agrees-about-safe-spaces.

59. National Center for PTSD, "Violence and Abuse," *US Department of Veterans Affairs*, September 14, 2023, https://www.ptsd.va.gov/understand/types/violence_abuse.asp.

60. Cory J. Clark, Matias Fjeldmark, Louise Lu, Roy F. Baumeister, Stephen Ceci, Komi Frey, Geoffrey Miller, Wilfred Reilly, Dianne Tice, William von Hippel, Wendy M. Williams, Bo M. Winegard, and Philip E. Tetlock, "Taboos and Self-Censorship Among U.S. Psychology Professors," *Perspectives on Psychological Science* (2024): 1–17.

61. Victoria M. E. Bridgland, Payton J. Jones, and Benjamin W. Bellet, "A Meta-Analysis of the Efficacy of Trigger Warnings, Content Warnings, and Content Notes," *Clinical Psychological Science* 12, 4 (2023): p. 16.

62. Lyell Asher, "How Ed Schools Became a Menace," *The Chronicle of Higher Education*, April 8, 2018, https://www.chronicle.com/article/how-ed-schools-became-a-menace/.

63. Center for Teaching and Learning, "Ungrading: Reimagining Assessment of Student Learning," *Columbia University*, no date, https://ctl.columbia.edu/faculty/sapp/ungrading/.

64. Rick Hess and Joe Feldman, "What Many Advocates—and Critics—Get Wrong about Equitable Grading," *Education Week*, January 29, 2024, https://www.edweek.org/leadership/opinion-what-many-advocates-and-critics-get-wrong-about-equitable-grading/2024/01.

65. Foundation for Individual Rights and Expression, "VICTORY: UCLA Reinstates Professor Suspended for Email on Why He Wouldn't Change Exam, Grading for Black Students," September 15, 2020, https://www.fire.org/news/victory-ucla-reinstates-professor-suspended-email-why-he-wouldnt-change-exam-grading-black.

66. Zack K. De Piero v. Pennsylvania State University, et.al., January 11, 2024, US District Court for the Eastern District of Pennsylvania Case 2:23-cv-02281-WB, available at https://www.fairforall.org/wp-content/uploads/2024/01/2024-01-11-31-Opinion-on-Motion-to-Dismiss.pdf.

67. Wikipedia, "Progressive Stack," April 13, 2023, https://en.wikipedia.org/wiki/Progressive_stack.

68. Kevin Gannon, "The Progressive Stack and Standing for Inclusive Teaching," *The Tattooed Professor*, October 20, 2017, https://thetattooedprof.com/2017/10/20/the-progressive-stack-and-standing-for-inclusive-teaching/.

69. Gannon, "The Progressive Stack and Standing for Inclusive Teaching."

70. National Equity Project, "Developing Community Agreements," no date, https://www.nationalequityproject.org/tools/developing-community-agreements. Ellipsis and bracketed material are in the original.

71. Center for Engaged Pedagogy, "Crafting Community Agreements: Overview," *Barnard College*, no date, https://cep.barnard.edu/crafting-community-agreements.

72. For one dissenting perspective on land acknowledgments, see Noah Smith, "No, You are Not on Indigenous Land," *Noahpinion*, November 30, 2024, https://www.noahpinion.blog/p/no-you-are-not-on-indigenous-land.

73. Josh Moody, "Land Acknowledgements Spur Controversy," *Inside Higher Ed*, February 22, 2022, https://www.insidehighered.com/news/2022/02/23/professors-land-acknowledgment-sparks-controversy. For a more humorous take on land acknowledgements, see Rob Henderson, *X*, October 13, 2023, https://x.com/robkhenderson/status/1712842785882055081?s=20.

74. Moody, "Land Acknowledgments Spur Controversies."

75. Center for Belonging and Social Change, "Land Acknowledgment," Ohio State University Office of Student Life, 2023, https://cbsc.osu.edu/about-

us/land-acknowledgement. In November 2023, I looked for this acknowledgement on the College of Arts and Sciences website but could no longer find it. It continued to appear on the websites of the Center for Belonging and Social Change and the department of Women's, Gender and Sexuality Studies. The Center for Belonging lists the authors of the statement: "Statement written by Dr. Melissa Beard Jacob (Sault St. Marie Tribe of Chippewa Indians) 2018. Updated and Edited by Madison Eagle (Cherokee and Shawnee) 2022."

76. University of Denver, Office of Teaching and Learning, "Inclusive Teaching Practices," 2022, https://operations.du.edu/inclusive-teaching/inclusive-pedagogy. Emphasis is added.

77. Foundation for Individual Rights and Expression, "Bias Response Team Report 2017," no date, https://www.thefire.org/sites/default/files/2022/09/Bias%20Response%20Team%20Report%202017.pdf.

78. Truman State University, "Bias-Related Incident Response," no date, https://titleix.truman.edu/reporting-bias-related-incident/. Emphasis is added.

79. Office for Institutional Equity and Title IX, "Bias Incident," *Carnegie Mellon University*, 2024, https://www.cmu.edu/title-ix/how-to-report-+-options-for-resolution/ccbrp/index.html. Emphasis is added.

80. By 2024, this information had disappeared from the Department of Psychology webpage. In its place was a "Bias Reporting" button under the "Diversity" tab, which linked to the University of Washington's Reporting Bias Incidents page. On that page, students are informed that the university "values and honors diverse experiences and perspectives" and that "members of [the] community might hold and express sometimes-unpopular views." University of Washington, "Reporting Bias Incidents," 2024, https://www.washington.edu/bias/.

81. Department of Psychology, "Bias Reporting Annual Report: 2020–2021," *University of Washington*, no date, https://psych.uw.edu/storage/diversity/Bias%20Reporting%20Annual%20Report-2021.pdf; Department of Psychology, "Bias Reporting Annual Report: 2021–2022," *University of Washington*, no date, https://psych.uw.edu/storage/diversity/Bias%20Reporting%20Annual%20Report-2022.pdf?v2.

82. Colorado State University, "What is the Bias Reporting System?" 2024, https://biasreporting.colostate.edu/.

83. The incident of "bias" involving a student reading *Mein Kampf* occurred at Stanford University. I confess to having assigned sections of Hitler's book to students in Political Ideologies classes. If Bias Response Teams had existed in the late 1980s and early 1990s, I might have found myself being "educated" about bias.

84. Office of the Provost, "Northwestern Principles of Inclusive Teaching,"

Northwestern University, November 2021, northwestern.edu/searle/docs/inclusive-teaching.pdf. Emphasis is added.

85. Rob Kurzban, "The Sword of Safetyism," *Aporia*, December 1, 2023, https://www.aporiamagazine.com/p/the-sword-of-safetyism.

3 Moralizing Politics

1. Center for Cultural Studies, "Left Conservatism: A Workshop," *University of California Santa Cruz,* 2018, https://culturalstudies.ucsc.edu/past-conferences/2836-2/.

2. Sheri Berman offers this pithy summary of what contemporary social democrats aim for: "promoting capitalism's upsides while protecting citizens from its downsides." See Sheri Berman, "Can Social Democrats Save the World (Again)?" *Foreign Policy,* January 15, 2020, https://foreignpolicy.com/2020/01/15/social-democracy-save-world-again-socialism/.

3. Richard Hanania, "Towards an Enlightened Centrism," *Richard Hanania's Newsletter*, June 23, 2023, https://www.richardhanania.com/p/towards-an-enlightened-centrism.

4. Arthur M. Schlesinger Jr., "Not Left, Not Right, But a Vital Center," *New York Times*, April 4, 1948, https://archive.nytimes.com/www.nytimes.com/books/00/11/26/specials/schlesinger-centermag.html.

5. Angela Nagle, *Kill All Normies: Online Culture Wars from 4Chan and Tumblr to Trump and the Alt-Right* (Winchester, UK: Zer0 Books, 2017).

6. John Locke, "A Letter Concerning Toleration," in Roger S. Gottlieb, editor, *Liberating Faith: Religious Voices for Justice, Peace, and Ecological Wisdom* (Lanham, Maryland: Rowman and Littlefield, 2003), p. 79; Mill, *On Liberty and Other Writings*, p. 21.

7. *Mill*, On Liberty and Other Writings, p., 20.

8. Jonathan Haidt and Zach Rausch, "What We Learned in 2023 about Gen Z's Mental Health Crisis," *After Babel*, December 31, 2023, https://www.afterbabel.com/p/best-of-2023.

9. Coleman Hughes, "A Case for Color Blindness," *TED*, April 2023, https://www.ted.com/talks/coleman_hughes_a_case_for_color_blindness?subtitle=en&trigger=30s.

10. Dylan Selterman links to research critical of color blindness cited by the psychologist Adam Grant. See Dylan Selterman, "Mismeasuring Racial Colorblindess," *Psychology Today*, December 21, 2023, https://www.psychol-

ogytoday.com/us/blog/the-resistance-hypothesis/202312/mismeasuring-racial-colorblindness; John Iceland and Eric Silver, "When All You Have is a Hammer: How Social Justice Distorts What We Know about Racial Disparities," *Theory and Society*, published online July 15, 2024, https://link.springer.com/article/10.1007/s11186-024-09568-1.

11. Jesse Singal, "Organizational Leaders Like Chris Anderson Should Stop Indulging Their Most Hysterical Employees," *Singal-Minded*, September 29, 2023, https://jessesingal.substack.com/p/organizational-leaders-like-chris.

12. Coleman Hughes, "My Last Word on TED," *Coleman's Corner*, October 4, 2023, https://colemanhughes.substack.com/p/my-last-word-on-ted.

13. Dawne Moon, *God, Sex, and Politics: Homosexuality and Everyday Theologies* (Chicago, Illinois, University of Chicago Press, 2004), p. 2.

14. Jill Filopovic, "Say Plainly What the Protesters Want," *The Atlantic*, May 6, 2024, https://www.theatlantic.com/ideas/archive/2024/05/israel-gaza-war-protest-movement/678303/.

15. Lukianoff and Haidt, *The Coddling of the American Mind*. Lukianoff and Haidt's concept of safetyism was given empirical support in Jared B. Celniker, Megan M. Ringel, Karli Nelson, and Peter H. Ditto, "Correlates of 'Coddling': Cognitive Distortions Predict Safetyism-Inspired Beliefs, Belief that Words Can Harm, and Trigger Warning Endorsement in College Students," *Personality and Individual Differences* 185 (2022): 1–21.

16. See Steven Collis, "On the Mission of Academic Institutions," *Reason*, September 13, 2024, https://reason.com/volokh/2024/09/13/on-the-missions-of-academic-institutions/.

17. One of the most rigorous theoretical taxonomies of oppression was developed by the political theorist Iris Marion Young in *Justice and the Politics of Difference* (Princeton, New Jersey: Princeton University Press, 1990). However, the literature on these matters is voluminous.

18. Carol Gilligan, *In a Different Voice: Psychological Theory and Women's Development* (Cambridge, Massachusetts: Harvard University Press, 1982).

19. Nel Noddings, *A Feminine Approach to Ethics and Moral Education* (Berkeley, California: University of California Press, 1984).

20. Joan Tronto, *Moral Boundaries: A Political Argument for an Ethic of Care* (New York: Routledge, 1993).

21. The quote is from Honor Ford-Smith and Beverley Hanson, "Justice as a Labor of Care: Self-Care, Collective Entanglement, and Feminist Activism in Caribbean Spaces," *Palimpsest* 11, 1 (2022): 42–65.

22. College of Arts and Sciences Global Arts and Humanities, "Announcing the Society of Fellows 2024–25 Theme: CARE | CULTURE | JUSTICE,"

The Ohio State University, October 26, 2023, https://globalartsandhumanities.osu.edu/news/announcing-society-fellows-2024-25-theme-care-culture-justice.

23. Carol Horton, "What's Woke? #3: Toxic Femininity and Surveillance Capitalism," *Liberal Confessions*, April 20, 2023, https://carolhorton.substack.com/p/whats-woke-3-toxic-femininity-and.

24. Rob Kurzban, "The Sword of Safetyism," *Aporia*, December 1, 2023, https://www.aporiamagazine.com/p/the-sword-of-safetyism. Emphasis is in the original.

25. Haidt, *The Righteous Mind*, pp. 197; 213; 28–9. Emphasis is in the original.

26. Cathy Young, "Our Nasty, Stupid, Frivolous Cancel Culture Fights (That We're Lucky Enough to Have)," *The Bulwark*, March 22, 2022, https://www.thebulwark.com/p/our-nasty-stupid-frivolous-cancel-culture-fights-that-were-lucky-enough-to-have.

27. Nick Haslam, Brodie C. Dakina, Fabian Fabianoa, Melanie J. McGrath, Joshua Rhee, Ekaterina Vylomova, Morgan Weaving and Melissa A. Wheeler, "Harm Inflation: Making Sense of Concept Creep," *European Review of Social Psychology* 31, 1 (2020): pp 254; 256; 277; 279.

28. Yoel Inbar, Michael Inzlicht, and Alexa Tullett, *Two Psychologists Four Beers*, Fireside, https://www.fourbeers.com/.

29. Yoel Inbar, "Episode 263: Free Yoel," *Very Bad Wizards*, hosted by Tamler Sommers and David Pizarro, *Very Bad Media*, June 27, 2023, https://verybadwizards.com/episode/episode-263-free-yoel.

30. Yoel Inbar Letter, https://docs.google.com/document/d/1gmGjIin-4r2W1wkgQNyN89BYmosytigv4GbF0AmdVucc/edit?tab=t.0. This version of the letter redacts the student signatories' names. Although the signatories' names are available online, some students wanted to shield their identities.

31. Megan Zahneis, "This Professor Criticized Diversity Statements. Did It Cost Him a Job Offer?" *The Chronicle of Higher Education*, June 28, 2023, https://www.chronicle.com/article/this-professor-criticized-diversity-statements-did-it-cost-him-a-job-offer.

32. University of Toronto, Department of Psychology, "Yoel Inbar, Associate Professor," https://www.psych.utoronto.ca/people/directories/all-faculty/yoel-inbar.

33. Yoel Inbar, David A. Pizarro, and Paul Bloom, "Conservatives are More Easily Disgusted Than Liberals," *Cognition and Emotion* 23, 4 (2008).

34. I rely in this discussion on Burack, *Sin, Sex, and Democracy*, pp. 124–30.

35. Mill, *On Liberty and Other Writings*, p. 82.

36. Andrew von Hirsch, "Extending the Harm Principle: Remote Harms and Fair Imputation," in *Harm and Capability*, edited by A.P. Simester and A.T.H. Smith (Oxford: Oxford University Press, 1996), pp. 265–271.

37. Eduardo Cuevas, John Bacon, and Jorge L. Ortiz, "Columbia Suspends Protesting Students; Demonstrators Take Over University Building: Updates," *USA Today*, April 29, 2024, https://www.usatoday.com/story/news/nation/2024/04/29/college-campus-protests-israel-gaza-live-updates/73496649007/.

38. Tyler Austin Harper, "America's Colleges are Reaping What They Sowed," *The Atlantic*, May 2, 2024, https://www.theatlantic.com/ideas/archive/2024/05/college-activism-hypocrisy/678262/.

39. Helen Pluckrose, *X*, May 13, 2024, https://x.com/HPluckrose/status/1789956717028975065).

40. James Bennet, "When the New York Times Lost Its Way," *The Economist*, December 14, 2023, https://www.economist.com/1843/2023/12/14/when-the-new-york-times-lost-its-way.

41. Julie Stone Peters, "In Praise of the Academic Cliché," *The Chronicle of Higher Education*, June 10, 2022, https://www.chronicle.com/article/in-praise-of-the-academic-cliche?sra=true.

42. Joe Forgas, "The Current State of Social Psychology," *Unsafe Science*, July 25, 2023, https://unsafescience.substack.com/p/the-current-state-of-social-psychology.

43. Jeff Bloodworth, "How the New Left Damaged Democrats in the 1960s and 1970s," *The Liberal Patriot*, February 5, 2024, https://www.liberalpatriot.com/p/how-the-new-left-damaged-democrats.

44. American Association of Physics Teachers, "Drying 'White Tears': Interrogating Whiteness and Racism in a Multiracial Classroom," no date, https://www.aapt.org/Conferences/SM2019/upload/Diversity-Workshops-2.pdf; Cell biology at Davidson College: Steve McGuire, *X*, February 27, 2024, https://x.com/sfmcguire79/status/1762562030093881448.

45. Jennifer Schuessler, "An Open Letter on Free Expression Draws a Counterblast," *New York Times*, July 10, 2020, https://www.nytimes.com/2020/07/10/arts/open-letter-debate.html; Adam Rubenstein, "I Was a Heretic at The New York Times," *The Atlantic*, February 26, 2024, https://www.theatlantic.com/ideas/archive/2024/02/tom-cotton-new-york-times/677546/; Jesse Singal, "Why is the Same Misleading Language about Youth Gender Medicine Copied and Pasted into Dozens of CNN.com Articles?" *Singal Minded*, March 22, 2024, https://jessesingal.substack.com/p/why-is-the-same-misleading-language.

46. Steve Kaagan and John Hagan, "Learning From an Intergenerational Blowup Over Social Justice," *Stanford Social Innovation Review*, January 4, 2024, https://ssir.org/articles/entry/an_intergenerational_social_justice_meltdown.

47. Carrie Robison and Aaron Terr, "California Library Violates First Amendment, Boots Speakers for Referring to Transgender Women as 'Biological Men,'" *Foundation for Individual Rights and Expression*, August 24, 2023, https://www.fire.org/news/california-library-violates-first-amendment-boots-speakers-referring-transgender-women; Michael Dudley and Amy Girard, "Library Bureaucracy as 'Scold's Bridle': Epistemic Injustice, Linguistic Muting, and the Silencing of Women," *Heterodoxy in the Stacks*, September 6, 2023, https://hxlibraries.substack.com/p/library-bureaucracy-as-scolds-bridle; Monica Harris, "The Unjust Firing of Ontario Librarian who Challenged DEI Orthodoxy," *National Post*, March 22, 2024, https://nationalpost.com/opinion/monica-harris-the-unjust-firing-of-ontario-librarian-who-challenged-dei-orthodoxy.

48. Lyell Asher, "How Ed Schools Became a Menace," *The Chronicle of Higher Education*, April 8, 2018, https://www.chronicle.com/article/how-ed-schools-became-a-menace/; Francesca Block, "How U.S. Public Schools Teach Antisemitism," *The Free Press*, December 19, 2023, https://www.thefp.com/p/how-us-public-schools-teach-antisemitism.

49. Janet Burroway, "Slouching Toward Sensitivity," *The Chronicle of Higher Education*, November 28, 2023, https://www.chronicle.com/article/slouching-toward-sensitivity; Coalition for Diversity and Inclusion in Scholarly Communications, "Toolkits for Equity," 2024, https://c4disc.org/toolkits-for-equity/; Elizabeth Kaye Cook and Melanie Jennings, "Scenes from the Literary Blacklist," *Persuasion*, September 13, 2024, Scenes From The Literary Blacklist (persuasion.community).

50. Camilo Ortiz, "Activist Therapists are Driving People Away from Therapy. Here's What Can be Done," *Iohud*, September 28, 2023, https://www.lohud.com/story/opinion/2023/09/28/activist-therapists-driving-people-away-from-psychotherapy/70727486007/; Pamela Paul, "Is This Social Work or Social Indoctrination?" *New York Times*, December 7, 2023, https://www.nytimes.com/2023/12/07/opinion/social-work-columbia-ideology.html; Lisa Selin Davis, "How Therapists Became Social Justice Warriors," *The Free Press*, May 17, 2023, https://www.thefp.com/p/how-therapists-became-social-justice-warriors.

51. Ann Bauer, "What Independent Bookshops Really Sell," Persuasion, March 6, 2024, https://www.persuasion.community/p/what-independent-bookshops-really/comments.

52. Greg Lukianoff and Rikki Schlott, *The Canceling of the American Mind* (New York: Simon and Schuster, 2023).

53. Randall Balmer, *Thy Kingdom Come: An Evangelical's Lament* (New York: Basic Books, 2006), p. 8.

54. Jeffrey M. Jones and Lydia Saad, "Democrats Lose Ground with Black and Hispanic Adults," *Gallup*, February 7, 2024, https://news.gallup.com/poll/609776/democrats-lose-ground-black-hispanic-adults.aspx.

55. Besheer Mohamed, Kiana Cox, Jeff Diamant and Claire Gecewicz, "Faith Among Black Americans," *Pew Center*, February 16, 2021, https://www.pewresearch.org/wp-content/uploads/sites/20/2021/02/PF_02.16.21_Black.religion.report.pdf.

56. Haidt, *The Righteous Mind.*

57. Simon Sebag Montefiori, "The Decolonization Narrative is Dangerous and False," *The Atlantic*, October 27, 2023, https://www.theatlantic.com/ideas/archive/2023/10/decolonization-narrative-dangerous-and-false/675799/

58. Mo Husseini, "Mo Husseini," *Medium*, no date, https://mo-husseini.medium.com/.

59. Mo Husseini, "50 Completely True Things," *Medium*, May 2, 2024, https://mo-husseini.medium.com/50-completely-true-things-1ce672087b28.

60. Caitlin Flanagan, "Colleges are Lying to Their Students," *The Atlantic*, February 2, 2024, https://www.theatlantic.com/ideas/archive/2024/02/thinking-yourself/677321/.

61. Zora Neale Hurston, *Their Eyes Were Watching God* (New York: Harper & Row, 1990), p. 23.

62. Travis Proulx, Vlad Costin, Elena Magazin, Natalia Zarzeczna, and Geoffrey Haddock, "The Progressive Values Scale: Assessing the Ideological Schism on the Left," *Personality and Social Psychology Bulletin* 49, 8 (2023): p. 1269.

63. See Cory Clark, Lee Jussim, Komi Frey [+ 35 authors], William von Hippel, "Prosocial Motives Underlie Scientific Censorship by Scientists: A Perspective and Research Agenda," *PNAS*, November 20, 2023, https://www.pnas.org/doi/10.1073/pnas.2301642120.

64. For strategic Christian conservative co-belligerence, see Francis Schaeffer, *Plan for Action: An Action Alternative Handbook for Whatever Happened to the Human Race?* (New York: Flemming H. Revell, 1980).

65. Burack, *Tough Love.*

66. Society for Personality and Social Psychology, "Diversity, Equity, Inclusion, or Anti-Racism Statements," 2024, https://spsp.org/events/annual-convention/submissions/diversity-equity-inclusion-antiracism-statements.

67. Lee Jussim, "Mandatory Diversity, Equity, and Inclusion Statements

at SPSP," *Unsafe Science*, August 7, 2022, https://unsafescience.substack.com/p/mandatory-diversity-equity-and-inclusion.

68. Mark Edmundson, "The Good People," *Liberties*, Summer 2023, https://libertiesjournal.com/articles/good-people-the-new-discipline/.

69. McWhorter, *Woke Racism*, pp. 18; 21.

70. Helen Dale and Lorenzo Warby, "Social Justice as Social Leverage," *Not on Your Team But Always Fair*, December 29, 2022, https://www.notonyourteam.co.uk/p/social-justice-as-social-leverage.

71. Cambridge Dictionary, "Indoctrination," 2024, https://dictionary.cambridge.org/us/dictionary/english/indoctrination.

72. National Women's Studies Association, "Deadline Extension/NWSA Recommits to BDS and Feminist Accountability," April 30, 2024, email.

73. Peter Weir, director, *Dead Poets Society* (Touchstone Pictures, 1989).

74. Rita Koganzon, "The Coddling of the American Undergraduate," *The Chronicle of Higher Education*, March 21, 2024, https://www.chronicle.com/article/the-coddling-of-the-american-undergraduate.

75. McWhorter, *Woke Racism*.

76. Len Gutkin, "Are Presidents Finally Quitting the Pulpit?" *The Chronicle of Higher Education*, October 23, 2023, https://www.chronicle.com/newsletter/the-review/2023-10-23.

77. Sarah Haider, "The Woke Have Won, and Decisively," *Hold That Thought*, May 29, 2023, https://newsletter.sarahhaider.com/p/the-woke-have-won-and-decisively.

78. Ian Buruma, "Doing the Work: The Protestant Ethic and the Spirit of Wokeness," *Harpers*, February 2022, https://harpers.org/archive/2023/07/protestant-ethic-and-the-spirit-of-wokeness/.

79. Andrew Doyle, *The New Puritans: How the Religion of Social Justice Captured the Western World* (London: Hachette, 2022).

80. Colette Colfer, "A New Religion," *Women's Space Ireland*, April 26, 2022, https://womensspaceireland.ie/articles/a-new-religion/.

81. Vincent Lloyd, "A Black Professor Trapped in Anti-Racist Hell," *Compact*, February 10, 2023, https://compactmag.com/article/a-black-professor-trapped-in-anti-racist-hell.

82. Wilfred Reilly, "On Seeking Truth," *Unsafe Science*, June 20. 2024, https://unsafescience.substack.com/p/on-seeking-truth. Ellipsis is in the original.

83. Harriet Alexander, Alex Hammer, and James Gordon, "University of

Cincinnati Backflips After Reprimanding Gender Studies Professor, 28, Who Gave Student ZERO Grade for Using Phrase 'Biological Women,'" *Daily Mail*, July 9, 2023, https://www.dailymail.co.uk/news/article-12279155/University-Cincinnati-backflips-reprimanding-gender-studies-professor-gave-student-ZERO-grade.html.

84. Department of Women's, Gender and Sexuality Studies, "What's So Scary about Gender Studies?" *The Ohio State University*, 2023, https://wgss.osu.edu/events/whats-so-scary-about-gender-studies. The "event was made possible by support from the Mellon Foundation."

85. Helen Dale and Lorenzo Warby, "Social Justice as Social Leverage," *Not On Your Team but Always Fair*, December 29, 2022, https://www.notonyourteam.co.uk/p/social-justice-as-social-leverage.

86. James Miller, "Is Bad Writing Necessary?" *Lingua Franca*, December/January 2000, http://linguafranca.mirror.theinfo.org/9912/writing.html.

87. Of course, there's George Orwell, *1984* (New York: Signet Classic, 1961). But see also George Orwell, "Politics and the English Language," *Orwell Foundation*, 2024, https://www.orwellfoundation.com/the-orwell-foundation/orwell/essays-and-other-works/politics-and-the-english-language/. I haven't taken all of Orwell's excellent suggestions on writing.

88. Freddie deBoer, "Where Am I? How Did I Get Here?" *Freddie deBoer Substack*, December 26, 2023, https://freddiedeboer.substack.com/about.

89. Freddie deBoer, "How Elites Ate the Social Justice Movement," *The Free Press*, October 2, 2023, https://www.thefp.com/p/how-elites-ate-the-social-justice.

90. Simon Sebag Montefiore, "The Decolonization Narrative is Dangerous and False," *The Atlantic*, October 27, 2023, https://www.theatlantic.com/ideas/archive/2023/10/decolonization-narrative-dangerous-and-false/675799/.

91. See any episode of RuPaul Andre Charles' *Logo TV* series, *Drag Race*.

92. Stanford University, "Elimination of Harmful Language Initiative," no date, available at https://s.wsj.net/public/resources/documents/stanfordlanguage.pdf.

93. Giulia Heyward, "A USC Office Removes 'Field' from its Curriculum, Citing Possible Racist Connotations," *University of Southern California*, January 14, 2023, https://www.npr.org/2023/01/14/1148470571/usc-office-removes-field-from-curriculum-racist.

94. Bari Weiss and Roland Fryer, "Weekend Listening: From McDonalds Drive-Through to Star Harvard Professor," *The Free Press*, February 18, 2024, https://www.thefp.com/p/roland-fryer-bari-weiss-honestly-utax-harvard.

95. Matt Lavietes, "Johns Hopkins Pulls 'Lesbian' Definition after Uproar

over Use of 'Non-Men' Instead of 'Women,'" *NBC News*, June 14, 2023, https://www.nbcnews.com/nbc-out/out-news/johns-hopkins-pulls-lesbian-definition-uproar-use-non-men-instead-wome-rcna89307.

96. See, for example, Susan Opotow, "Moral Exclusion and Injustice: An Introduction," *Journal of Social Issues* 46, 1 (1990): 1–20.

97. Lindsey Bever, "Students Were Told to Select Gender Pronouns. One Chose 'His Majesty' to Protest 'Absurdity,'" *Washington Post*, October 7, 2016, https://www.washingtonpost.com/news/education/wp/2016/10/07/a-university-told-students-to-select-their-gender-pronouns-one-chose-his-majesty/.

98. Office of Institutional Equity, "Guidance on Use of Chosen/Preferred Names and Pronouns," *The Ohio State University*, no date, https://equity.osu.edu/policies-and-standards/guidance-use-chosen-preferred-names-and-pronouns.

99. Human Rights Campaign, "Pronouns 101," *The Ohio State University*, no date, https://lgbtq.osu.edu/documents/hrc-acaf-pronouns-101-1.pdf.

100. Anne Ryman and Matt Wynn, "For Anti-Abortion Activists, Success of 'Heartbeat' Bills was 10 Years in the Making," *The Center for Public Integrity*, June 20, 2019, https://publicintegrity.org/politics/state-politics/copy-paste-legislate/for-anti-abortion-activists-success-of-heartbeat-bills-was-10-years-in-the-making/.

101. Steven Brint, "The Political Machine Behind the War on Academic Freedom," *The Chronicle of Higher Education*, August 28, 2023, https://www.chronicle.com/article/the-political-machine-behind-the-war-on-academic-freedom.

102. *Nicholas Meriwether v. Francesca Hartop*, et.al., No 20–3289 Sixth Circuit Court of Appeals March 26, 2021, https://www.opn.ca6.uscourts.gov/opinions.pdf/21a0071p-06.pdf

103. Aaron Corpora, "Ohio Professor's Pronoun-Use Lawsuit Delivers First Amendment Victory," *Foundation for Individual Rights and Expression*, April 22, 2022, https://www.thefire.org/news/ohio-professors-pronoun-use-lawsuit-delivers-first-amendment-victory.

4 Enemies of the People

1. I've only been able to confirm this memory from one reference: Democratic Underground, "What is the Biggest Difference Between DU and Freerepublic?" 2011, https://www.democraticunderground.com/discuss/duboard.php?az=view_all&address=364x2579397.

2. Simon Sebag Montefiore, "The Decolonization Narrative is Dangerous and False," *The Atlantic*, October 27, 2023, https://www.theatlantic.com/ideas/archive/2023/10/decolonization-narrative-dangerous-and-false/675799/.

3. Nathan Honeycutt, Sean T. Stevens, and Eric Kaufmann, "The Academic Mind in 2022: What Faculty Think About Free Expression and Academic Freedom on Campus," *Foundation for Individual Rights and Expression*, 2023, https://www.thefire.org/research-learn/academic-mind-2022-what-faculty-think-about-free-expression-and-academic-freedom.

4. Steven Zhou and Nicole Barbaro, "2022 Campus Expression Survey Report," *Heterodox Academy*, March 22, 2023, https://heterodoxacademy.org/reports/2022-campus-expression-survey-report/.

5. Elisabeth Noelle-Neumann, "The Theory of Public Opinion: The Concept of the Spiral of Silence," in J. A. Anderson, editor, *Communication Yearbook* (Sage Publications, 1991), pp. 257; 259.

6. Pippa Norris, "Cancel Culture: Heterodox Self-Censorship or the Curious Case of the Dog-Which-Didn't Bark," *Harvard Kennedy School*, July 2023, https://www.hks.harvard.edu/publications/cancel-culture-heterodox-self-censorship-or-curious-case-dog-which-didnt-bark.

7. Izabella Tabarovsky, "The American Soviet Mentality," *Tablet*, June 15, 2020, https://www.tabletmag.com/sections/news/articles/american-soviet-mentality; Anna Krylov: "From Russia With Love: Science and Ideology, Then and Now," *Heterodox STEM*, November 28, 2022, https://hxstem.substack.com/p/from-russia-with-love-science-and; Anna Krylov and Jay Tanzman, "Fighting the Good Fight in an Age of Unreason—A New Dissident Guide," *Heterodox STEM*, October 1, 2023, https://hxstem.substack.com/p/fighting-the-good-fight-in-an-age; Joseph Paul Forgas, "The Tribal Threat to Liberal Democracy," *Quillette*, February 18, 2022, https://quillette.com/2022/02/18/the-tribal-threat-to-liberal-democracy/; Alexander Barvinok, "Leaving the AMS," *American Mathematical Society*, August 2023, https://www.ams.org/journals/notices/202307/noti2736/noti2736.html; Xiao Li, "America's Cultural Revolution is Just Like Mao's," *UnHerd*, July 6, 2020, https://unherd.com/2020/07/americas-cultural-revolution-is-familiar-to-the-chinese/.

8. Anne Applebaum, "The New Puritans," *The Atlantic*, August 21, 2021, https://www.theatlantic.com/magazine/archive/2021/10/new-puritans-mob-justice-canceled/619818/.

9. Renata Salecl, *The Spoils of Freedom: Psychoanalysis, Feminism and Ideology after the Fall of Socialism* (New York: Routledge, 1994), pp. 42–43; 48.

10. Timur Kuran, "Preference Falsification, Policy Continuity and Collective Conservatism," *The Economic Journal* 97, 387 (1987): 642–43.

11. Glenn C. Loury, "Self-Censorship in Public Discourse: A Theory of

'Political Correctness' and Related Phenomena," *Rationality and Society* 6, 4 (1994): pp. 430; 435; 436.

12. Richard Hanania, "Does Apologizing Work? An Empirical Test of the Conventional Wisdom," *Behavioural Public Policy* 6, 4 (2022): 516–29.

13. Anne Applebaum, "The New Puritans," *The Atlantic*, August 21, 2021, https://www.theatlantic.com/magazine/archive/2021/10/new-puritans-mob-justice-canceled/619818/; Gallaudet University, "How to Write Apologies," 2024, https://gallaudet.edu/student-success/tutorial-center/english-center/writing/how-to-write-letters/how-to-write-apologies/.

14. Sami R. Yousif, Rosie Aboody, and Frank C. Keil, "The Illusion of Consensus: A Failure to Distinguish Between True and False Consensus," *Psychological Science* 30, 8 (2019): 1195–1204.

15. Eric Hoffer, *The True Believer: Thoughts on the Nature of Mass Movements* (New York: Perennial Classics, 2002), p. 79.

16. Carole Hooven, "Academic Freedom is Social Justice," *Tablet*, June 21, 2023, https://www.tabletmag.com/sections/arts-letters/articles/academic-freedom-social-justice.

17. Foundation for Individual Rights and Expression, "Scholars Under Fire Database," no date, https://www.fire.org/research-learn/scholars-under-fire?range=10&orderdir=desc&orderby=year.

18. Foundation for Individual Rights and Expression, Subscriber mail, January 24, 2023.

19. Eric Kaufmann, "The Rise of Campus Antisemitism Should Come as No Surprise," *UnHerd*, December 6, 2023, https://unherd.com/newsroom/the-rise-of-campus-antisemitism-should-come-as-no-surprise/?edition=us.

20. Julia Schaletzky, "College Presidents are Lying about Free Speech," *Tablet*, December 11, 2023, https://www.tabletmag.com/sections/arts-letters/articles/college-presidents-are-lying-about-free-speech.

21. See Len Gutkin, "The Review: Diversity's Intellectual History," *The Chronicle of Higher Education*, May 13, 2024, https://www.chronicle.com/newsletter/the-review/2024-05-13.

22. Laura Kipnis, "Why are Scholars Such Snitches?" *The Chronicle of Higher Education*, March 17, 2022, https://laurakipnis.com/wp-content/uploads/2022/03/Chronicle.pdf.

23. Michel Foucault, *Discipline and Punish : The Birth of the Prison* (New York: Vintage, 1979), pp. 14; 25; 29.

24. Kathleen Stock, "The Reason White Male Academics Can't Get Jobs," *UnHerd*, May 31, 2024, https://unherd.com/2024/05/the-reason-white-male-

academics-cant-get-jobs/.

25. Matt Berg, "Georgetown Invited Navalny's Kid to Commencement. 'Chaos' Followed," *Politico*, May 19, 2023, https://www.politico.com/news/2023/05/19/georgetown-invited-navalnys-kid-to-commencement-chaos-followed-00097954.

26. Laura Kipnis, "Why are Scholars Such Snitches?"

27. Applebaum, "The New Puritans."

28. Joseph Heath, "A Simple Theory of Cancel Culture," *In Due Course*, December 2, 2023, https://josephheath.substack.com/p/a-simple-theory-of-cancel-culture.

29. Izabella Tabarovsky, "What My Soviet Life Taught Me About Censorship," *Quillette*, May 17, 2024, https://quillette.com/2024/05/17/what-my-soviet-life-taught-me-about-censorship/. Emphasis is in the original.

30. National Communication Association, "Political Party Affiliation Among Academic Faculty," March 2017, https://www.natcom.org/sites/default/files/publications/NCA_C-Brief_2017_March.pdf.

31. Peter Wood, "American Association of University Professors Abandons Scholars Under Siege," *National Association of Scholars*, December 2, 2015, https://www.nas.org/blogs/article/american_association_of_university_professors_abandons_educators_under_siege.

32. Ethan Young, "Leaked Documents Shed New Light on Recommended Amy Wax Sanctions, Her Appeal to Penn," *The Daily Pennsylvanian*, February 29, 2024, https://www.thedp.com/article/2024/02/amy-wax-hearing-leaked-documents-penn.

33. Cathy Young, "When Anti-Woke Becomes Pro-Trump," *Persuasion*, November 1, 2024, https://www.persuasion.community/p/when-anti-woke-becomes-pro-trump; Yascha Mounk, "How to Argue Against Identity Politics Without Turning into a Reactionary," *New York Times*, September 22, 2023, https://www.nytimes.com/2023/09/22/opinion/identity-politics.html.

34. Vamık D. Volkan, *The Need to Have Enemies and Allies: From Clinical Practice to International Relationships* (Northvale, New Jersey: Jason Aronson, 1988), p. 104.

35. Haidt, *The Righteous Mind*, p. 164.

36. Haidt, *The Righteous Mind*, p. 14. Emphasis is in the original.

37. Len Gutkin, "The Review: Discipline and Punish," *The Chronicle of Higher Education*, November 21, 2022, https://www.chronicle.com/newsletter/the-review/2022-11-21.

38. Jacob Ware, "How Far-Right Terrorists Choose Their Enemies,"

Foreign Policy, February 9, 2022, https://foreignpolicy.com/2022/02/09/far-right-terrorism-extremism-target-selection-jihad-enemy/.

39. Nellie Bowles, "The Day I Stopped Canceling People," *The Free Press*, May 10, 2024, https://www.thefp.com/p/nellie-bowles-morning-after-the-revolution.

40. Kathleen Stock, *Material Girls: Why Reality Matters for Feminism* (London: Fleet, 2022), pp. 1; viii.

41. Kipnis, "Why are Scholars Such Snitches?"

42. Xiao Li, "America's Cultural Revolution is Just Like Mao's," *UnHerd*, July 6, 2020, https://unherd.com/2020/07/americas-cultural-revolution-is-familiar-to-the-chinese/.

43. McWhorter, *Woke Racism*, p. 13.

44. Emily Ekins, "The State of Free Speech and Tolerance in America," *Cato Institute*, October 31, 2017, https://www.cato.org/survey-reports/state-free-speech-tolerance-america.

45. Ezra Klein and Michael Lind, "The End of the Obama Coalition," *New York Times*, November 13, 2024, https://www.nytimes.com/2024/11/13/opinion/obama-ezra-klein-podcast-michael-lind.html.

46. An excellent overview of movements' strategies and tactics is provided by Clifford Bob, *The Global Right Wing and the Clash of World Politics* (Cambridge: Cambridge University Press, 2012).

47. Jeannie Suk Gersen, "The Trouble with Teaching Rape Law," *The New Yorke*r, December 15, 2014, https://www.newyorker.com/news/news-desk/trouble-teaching-rape-law.

48. Aaron Sibarium, "Law School Administrators Huddle to Circumvent Affirmative Action Ban," *The Washington Free Beacon*, August 23, 2023, https://freebeacon.com/campus/law-school-administrators-huddle-to-circumvent-affirmative-action-ban/.

49. Aaron Hutchins, "Inside Lindsay Shepherd's Controversial Battle over Free Speech on Campus," *Maclean's*, December 11, 2017, https://macleans.ca/lindsay-shepherd-wilfrid-laurier/.

50. stking, "Traphouse," *Urban Dictionary*, February 26, 2015, https://www.urbandictionary.com/define.php?term=traphouse; Aaron Terr, "How Yale Law School Pressured a Law Student to Apologize for a Constitution Day 'Trap House' Invitation," *Foundation for Individual Rights and Expression*, October 14, 2021, https://www.thefire.org/news/how-yale-law-school-pressured-law-student-apologize-constitution-day-trap-house-invitation.

51. Terr, "How Yale Law School Pressured a Law Student."

52. I use passive voice because the report from which these details are culled is heavily redacted. As a result, it's hard to discern who did what.

53. Monica Reynoso and Andy Schwich, "Institutional Intake Report Case No. EV2023061355," *University of Washington*, Sep 22, 2023, https://www.nas.org/storage/app/media/New%20Documents/-REDACTED-Psychology-Report.pdf.

54. John D. Sailer, "University of Washington Violated Non-Discrimination Policy, Internal Report Finds," *National Association of Scholars*, December 31, 2023, https://www.nas.org/blogs/article/university-of-washington-violated-non-discrimination-policy-internal-report-finds/.

55. Ryan Quinn, "'Let's Talk About Sex?' or 'Let's Platform Transphobia'? Association Cancels a Panel," *Inside Higher Ed*, October 4, 2023, https://www.insidehighered.com/news/faculty-issues/diversity-equity/2023/10/04/anthropological-assoc-cancels-lets-talk-about-sex. See also Retraction Watch, "Anthropology Groups Cancel Conference Panel on Why Biological Sex is 'Necessary' for Research," September 27, 2023, https://retractionwatch.com/2023/09/27/anthropology-groups-cancel-conference-panel-on-why-biological-sex-is-necessary-for-research/.

56. Colleen Flaherty, "Much More Than Bones," *Inside Higher Ed*, February 14, 2022, https://www.insidehighered.com/news/2022/02/15/anthropologist-says-shes-being-punished-views-bones. The book is Elizabeth Weiss and James W. Springer, *Repatriation and Erasing the Past* (Gainesville, Florida: University Press of Florida, 2020).

57. There are other such cases, See, for example, Lee Jussim, "The Censorious Society for Personality and Social Psychology," *Unsafe Science*, February 13, 2024, https://unsafescience.substack.com/p/the-censorious-society-for-personality.

58. Sam Kahn, "Woke is Here to Stay," *Persuasion*, October 10, 2024, https://www.persuasion.community/p/woke-is-here-to-stay.

59. The Ohio State University, "Shared Values Initiative," 2023, https://oaa.osu.edu/shared-values-initiative.

60. Blake Smith, "Do Administrators Think They're Spiritual Healers?" *The Chronicle of Higher Education*, October 12, 2022, https://www.chronicle.com/article/do-administrators-think-theyre-spiritual-healers.

61. Office of Institutional Equity, "Guidelines to Ensure Equal Opportunity in University Programs, Activities and Resources," *The Ohio State University*, no date. Emphasis is added.

62. Foundation for Individual Rights and Expression, "Spotlight on Speech Codes 2024," January 2024, https://www.fire.org/sites/default/files/2024/01/

Speech%20Code%20Report_2024_final.pdf.

63. Bryan Caplan, "George Mason's Orwellian 'Just Societies' Requirement," *The James G. Martin Center for Academic Renewal*, March 1, 2024, https://jamesgmartin.center/2024/03/george-masons-orwellian-just-societies-requirement/.

64. Jessica Hehman and Catherine Salmon, "How Institutional Review Boards Can Be (and Are) Weaponized Against Academic Freedom," *Unsafe Science*, June 30, 2024, https://unsafescience.substack.com/p/how-institutional-review-boards-can.

65. Stone Age Herbalist, "The Rise of Archeologists Anonymous," *UnHerd*, December 3, 2022, https://unherd.com/2022/12/the-rise-of-archaeologists-anonymous/. See also Spencer, "The Politics of Prehistoric," *Social Stigma,* October 22, 2023, https://socialstigma.substack.com/p/the-politics-of-prehistoric.

66. House of Representatives, Committee on Oversight and Reform, "Hearing with Michael Cohen, Former Attorney to President Donald Trump," *US Government*, February 27, 2019, https://www.congress.gov/116/chrg/CHRG-116hhrg35230/CHRG-116hhrg35230.pdf, p. 106.

67. Jay Caspian Kang, "Identity Crisis," *New Yorker*, February 26, 2024, https://www.newyorker.com/magazine/2024/03/04/a-professor-claimed-to-be-native-american-did-she-know-she-wasnt.

5 Critical Thinking

1. Family Research Council Action, "Values Voter Summit: Election 2016," September 9–11, 2016, conference program.

2. Cynthia Burack, field notes, Values Voter Summit, Washington, DC, 2016.

3. Hugo Mercier and Dan Sperber, "Why do Humans Reason? Arguments for an Argumentative Theory," *Behavioral and Brain Sciences* 34 (2011): 57 –111.

4. Sean T. Stevens, "2024 College Free Speech Rankings," *College Pulse, Foundation for Individuals Rights and Expression*, 2023, https://www.fire.org/sites/default/files/2023/09/CFSR%202024_final_updated.pdf.

5. Tyler J. VanderWeele, "Moral Controversies and Academic Public Health: Notes on Navigating and Surviving Academic Freedom Challenges," *Global Epidemiology*, December, 2023, https://www.sciencedirect.com/science/article/pii/S2590113323000226.

6. Tyler J. VanderWeele, "Higher Education Has a Viewpoint Diversity Problem. Here's How to Respond," *The Harvard Crimson*, February 12, 2024, https://www.thecrimson.com/column/council-on-academic-freedom-at-harvard/article/2024/2/12/VanderWeele-harvard-viewpoint-diversity/; Tyler J. VanderWeele, "Viewpoint Diversity in Public Health," *Frontiers* 30 (2023): 1–5.

7. Max Horkheimer, *Critical Theory: Collected Essays* (New York, Continuum, 2002), p. 246.

8. "Faculty for Yale," no date, https://campuspress.yale.edu/facultyforyale/.

9. Len Gutkin, "The Review: Rival Factions Vie for Yale's Soul," *Chronicle of Higher Education*, February 20, 2024, https://www.chronicle.com/newsletter/the-review/2024-02-20.

10. Stanford Encyclopedia of Philosophy, "Critical Thinking," *Stanford University*, October 12, 2022, https://plato.stanford.edu/entries/critical-thinking/.

11. Patrick J. Casey, "The Reeducation of DEI," *Inside Higher Ed*, May 7, 2024, https://www.insidehighered.com/opinion/views/2024/05/07/reeducation-dei-opinion.

12. Frank Bruni, "The Most Important Thing I Teach My Students Isn't on the Syllabus," *New York Times*, April 20, 2024, https://www.nytimes.com/2024/04/20/opinion/students-humility-american-politics.html.

13. Hannah Arendt, *Lectures on Kant's Political Philosophy* (Chicago: University of Chicago Press, 1982), pp. 42–44.

14. Cynthia Burack, *Tough Love*, p. 90.

15. See Hannah Arendt, "'What Remains? The Language Remains': A Conversation with Günter Gaus," in Peter Baehr, editor, *The Portable Hannah Arendt* (New York: Penguin, 2000), pp. 16–19.

16. Hannah Arendt, *Eichmann in Jerusalem: A Report on the Banality of Evil* (New York: Viking, 1965).

17. Richard Hofstadter, quoted in George Packer, "The Campus-Left Occupation that Broke Higher Education," *The Atlantic*, April 25, 2024, https://www.theatlantic.com/ideas/archive/2024/04/campus-left-university-columbia-1968/678176/.

18. William Deresiewicz, "How Pseudo-Intellectualism Ruined Journalism," *Persuasion*, March 8, 2024, https://www.persuasion.community/p/how-pseudo-intellectualism-ruined.

19. *Anthony Novak v. City of Parma, Ohio*, Brief amicus curiae of *The Onion*, Oct 2022, https://www.supremecourt.gov/Docket-

PDF/22/22-293/242596/20221006144840674_Novak%20Parma%20 Onion%20Amicus%20Brief.pdf; *Anthony Novak v. City of Parma, Ohio*, Brief amicus curiae of *The Babylon Bee*, Oct 28, 2022, https://www.supremecourt.gov/ DocketPDF/22/22-293/244213/20221028092221628_Babylon%20Bee%20 -%20Amicus%20Brief.pdf.

20. Hannah Natanson, "Students Hated 'To Kill a Mockingbird.' Their Teachers Tried to Dump It," *Washington Post*, November 3, 2023, https://www.washingtonpost.com/education/2023/11/03/to-kill-a-mockingbird-book-ban-removal-washington/.

21. Ayaan Hirsi Ali, *The Caged Virgin: An Emancipation Proclamation for Women and Islam* (New York: Free Press, 2006); Jeanine Cummins, *American Dirt* (New York: Flatiron Books, 2020).

22. Abigail Shrier, "Does the ACLU Want to Ban My Book?" *Wall Street Journal*, November 15, 2020, https://www.wsj.com/articles/does-the-aclu-want-to-ban-my-book-11605475898.

23. Prof. Grace Lavery, *X*, November 14, 2020, https://twitter.com/graceelavery/status/1327743400553172997.

24. Abigail Shrier, *Irreversible Damage: The Transgender Craze Seducing Our Daughters* (Washington, DC: Regnery, 2021).

25. I reprint this essay with permission from the student.

26. Heather Mac Donald, "Hysterics for Hamas," *City Journal*, May 9, 2024, https://www.city-journal.org/article/hysterics-for-hamas.

27. JPE Harper-Scott, "Why I Left Academia," no date, https://jpehs.co.uk/why-i-left-academia/.

28. Emma Pettit, "How a Heated Q&A on Israel and Hamas Led to a Department Chair's Resignation," *The Chronicle of Higher Education*, October 30, 2023, https://www.chronicle.com/article/how-a-fiery-q-a-on-israel-and-hamas-led-to-a-department-chairs-resignation.

29. Pettit, "How a Heated Q&A on Israel and Hamas Led to a Department Chair's Resignation."

30. Yo-Yo Ma, *Beginner's Mind* (Newark, New Jersey: Audible, 2023).

Select Bibliography

Al-Gharbi, Musa. *We Have Never Been Woke: The Cultural Contradictions of a New Elite*. Princeton, New Jersey: Princeton University Press, 2024.

Altemeyer, Bob. *The Authoritarians*. 2024. https://theauthoritarians.org/.

American Association of University Professors. "1915 Declaration of Principles on Academic Freedom and Academic Tenure." no date. https://www.aaup.org/NR/rdonlyres/A6520A9D-0A9A-47B3-B550-C006B5B224E7/0/1915Declaration.pdf.

American Association of University Professors."1940 Statement of Principles on Academic Freedom and Tenure." no date. https://www.aaup.org/sites/default/files/1940%20Statement.pdf.

Applebaum, Anne. "The New Puritans." *The Atlantic*. August 21, 2021. https://www.theatlantic.com/magazine/archive/2021/10/new-puritans-mob-justice-canceled/619818/.

Barkun, Michael. "Conspiracy Theories as Stigmatized Knowledge." *Diogenes* 62, nos 3–4 (2015): 114–20.

Bipartisan Policy Center. "Campus Free Expression: A New Roadmap." November 2021. https://bipartisanpolicy.org/download/?file=/wp-content/uploads/2021/11/BPC-Report-Campus-Free-Expression_A-New-Roadmap.pdf.

Bob, Clifford. *The Global Right Wing and the Clash of World Politics*. Cambridge: Cambridge University Press, 2012.

Bridgland, Victoria M. E., Payton J. Jones, and Benjamin W. Bellet. "A Meta-Analysis of the Efficacy of Trigger Warnings, Content Warnings, and Content Notes." *Clinical Psychological Science* 12, no 4 (2023): 1–21.

Brown, Wendy. "The Impossibility of Women's Studies." *Differences* 9, no 3 (1997): 79–101.

Burack, Cynthia. *Because We Are Human: Contesting US Support for Gender and Sexuality Human Rights*. Albany, New York: State University of New York Press, 2018.

Burack, Cynthia. *Sin, Sex, and Democracy: Antigay Rhetoric and the Christian Right*. Albany, New York: State University of New York Press, 2008.

Burack, Cynthia. *Tough Love: Sexuality, Compassion, and the Christian Right*. Albany, New York: State University of New York Press, 2013.

Canovan, Margaret. "'Trust the People!' Populism and the Two Faces of Democracy." *Political Studies* 47 no 1 (1999): 2–16.

Kimberlé Crenshaw, "Demarginalizing the Intersection of Race and Sex: A Black Feminist Critique of Antidiscrimination Doctrine, Feminist Theory, and Antiracist Politics." In *Feminist Legal Theory: Readings in Law and Gender*. Edited by Katharine T. Bartlett and Rosanne Kennedy, 57–80. Boulder, Colorado: Westview Press, 1991.

Dale, Helen and Lorenzo Warby, "Social Justice as Social Leverage." *Not On Your Team but Always Fair*. December 29, 2022. https://www.notonyourteam.co.uk/p/social-justice-as-social-leverage.

Dawkins, Richard. "How Can We Have a Proper Debate When We No Longer Speak the Same Language?" *Evening Standard*. August 15, 2023. https://www.standard.co.uk/comment/comment/freedom-speech-debate-language-trans-differing-richard-dawkins-b1100729.html.

deBoer, Freddie. "How Elites Ate the Social Justice Movement." *The Free Press*. October 2, 2023. https://www.thefp.com/p/how-elites-ate-the-social-justice.

Gutkin, Len. "Are Presidents Finally Quitting the Pulpit?" *The Chronicle of Higher Education*. October 23, 2023. https://www.chronicle.com/newsletter/the-review/2023-10-23.

Harding, Sandra. "Rethinking Standpoint Epistemology: What is 'Strong Objectivity'?" In *Feminist Epistemologies*. Edited by Linda Alcoff and Elizabeth Potter, 49–82. New York: Routledge, 1993.

Haslam, Nick, Brodie C. Dakina, Fabian Fabianoa, Melanie J. McGrath, Joshua Rhee, Ekaterina Vylomova, Morgan Weaving and Melissa A. Wheeler, "Harm Inflation: Making Sense of Concept Creep." *European Review of Social Psychology* 31 no 1 (2020): 254–286.

Hawkins, Stephen and Taran Raghuram. "American Fabric: Identity and Belonging." *More in Common*. December 2020. moreincommon_americanfabricreport.pdf.

Henrich, Joseph, Steven J. Heine, and Ara Norenzayan. "Most People are Not WEIRD." *Nature* 466 no 29 (2010): 29.

Hoffer, Eric. *The True Believer: Thoughts on the Nature of Mass Movements.* New York: Perennial Classics, 2002.

Honeycutt, Nathan, Sean T. Stevens, and Eric Kaufmann, "The Academic Mind in 2022: What Faculty Think About Free Expression and Academic Freedom on Campus." *Foundation for Individual Rights and Expression.* 2023. https://www.thefire.org/research-learn/academic-mind-2022-what-faculty-think-about-free-expression-and-academic-freedom.

Ignatieff, Michael. "Why the Populist Right Hates Universities." *The Atlantic.* August 6, 2023. https://www.theatlantic.com/ideas/archive/2023/08/viktor-orban-illiberalism-ron-desantis-universities/674915/.

James Madison Program in American Ideals and Institutions, "Princeton Principles for a Campus Culture of Free Inquiry." 2024. https://jmp.princeton.edu/princeton-principles-campus-culture-free-inquiry.

Jussim, Lee. "Mandatory Diversity, Equity, and Inclusion Statements at SPSP." *Unsafe Science.* August 7, 2022. https://unsafescience.substack.com/p/mandatory-diversity-equity-and-inclusion.

Jussim, Lee. "On Seeking Truth." *Unsafe Science.* June 20, 2024. https://unsafescience.substack.com/p/on-seeking-truth.

Kipnis, Laura. "Why are Scholars Such Snitches?" *Chronicle of Higher Education.* March 22, 2022. https://www.chronicle.com/article/academe-is-a-hotbed-of-craven-snitches.

Koestler, Arthur. "Arthur Koestler." In *The God That Failed.* Edited by Richard H. Crossman. New York: Columbia University Press, 2001.

Kuran, Timur. "Preference Falsification, Policy Continuity and Collective Conservatism." *The Economic Journal* 97 no 387 (1987): 642–665.

Lakoff, George. *Moral Politics: What Conservatives Know that Liberals Don't.* Chicago, Illinois: University of Chicago Press, 1996.

Lloyd, Vincent. "A Black Professor Trapped in Anti-Racist Hell," (*Compact,* February 10, 2023) https://compactmag.com/article/a-black-professor-trapped-in-anti-racist-hell.

Loury, Glenn C. "Self-Censorship in Public Discourse: A Theory of 'Political Correctness' and Related Phenomena," *Rationality and Society* 6 no 4 (1994): 428–61.

Lukianoff, Greg and Jonathan Haidt. *The Coddling of the American Mind: How Good Intentions and Bad Ideas are Setting Up a Generation for Failure.* New York: Penguin Press, 2018.

McWhorter, John. *Woke Racism: How a New Religion Has Betrayed Black America.* New York: Portfolio, 2021.

Mill, John Stuart. *On Liberty and Other Writings*. Cambridge: Cambridge University Press, 1994.

Miller, James. "Is Bad Writing Necessary?" (*Lingua Franca*, December/January 2000) http://linguafranca.mirror.theinfo.org/9912/writing.html.

Montefiore, Simon Sebag. "The Decolonization Narrative is Dangerous and False," *The Atlantic*. October 27, 2023. https://www.theatlantic.com/ideas/archive/2023/10/decolonization-narrative-dangerous-and-false/675799/.

Moon, Dawne. *God, Sex, and Politics: Homosexuality and Everyday Theologies*. Chicago, Illinois, University of Chicago Press, 2004).

Mounk, Yascha. *The Identity Trap: A Story of Ideas and Power in Our Time*. New York: Penguin Random House, 2023.

Müller, Jan-Werner. *What Is Populism?* Philadelphia, Pennsylvania: University of Pennsylvania Press, 2016.

Noelle-Neumann, Elisabeth. "The Theory of Public Opinion: The Concept of the Spiral of Silence." In *Communication Yearbook*. Edited by J. A. Anderson, editor, 256–308. Thousand Oaks, California: Sage Publications, 1991.

Norris, Pippa. "Cancel Culture: Heterodox Self-Censorship or the Curious Case of the Dog-Which-Didn't Bark." *Harvard Kennedy School*. July 2023. https://www.hks.harvard.edu/publications/cancel-culture-heterodox-self-censorship-or-curious-case-dog-which-didnt-bark.

Nussbaum, Martha C. *Cultivating Humanity: A Classical Defense of Reform in Liberal Education*. Cambridge, Massachusetts: Harvard University Press, 1997.

Orwell, George. *1984*. New York: Signet Classic, 1961.

Patai, Daphne and Noretta Koertge, *Professing Feminism: Cautionary Tales from the Strange World of Women's Studies*. New York: Basic Books, 1994.

Patel, Eboo. "How Colleges Can Prepare for a Chaotic Fall." *The Chronicle of Higher Education*. June 21, 2024. https://www.chronicle.com/article/how-colleges-can-prepare-for-a-chaotic-fall.

Pew Research Center. "Beyond Red vs. Blue: The Political Typology." November 9, 2021. https://www.pewresearch.org/politics/2021/11/09/beyond-red-vs-blue-the-political-typology/.

Pluckrose, Helen and James Lindsay. *Cynical Theories: How Activist Scholarship Made Everything about Race, Gender, and Identity*. Durham, North Carolina: Pitchstone Publishing, 2020.

Proulx, Travis. Vlad Costin, Elena Magazin, Natalia Zarzeczna, and Geoffrey Haddock. "The Progressive Values Scale: Assessing the Ideological Schism on the Left." *Personality and Social Psychology Bulletin* 49 no 8 (2023): 1248–1272.

Rosenfield, Kat. "The Many Faces of Literary Censorship." *Persuasion*, March 28, 2022. https://www.persuasion.community/p/literary-censorships-evolving-landscape.

Sailer, John D., "Inside Ohio State's DEI Factory." *Wall Street Journal*, November 20, 2023. https://www.wsj.com/opinion/inside-ohio-states-dei-factory-faculty-report-diversity-hiring-cefd804d.

Salecl, Renata. *The Spoils of Freedom: Psychoanalysis and Feminism After the Fall of Socialism*. London, UK: Routledge, 1994.

Schrier, Abigail. *Irreversible Damage: The Transgender Craze Seducing Our Daughters*. Washington, DC: Regnery, 2021.

Singal, Jesse. "This is What a Modern-Day Witch Hunt Looks Like." *New York Magazine*, May 2, 2017. https://nymag.com/intelligencer/2017/05/transracialism-article-controversy.html.

Stock, Kathleen. *Material Girls: Why Reality Matters for Feminism*. London: Fleet, 2022.

Tabarovsky, Izabella. "What My Soviet Life Taught Me About Censorship." *Quillette*, May 17, 2024. https://quillette.com/2024/05/17/what-my-soviet-life-taught-me-about-censorship/.

University of Chicago. "Kalven Committee: Report on the University's Role in Political and Social Action." no date. https://provost.uchicago.edu/sites/default/files/documents/reports/KalvenRprt_0.pdf.

University of Chicago, "Report of the Committee on Freedom of Expression." 2014. https://provost.uchicago.edu/sites/default/files/documents/reports/FOECommitteeReport.pdf.

Young, Cathy. "The Rising Threat on Campuses." *Persuasion*. March 12, 2021 https://www.persuasion.community/p/the-rising-threat-on-campuses.

Young, Cathy. "Our Nasty, Stupid, Frivolous Cancel Culture Fights (That We're Lucky Enough to Have." *The Bulwark* March 22, 2022. https://www.thebulwark.com/p/our-nasty-stupid-frivolous-cancel-culture-fights-that-were-lucky-enough-to-have.

Index

About the Author

Cynthia Burack is a first-generation college grad and retired academic. She lives in Washington, DC, her chosen hometown.

www.ingramcontent.com/pod-product-compliance
Lightning Source LLC
Jackson TN
JSHW081925070826
106393JS00006B/33
9781634312806